Afghanistan and Super Powers

Mohammad Khalid Ma'aroof

Commonwealth

Afghanistan and Super Powers

Edition : 2027

ISBN : 81-7169-043-2

Published by :
COMMONWEALTH PUBLISHERS (P) LTD.
4831/24, Govind Lane,
Ansari Road, Darya Ganj,
New Delhi - 110002
Ph. : 23242541, 23272541
e-mail : commonwealthpublishers2016@gmail.com

Distributed by :
ARJUN PUBLISHING HOUSE
4831/24, Govind Lane,
Ansari Road, Darya Ganj,
New Delhi - 110002
Ph. : 23242541, 23272541
e-mail : arjunbooks2001@gmail.com
arjunpubhouse@gmail.com

Laser Typesetting by :
Dimple Computers
Delhi

Printed at :
Milan Enterprises
Delhi

Preface

The traditional adage that nations make history is truly applicable to Afghanistan where brave people have rewritten the history in this decade and set a precedence. In a multipolar world strewn with power rivalry between the Super Powers the survival of a small nation presents an interesting study of interaction of geopolitical forces in international relations. Such a study assumes added significance when it pertains to Afghanistan which has been subject to Super Power rivalry since centuries and, since December 1979, it has been the victim of Soviet invasion. Afghanistan, which shares common border with Soviet Union, had been subject to Anglo-Russian rivalry for about fifteen decades. In the wake of the emergence of cold war in the immediate aftermath of the conclusion of the Second World War, the Soviet-United States rivalry also spread its tentacles towards Afghanistan but, like the past, the rulers of Afghanistan maintained the independence, sovereignty and territorial integrity of Afghanistan by pursuing the policy of strict neutrality and genuine non-alignment.

However, the traumatic political events leading to the advent of Soviet-backed communist *coup* in Kabul in April 1978 had triggered the process of rapid Soviet infiltration into Afghanistan which culminated in the Soviet invasion of that country in December 1979. Since then hundreds of thousands of Soviet troops had been stationed in Afghanistan and they could not succeed in their sinister designs to annex it but under the pretext of Geneva accord, pulled back by 15 February, 1989. The Soviet invasion was opposed by the people of Afghanistan. Six millions Afghans are living as refugees in Pakistan, Iran and other countries. The Afghan freedom fighters, also known as Afghan Mujahideen, gave a tough resistance to the occupying forces who finally withdrew and now Afghan Freedom fighters are engaged in liberating Afghanistan from the Kabul regime.

The Soviet invasion of Afghanistan and the continued presence of Soviet troops in that country and their subsequent wtthdrawal had been the focus of strategic thinkers, policy makers, academicians, journalists and freedom loving people throughout the world. The resultant impact had been the appearance of plethora of literature on various aspects of Afghanistan. The bulk of literature available on the subject deals with the analysis of the developments leading to the Soviet invasion of Afghanistan. This literature comprises the works of Western academicians and Journalists who have written research-oriented books and articles. A close scrutiny of the available literature reveals that many pertinent questions have remained unanswered. The questions like when a Super Power invades a non-aligned country like Afghanistan, and how the other Super Power reacts to it, how a small and non-aligned country like Afghanistan can exist in the wake of severe Super Power rivalry; and how the international community has responded in the wake of Soviet invasion of Afghanistan. All these questions have been deeply examined in the present study which is the revised, enlarged and updated version of the author's Ph.D. thesis.

I am intellectually indebted to Abdur Rahman Pazhwak, the outstanding statesman and seasoned diplomat of Afghanistan who has served as Permanent Afghan Representative to the United Nations, as Afghan Ambassador to the United Kingdom, West Germany and India, for the valuable comments on the various complex aspects of Afghanistan's foreign policy. I have also greatly benefitted from his writings.

Despite his preoccupations, he has been kind enough to answer some of my queries which have unfolded unto me the great reservoir of his dispassionate analysis and deep understanding of Afghan diplomacy. The impact of his learning looms large in the present study.

The author also owes his intellectual debt to Dr. Akhtar Majeed, and Director, Centre far strategic studies Associate Professor, Department of Political Science, Aligarh Muslim University, for his able guidance and constant encouragement. The author is also grateful to Dr. S.A.H. Bilgrami, Professor (Retd.), Department of Political Science, Aligarh Muslim University, for his keen interest and encouragement. My thanks also go to my other teachers at the AMU whose profound knowledge and experience enabled me to sharpen my tools of learning.

I am also beholden to Dr. Zamin Momand, an expert on Afghan diplomacy, currently with the Voice of America, Washington, DC, for his constant encouragement and valuable comments on various aspects of Afghan diplomacy. I feel obliged to Dr. Zakaria Ferotan, now in Canada for his cooperation. I owe my thanks to Dr. Chaibai Mostamandi, renowned archaeologist of Afghanistan and Mrs. Meria Mcstamandi, both now in the United States for their affection and encouragement. My sincere thanks also go to Mohammad Hassan Wolasmal, editor of former *Afghan Mujahid* now known as *Mujahid Woles*, whose writings have been a source of constant inspiration for me. I am also indebted to Dr. Miratta Mugalzai, former Assistant Professor, Faculty of Medicine, Nangarhar University, and now working with Afghan freedom fighters, for his kind cooperation. I am deeply indebted to Professor Shirindal Gardiwal, Professor in Pushtu Department, School of Languages, Jawaharlal Nehru University, New Delhi, for his affection and cooperation. My sincere thanks also go to Dr. Arshad Mahmood, M.D., an Indian friend who stood by me through thick and thin. I am also immensely obliged to my senior Afghan colleagues—Dr. Qudus, M.D., and Taj Mohammad Akbar for their affection and encouragement.

I am also intellectually beholden to Professor M.L. Sondhi, Professor and Chairman of the Centre for International Politics and Diplomacy, School of International Studies, JNU, New Delhi, for his valuable suggestions. I also feel obliged to Professor Ram Rahul Sheel, an expert on Central Asia, for his valuable comments when the present study was at the draft stage. My thanks also go to Dr. Ram Avtar Sharma of Delhi University for his benign cooperation.

My sincere thanks go to the librarians and other members of the staff of Maulana Azad Library, AMU, Aligarh, National Archives of India, New Delhi, Sapru House Library, IDSA Library, JNU Library, American Centre Library, UN Information Centre, all in New Delhi, who generously helped in making the adequate material available to me.

Finally a word about the spellings of Afghan names. The name of A.R. Pazhwak is spelled out as Abdur Rahman Pazhwak and as Abdul Rahman Pazhwak. Both spellings are commonly used. Besides the name "Mahmood" is generally written as Mahmood or Mahmud but for the purposes of the present study, the spellings retained are as "Mahmud." Similarly, the word Mohammad is also spelled as Mohammed, but the former spellings have been retained for the purpose of present study. My sincere thanks go to Mr. B.R. Verma, for Common Wealth Publishers for his constant interest and meticulous efforts in bringing out the book within a short span of time.

(MOHAMMAD KHALID MA'AROOF)

Contents

CHAPTER I

HISTORICAL BACKGROUND

An analysis of the evolution of Afghan foreign policy since the emergence of modern Afghanistan in 1747 till the conclusion of the Second World War, with special reference to Afghanistan's relations with the contemporary great powers—Russia and Britain—and Afghan response to them including the challenges posed by Anglo-Russian rivalry and its impact on Afghan foreign policy is helpful in ascertaining the full gamut of Afghanistan's past and present history.

The word "Afghan" is the national name of all the peoples of Afghanistan which symbolizes an indivisible unit under all historical, economic and social conditions in the heart of Asia.[1] According to Hasan Kawun Kakar, a noted Afghan scholar, Afghanistan has had three principal names—*Aryana* in antiquity, Khurasan in the medieval era and Afghanistan in modern times.[2] Modern Afghanistan is almost co-extensive with the land mentioned in the old Greek as Ariana, in the old Persian as Airya or Airyana, in Sanskrit as Arya-Vartta or Arya-Varsha and in Zend as Eriene-Veejo. Situated between India and Persia, Aryana was a geographical and cultural rather than political name.[3] The name Aryana lasted for about 1,500 years from 1000 B.C. to the fifth century of the Christian Era. The world *Khurasan*, denoting the "land of the rising sun" gained currency during the second century of the Christian

Era. According to Mir Ghulam Muhammad Ghobar, an eminent Afghan historian, "for fourteen centuries Khurasan was applied initially to parts of Afghanistan and later to the whole country and is still in use for a small region to the northwest of it.[4] Even upto the nineteenth century the name *Khurasan*, signifying Afghanistan was in vogue along with the words *Pashtunkhwa* and *Sarhad*.[5] Thus it was only toward the end of the nineteenth century that "the apellation Afghanistan replaced the word Khurasan completely."[6] According to Hasan K. Kakar, Afghanistan is not a new name and "it is generally believed to have appeared with the accession of Ahmad Shah Durrani in 1747."[7] According to A.R. Pazhwak, "to discover the original name of Afghanistan, it is necessary to study the earlier records which reveal that it was then called 'Aryana'."[8] According to available evidence the word "Afghanistan" was applied in a political sense to a land for the first time in the third decade of the fourteenth century by Saifi Herawi.[9] A detailed analysis of this etymological controversy is beyond the scope of the present study and it deems suffice to say that Afghanistan is an ancient country whose history dates back to over five thousand years.

The anthropological excavations undertaken in the early decades of the present century in Afghanistan revealed that Palaeolithic man probably lived in the caves of northern Afghanistan as long as 50,000 years ago. According to Louis Dupree, "Post-World War II excavations in South-central Afghanistan point to intimate relationships with the Indus Valley Civilization fourth-second millennia B.C."[10]

References to Afghanistan recur in the ancient Vedic literature and subsequent travelogues of foreign travellers. The reference to Afghanistan as Avagana occurs in Varaha Mishra's *Bhrita Sanhita*. This view has been supported by A. Foucher, a noted French scholar.[11] The works of Al Beiruni and Hsuen Tsang also mention about Afghanistan.

The advent of Islamic during the seventh century in Afghanistan proved instrumental in overhauling the entire culture and civilization of Afghanistan.[12] Islam which brought about an overall change in the social, cultural and historical development of Afghanistan also forged a new religious and cultural bonds—bonds that to a certain extent overrode the prevalent ethn ic diversities.[13]

The advent of Islam in Afghanistan was followed by the conquest by Arabs who reached Kabul and Kandhar during the seventh century. The Muslim conquest brought Afghanistan within a greater political entity, stimulated trade in the region and preserved the country's geographic importance as a crossroad between India, Central Asia and the Mediterranean world.[14]

For about two centuries the local dynasties ruled over Afghanistan—Tahirids (820-70), and the Samanids (874-999). The closing years of the tenth century witnessed the advent of regime of Sabuk-tagin in Afghanistan who was succeeded by his son Mahmud Ghaznavi who ruled over Afghanistan till 1157 A.D. The Ghaznavi's empire extended over Kabul, Balkh, Badakhshan, Persian Khorasan and some parts of India.[15] Following the collapse of Ghaznavi rule, the central authority in Afghanistan passed on to the local forces.[16] The Mongol invasion brought economic disaster for Afghanistan during the thirteenth century. During the fourteenth century Afghanistan was invaded by Taimurlane and the early decades of the sixteenth century witnessed the establishment of Mughal rule in Kabul by Babur, a descendant of Timur, in 1504. Following the death of Babur which led to the collapse of Mughal rule in Afghanistan, the local tribes again vied for establishing their paramountcy in Afghanistan. During this period, Afghanistan was divided "between the empires of Persia and Mughal India, the northern tribes being under Mughal rule.[17] The Afghan nationalism found its early seedlings during the sixteenth and seventeenth centuries under the inspiration of Roshania movement and Khushal Khan Khattak (1613-89) who inspired the Afghan tribes to "defend their independence and strive for political unity."[18]

The geo-political situation in the region underwent a substantial change and the early period of eighteenth century witnessed the southern Afghan tribes led by Ghilzais rise in revolt against Persia which in later years spread to Herat and southeast of Persia. The first successful attempt to establish an autonomous Afghan State was made in 1709 when Mir Wais, a prominent Ghilzai chieftain rallied his tribe in a successful revolt against the Persian Empire.[19] However the revolt was quelled by the then Persian King, Nadir Shah, but Mir Wais succeed in establishing the rule of Ghilzai dynasty's rule in Afghanistan. The assassination of Persian King, Nadir Shah in 1747, provided an opportunity to the Abdalis under the leadership of Ahmad Khan Abdali to declare the independence of Afghanistan. During the same year, Ahmad Shah Abdali was made the King of Afghanistan. The succeeding pages present and analysis of Afghan foreign policy since its emergence as an independent modern State in 1747 till the conclusion of the Second World War with special reference to contemporary great powers. Adamec has divided the period between 1747 till the end of Second World War into the following four phases.

(A) The Period of Expansionism (1747 to 1800)

(B) The Period of Foreign Conflict (1800 to 1880)

(C) The Period of Defensive Isolationism (1880 to 1919)

(D) The Period of Defensive Neutral sm (1919 till the end of Second World War).[20]

Though Adamec calls the period from 1747 to 1800 as period of expansionism but actually it was the period of consolidation. Afghanistan had never been an imperial power at any stage of history. Hence for the purpose of present study, it is appropriate to call it as period of consolidation.

(A) The Period of Consolidation: 1747 to 1800

Ahmad Shah Abdali after assuming the reins of power, consolidated his position and took measures to strengthen his empire.

In this direction, he led eight expeditions into India. In their first expedition launched in 1748, however, the Afghan forces could not go beyond the Indus.[21] In his subsequent expeditions, the Afghan King was able to incorporate Punjab, Kashmir and Multan into his empire. At the time of his death in 1773, the Afghan empire of Ahmad Shah Abdali extended from Atrek river to the Indus and from Tibet to the Arabian Sea.[22] Timur Shah succeeded after the death of his father in 1773 a the new ruler of Afghanistan. Two decades of Timur Shah's rule over Afghanistan witnessed no major change in Afghan domestic and external policies but continuation of the legacy.

The closing years of the eighteenth century witnessed the rise of a powerful France evincing interest in the countries of South-west and Central Asia. The British, whose power in India had been in ascendency since the establishment of the East India Company in the beginning of the seventeenth century, were also planning to augment their political power and expand their trade and commerce in and beyond Afghanistan. This period also "witnessed the beginning of that interesting epoch when the diplomatic rivalries of the European powers became clear cut on the chess-board of Central Asia."[23]

Zaman Shah (1793-99) who succeeded Timur Shah as the King of Afghanistan continued the policy of his father and grandfather. The external threats to Afghanistan during this period had increased. The growing power and expansion of the British in India and Persian plans to reassert its sovereignty over Herat portended threat to Afghanistan. According to Vartain Gregorian, "Afghanistan thus entered the nineteenth century a politically disunited .. state."[24]

(B) The Period of Foreign Conflict: 1800-1880

The onset of the nineteenth century envisaged an era of foreign conflicts for Afghanistan. During the first decade of the nineteenth century, the British signed a treaty with the Sikh ruler of Punjab, Maharaja Ranjit Singh on 25 April, 1809 under which the British acquired a right of passage for their army through the Sikh territories in case of foreign aggression and the Sikhs undertook to help the British in their task of defence.[25] This treaty was motivated by two factors. In the first place, by the growing possibility of a French invasion of India in 1808 and, secondly, to check the growing Sikh power to secure the British power in India.

During this period, the British were facing threat to their power locally from Marathas and the Sikhs. In the scheme of of their defence strategy, the British made friendly gestures to the then Afghan ruler, Shah Shuja, and a British mission under Mountstuart Elphinstone left for Kabul on 13 October, 1808.[26] The Elphinstone Mission tried to raise the issue of French and Russian threat to Afghanistan as well as India and wanted Shah Shuja to contract an alliance but were reluctant to help the Afghan King in his internal challenge which threatened the throne.[27] However the Afaghans were shrewd enough to discover the British designs and regarded "an alliance for the purpose of repelling one enemy was imperfect and that true friendship between the two states could only be maintained by identifying their interests in all cases."[28]

Despite the differing approaches, the British India and Afghanistan signed a treaty in June 1809 in terms of which Afghanistan undertook to prevent the passage through Afghanistan of French and Persian troops on their way to India and the British Government pledged to pay the Afghans for their services against the confederacy. Besides Afghanistan was to exclude all Frenchmen from its territory.[29] However, following the defeat of Shah Shuja by Shah Mahmud, the treaty became almost a dead letter.

Afghanistan, because of its borders with Russia and Persia,[30] had assumed immense strategic importance in British defence strategy with regard to consolidation and protection of British rule in India. The Russians had started showing interest in Persia during this period. Besides, the growing French power was also deemed as a threat by the British. Consequently the

British signed two treaties in 1809 and 1814 with Persia. Under the terms of the Anglo-Persian Treaty of 1809, Persia agreed "not to permit any European force whatever to pass through Persia either towards India or towards the ports of that country."[31] Persia also promised to afford a force for the protection of British dominions in case of attack from Afghanistan or any other country. The British Government in return agreed to "afford to the Shah (Persian King) a force, or in lieu of it, a subsidy, with warlike ammunition such as guns, muskets etc…"[32] Similarly the Anglo-Persian treaty of 1814 envisaged for a Persian attack against Afghanistan in the event Afghans invaded India.[33]

On the other hand, Russia had gained considerable diplomatic, political and economic gains in the region by virtue of two treaties—the Treaty of Turkmanchai signed with Persia in 1828 and the Treaty of Adrianople signed with the Ottoman Empire in 1829. Under the terms of the Treaty of Turkmanchai, Persia surrendered its all territories west of the Caspian Sea to Russia. These developments proved instrumental in changing British strategy towards Iran as well as Afghanistan. It regarded any Persian encroachment or gain at the expense of Afghanistan as tantamount to an extension of Russia's political and economic gains on the doorstep of India.[34]

Lord Ellenborough, a then top ranking British official, had opined that Russia could enter India via Afghanistan. He further added: "Russian commerce would be utilized to prepare the way for Russian armies in Afghanistan."[35] Thus, the Russian factor was the major determinant of British policies towards Afghanistan and Persia. Lord Palmerston, the then British Foreign Secretary was of the view that "a pro-British power in Afghanistan could influence officers in Persia in which Russia was deeply interested."[36]

The British Governor-General in India, Lord Auckland, was advised by London to conclude political or commercial agreements with Afghanistan:

> The time has arrived when it will be right for you to interfere, decidedly in the affairs of Afghanistan. Such an interference would doubtless be requisite either to prevent the extension of Persian dominion in that quarter or to raise a timely barrier against impending encroachments of Russian influence.[37]

Consequently Lord Auckland sent his emissary Alexander Burnes to Kabul in November 1836 with the objective of securing political and commercial advantages without conceding any strategic concessions to Afghanistan.

The First Anglo-Afghan War

Realizing that the British were not going to get the desired concessions from the then Afghan ruler, Amir Dost Mohammad, they tried to cultivate Shah Shuja who was then living in exile in India with the promise to restore him his throne. Efforts were also made to enlist the support of Maharaja Ranjit Singh of Punjab. During that period, Persia was planning to invade Herat. However in November 1838, the British foiled Persian attempts to invade Herat and forced the latter to accept a hands-off policy in regard to Herat.[38] Subsequently the British also concluded a treaty with Shah Kamran, the ruler of Herat in August 1839,[39] thus making Herat an exclusive British sphere of influence. This move seemed to be the part of overall British policy of bringing Afghanistan under British sphere of influence in the wake of growing Russian influence in the neighbouring countries of Central Asia. The Russians, who had gained considerable economic stakes in Central Asia between 1758 and 1858, considered a pro-British or English dominated Afghanistan a serious threat to their interests in the region.[40] Thus both British and Russians were apprehensive of each other over Afghanistan.

In the meanwhile, in October 1838, the then Governor-Genreal of India, Lord Auckland, issued a "Manifesto" accusing the Afghan ruler, Dost Mohammad of taking measures prejudicial to the security and peace of Indian frontiers.[41] It was also planned to instal Shah Shuja as the ruler of Afghanistan with the help of British army. In November 1838, the British army launched expedition against Amir Dost Mohammad and in August 1839 Shah Shuja entered Kabul following the surrender of Dost Mohammad.

However the people of Afghanistan, despite their internal differences, could not tolerate the alien presence on their land. Consequently a countrywide revolt by the Afghans resulted in the annihilation of a British force of 4,500 men and supporting army of 12,000 and the murder of Shah Shuja.[42]

Despite this blowing defeat, the British forces again entered Afghanistan in the autumm of 1842 but were defeated again.[43] As a consequence of the British failure, Amir Dost Mohammad regained his throne in 1842. Prof. Bilgrami has opined that the first British defeat in the first Anglo-Afghan war "served as a good lesson to the British empire builders not to meddle in the affairs of the far-off lands and taught them to follow a policy of non-entanglement and non-interference."[44] However the British never learnt the lesson but repeated the same mistake by launching second and third war against Afghanistan as analysed in the succeeding pages.

Second Anglo-Afghan War

Until the death of Amir Dost Mohammad in 1863, the British followed a policy of non-intervention in the internal affairs of Afghanistan. In view of growing Persian pressure over Herat, the British Government lost no time in strengthening their position *vis-a-vis* Persia by increasing their bonds of friendship with Dost Mohammad Khan, the Amir of Afghanistan. Consequently, on 30 March 1855, a treaty was signed between the British Government and the Amir of Afghanistan under which the British undertook to respect the independence of Afghan territories, then in possession of Amir Dost Mohammad and promised not to interfere in the internal affairs of Afghanistan. In return, the Afghan Amir agreed to do the same and "pledged to be friend of friends and enemy of the enemies" of the

East India Company.[45] However the treaty did not impose any such stipulation on the British toward the Amir of Afghanistan. However the treaty was not based on reciprocal obligations which should have been essential as a guarantee for the royalty of the parties concerned.

Another treaty was signed between the Amir of Afghanistan and the British Government on 26 January, 1857.[46] Under the terms of the treaty, the Afghan Amir was offered a subsidy of Rupees one lakh per month during the period of hostilities with Persia. The Afghan Amir, Shah Mohammad Dost, however, declined to the stationing of British military mission and British officers in Afghanistan. In this regard, British Government agreed to send only a mission under Major H.B. Lumsden who was to stay at Kabul on the basis of mutual agreement between the two countries.[47]

There followed a period of internal dissensions in Afghanistan after the death of Amir Dost Mohammad. However, between 1869 and 1872, the British and the Afghans forged closer relations. Following the second Anglo-Sikh War of 1847, India and Afghanistan had become close to each other. In 1869, the then Afghan Amir, Sher Ali Khan paid a visit to India which resulted in the signing of Anglo-Afghan agreement under which the British declared their intention not to interfere in Afghan internal affairs and also undertook to support Afghanistan's independence.[48]

However the British Government was alarmed over the growing Russian advances in the Central Asian countries bordering Afghanistan. In 1864, Russians gained control of Khiva and Kookand, captured Tashkent in 1865 and annexed Samarkand in 1869 and then got Bukhara. These Russian advances were deemed a serious threat to British power in India A section of the British policy makers argued in favour of establishing a permanent British mission in Kabul and make clear to all that a pro-British and peaceful Afghanistan was of immense significance to British interests in India and the East.[49]

Until the beginning 1874, London favoured a policy of non-intervention in Afghanistan. In February 1874, Benjamin Disraeli's Government came to power in London and Lord Salisbury was appointed as the new Secretary of State for India. The new Government followed a "Forward Policy"[50] which meant that Britain could not preserve its interests in India while pursuing a non-interventionist policy in Afghanistan and demanded the establishment of a permanent British mission in Kabul. However, the then Afghan ruler. Sher Ali Khan was opposed to the appointment of a British mission in Kabul and argued that the religious sentiments of his "people at the time would impose too great a responsibility upon him in protecting a British agent in Afghanistan."[51]

Incidentally, during July-August 1878, a Russian Mission under General Stolietoff reached Afghanistan on its way to St. Petersburg. The British sources show that Amir Sher Ali Khan received the Russian Mission with honour.[52] These events provoked the British who launched an invasion on Afghanistan which culminated into the Second Anglo-Afghan War. The Afghan forces withdrew. Consequently Amir Sher Ali Khan went to Mazar-i-Sherif with a view to secure help from Russian forces which were then standing on the passes against the British. But the Russians declined.

Though the British had military advantage over Afghanistan, but at Maiwand, the English Army suffered a humiliating defeat at the hands of Ayub Khan, the son of Amir Sher Ali and the real brother of Yakub Khan who latter became Amir of Afghanistan. Amir Sher Ali Khan died at Mazar-i-Sherif on 21 February, 1879.[53]

Consequently the British imposed the Treaty of Gandamak signed in May 1879[54] on Afghanistan. Amir Yakub Khan, son of Amir Sher Ali, became the new ruler of Afghanistan. Under the Treaty of Gandamak, Afghan ruler agreed to the appointment of a British agent in Kabul and follow the advice of the British in the conduct of Afghan foreign relations. Sir Louis Cavagnari who took over as British envoy in Kabul was murdered in September 1879 which led to the British reprisals. These events led to the abdication of Amir Yakub Khan and in 1880, Amir Abdur Rahman, the nephew of Amir Sher Ali Khan took over as the new ruler of Afghanistan.

(C) The Period of Defensive Isolationism: 1880-1919

When Amir Abdur Rahman took over as the new ruler of Afghanistan in 1880, "Anglo-Afghan relations were burdened with the legacy of two wars, the loss of life and property and the illwill and distrust that resulted."[55] In his first foreign policy pronouncement, Amir Abdur Rahman informed the then chief British political officer in Afghanistan:

> ...As long as your Empire and that Russia exist, my countrymen, the tribes of Afghanistan should live quietly in ease and peace; and that these two States should find us true and faithful... and we hope of your friendship that, sympathizing with and assisting the people of Afghanistan, you will place them under the honourable protection of the two Powers....[56]

In the wake of acute Anglo-Russian rivalry, the Afghan Amir wanted Afghanistan to pursue an independent foreign policy by maintaining friendly relations with British India as well as Russia. However the British were reluctant to concede the Afghan demand. Lepel Griffin, while assuring the Afghan Amir about the British intention not to interfere in the internal affairs of Afghanistan, wrote: "...Your Highness can have no political relations with any foreign power except with the British Government...[57] This analysis makes it discernible that the British Government accepted the internal independence of Afghanistan while continuing its control over the foreign affairs of Afghanistan. However, Amir Abdur Rahman wanted to pursue an independent policy, both domestically and externally.

Ludwig W. Adamec has divided the foreign policy of Abdur Rahman into three categories:

(i) Assertion of National Independence;

(ii) Insistence on Isolationism; and

(iii) Promotion of a Balance of Power.[58]

The succeeding pages analyse these aspects.

(i) Assertion of National Independence

Amir Abdur Rahman always regarded himself as an independent ruler of an independent Afghanistan. In the light of the fact that British exerted control over Afghanistan's foreign relations, the Amir insisted that, after seeking the advice of the British Iadian Government, he could take an independent decision on any issue at hand.[59] The Amir wrote to the then chief British agent in Kabul, Lepel Griffin in 1880, "I desire nothing in lieu of services rendered nor do I demand favours in exchange for duties performed. But I have my claims on the desire of the Afghan nation."[60]

In a royal proclamation issued in 1887, he appealed to the Afghan's sense of honour, national dignity and patriotism, drawing their attention to the Anglo-Russian threats: "The country of Afghanistan is a mere spot under the compass of two infields . . . it is closely besieged; yet although imprisoned, men are always thinking of their release, you are indifferent to your bonds."[61] Amir Abdur Rahman united Afghanistan and retained powers and authority to himself. He also equipped the army with modern weapons.

(ii) Insistence on Isolationism

Afghanistan followed a consistent policy of isolationism during the reign of Amir Abdur Rahman. Because of the British control over Afghan foreign policy. Afghanistan was isolated from Persia and Russia and left the door for political relations open only to Britain. Even while dealing with the British, the Afghan Amir exercised and asserted his independence to decide the important issues. In place of a British envoy, the Afghan

Amir insisted on the appointment of a Muslim as British envoy to Kabul. In October 1881, the British Viceroy suggested the name of Mir Hashim Khan as the British envoy, but the Amir insisted on the appointment of Afzal Khan, which was to be approved by the British.[62]

As a part of the policy of isolationism, the Afghan Amir also refused to allow the British troops and officers to visit the strategic areas in Afghanistan. In 1884, when the Russians had reached Merv, the British tried to influence the Amir for the construction of rail links for the defence of Afghanistan but the Amir while appreciating the British suggestions refused to oblige. He protested the planned extension of the British rail roads to Chaman as "leading to no good."[63]

The Amir was all in favour of the induction of modern technology into Afghanistan but at the same time he feared that it would lead to the penetration of foreign influence.[64] He was also opposed to the stationing of British troops or adviser in Afghanistan. During 1887-88 when the Amir was faced with Ghilzai rebellion and revolt of Ishaq Khan, he proclaimed that the British were waiting at the border for his call to come to his help. In fact, he did not invite the British army. His purpose was only to warn his enemies and he was not inclined to invite foreign troops on Afghan soil.[65]

The independent thinking of Amir Abdur Rahman was noticed by the British. Lord Dufferin wrote to the Amir in 1886: ". . . your mind is constantly occupied by the idea of asserting your independence of all control in internal affairs, that you see interference in every British action."[66]

(iii) Promotion of Balance of Power

During the reign of Amir Abdur Rahman, the geopolitical situation in the neighbourhood of Afghanistan had assumed significant dimensions. Anglo-Russian rivalry was at its zenith. Both great powers were increasing and expanding the sphere of influence in Islamic countries—Afghanistan, Persia and Ottoman Empire.

Under these circumstances, Amir wanted Afghanistan to pursue a "middle course" policy of forging closer relations with neighbouring Islamic countries without annoying the either great power in the neighbourhood. According to Adamec: "Abdur Rahman's relations with the more or less independent Muslim populations of the East were influenced by Pan-Islamic considerations."[67]

According to Amir Abdur Rahman, the Russian policy was essentially that "rightly or wrongly, friendly or unfriendly, with peace or war, the Islamic kingdoms should be washed away from the face of the Asiatic continent."[68]

Amir Abdur Rahman was perhaps also convinced that the Russians were determined to annex Persia, Turkey and Afghanistan, by hook or crook. There were two possible ways of doing so. In the first place, Russians could directly befriend these countries and thus draw them to their orbit or on the other hand provoke these countries against Britain and eventually reach an understanding with the British in crushing them and thus dividing the booty.[69]

The Afghan Amir also recounted in his memoirs that the Russians were planning to attack India: "Russia expected that an attack on India would be accompanied by a general uprising in that country, followed by a quick Russian victory, since Britain, as a seapower, was no match for Russia on land."[70] In the wake of such geopolitical compulsions, Amir Abdur Rahman proposed the establishment of an Islamic alliance among Turkey, Persia and Afghanistan, which could separate the two great empires neither allowing Russia nor England to take any part of our dominions."[71] The Amir was convinced about the nefarious designs of both great power and added that no single power could usurp Afghanistan without invoking the hostility of the other. He felt that although "these neighbours are a cause of much anxiety to Afghanistan, yet, as they are pulling against each other, they are no less an advantage and protection for Afghanistan than a danger (and indeed) a great deal of safety of the Afghan Government depends upon the fact that neither of these two neighbours can bear to allow the other to annex an inch of Afghan territory."[72]

Thus, Amir Abdur Rahman kept Afghanistan politically intact by pursuing a policy of strict neutrality by warding off the internal or external interference by either great power. He also maintained the balance of power to the advantage of Afghanistan.

The Durand Line agreement signed between Amir Abdur Rahman and the British India in 1893 is analysed in the succeeding pages because of its recurring references in subsequent years.

Following the death of Amir Abdur Rahman in October 1901, his son, Habibullah succeeded as new Amir of Afghanistan during the same month. Amir Habibullah was faced with a critical foreign political challenge because both Russia and Britain desired a change in the political *status quo* of Afghanistan.[73] The Russians wanted to have direct relalions with the new Afghan Amir but the British were opposed to such a move and wanted to retain their hold over the conduct of Afghan foreign affairs.

The British Indian Government, while sending the condolence message to the new Amir over the demise of late Amir Abdur Rahman, hinted that a mission would be required to meet the new Amir to confirm the previous Anglo-Afghan agreements.[74] Britain also informed Russia that there prevailed a *status quo* even after the death of Amir Abdur Rahman.[75] However Amir Habibullah in his reply on 31 October, 1901, while ignoring the British hint, promised that he would honour the agreements made by his late father with the British Indian Government "so long as the illustrious British Government firmly adhere to them."[76]

However, the Russians wanted a change in the *status quo*. Even prior to the death of Abdur Rahman, the Russians had expressed such a desire on 1 February 1899, a Russian publication *Novoe Vremva* contained a hint in this regard:

> Russia, whose frontiers run more than 2000 versts with that of Afghanistan, cannot settle the most simple, but unavoidable, frontier question through her relations with the powers of this neighbouring state. For this purpose, we have to communicate with London, and London with Simla, and from Simla attempts begin to enter into negotiations with Kabul, which can easily lead to no result, as the Amir already for some time, and on every possible occasion, shows that he is not a vassal of England . . .[77]

It further suggested the stationing of representatives of both Russia and Britain in Kabul—a move which could help in removing the British distruct of a Russian invasion of India. In this regard, M. Lesar, Secretary at the Russian Embassy in London, informed the British Government on 6 February, 1900:

> Russo-Afghan relations have been defined by the Arrangement of 1872 and 1873, which Russia regards as still being in effect and as placing Afghanistan entirely outside her sphere of action. Although Russia's obligations onlybi nd her to refrain from political action, she has, except in the case of transient deviation from the correct standard of diplomatic action, consented in the past, from a feeling of friendly interest toward Great Britain, to forego even non-political relations . . . the moment would accordingly appear to have come when a definite step should be taken in the regularization of these relations. . .[78]

Thus it is evident from these pronouncements that Russia had predetermined to have direct relations with Kabul even prior to the taking over by Habibullah as the new Amir of Afghanistan.

There ensued a series of diplomatic negotiations between Russia and England in which London wanted to know Russian intentions of having direct relations with Kabul with a view to ascertain if a mutually satisfactory solution could be found. On 29 January, 1902, the British envoy in St. Petersburg conveyed a verbal declaration of his Government to the Russians that Britain did not wish to contend that "there was no force in the Russian arguments for direct communications on matters of local detail, but that as having charge of Afghan foreign relations, they held that arrangements for the purpose could only be made with their consent."[79] Ludwing W. Adamec feels that now it was left to Russia to formulate proposals as to the change of the *status quo* and to give guarantees that any relations would remain of a nonpolitical character.[80] However on 19 December, 1902, the *Novoe Vremav*, a Soviet publication, carried a statement of the Russian Foreign Office which stated:

> In regard to our relations to Afghanistan, it must be remarked that in this matter we made no request to the London Cabinet, but that we merely intimated our decision to enter into direct relations with Afghanistan in consequence of altered circumstances. No further explanations have taken place on this subject.[81]

Both Britain and Russia stuck to their respective positions which created an impasse. In the meanwhile, Russians initiated diplomatic offences resulting in a series of incidents. In September 1902, the Afghan officials noticed removal of boundary pillars at Meshed by the Russians. The Russian Government, however, expressed its willingness to reinstate the boundary pillars by a joint Russo-Afghan commission but Amir Habibullah declined the Russian suggestion.[82] The Afghan Amir, at that juncture, asked for the British advice and the latter offered to send a representative. However, the Russians rejected the idea of dealing with the British representative and went ahead with the task of restoring some of the pillars themselves. In the meantime Meshed area was hit by a famine and some Russians were reportedly selling wheat at cheap rates to the Afghans in the famine hit areas. Thus on the one pretext or the other, the Russians got an opportunity to deal and negotiate with local Afghan officials in Meshed and Herat.

In the wake of these developments the British Indian Government got alarmed and thought that a permanent British representative should be stationed at Herat. However this idea was shelved for the time being because the then Viceroy, Lord Curzon, cautioned the British against such a move since it would frighten the Amir who might resent Russian pressure just as much as he did British.[83]

As a follow up of these developments, the British impressed upon the Afghan Amir the need for the revision of Anglo-Afghan agreements signed earlier on the plea that those agreements were concluded with the late Amir Abdur Rahman as person, subject to renegotiations with every successor.[84] However, Amir Habibullah asserted that there was no need to renegotiate those agreements. Following prolonged discussions, the Amir finally agreed to accept a British mission in this regard at Kabul.

Consequently, a Brilish mission headed by Louis W. Dane reached Kabul on 12 December, 1904 to renegotiate the Anglo-Afghan agreements in force during the reign of late Amir Abdur Rahman. It came to be known as Dane Mission. The negotiations between the British officials and Afghan officials lasted until the end of March 1905. The main issue around which the discussions veered was the nature of Anglo-Afghan agreement of 1880 and its revision. The major British objective was both to get the Agreement of 1880 renewed with favourable modifications and resolve the vexing question of Russo-Afghan relations. However, Amir Habibullah's main objective was to remain independent and not to serve as a "mere pawn on the chess-board of Indian military defence."[85] Consequently, both the sides exchanged drafts of the proposed treaty. The copy of the British draft treaty was given by Dane to the Afghan Amir who objected to the word "*Siyasi*" as a translation for "Political" for his foreign relations. This shows that the Amir was conscious of not accepting any provision in the proposed treaty which could undermine the Afghan national interests,

The prolonged series of negotiations resulted in the conclusion of what became to be known as Habibullah-Dane Treaty on 21 March, 1905.[86] The Amir Habibullah was recognized by the British as the "Independent King of the State of Afghanistan and its Dependencies" and he was to be addressed as "His Majesty."[87] The treaty reaffirmed the annual subsidy granted in 1893, allowing the Amir to collect £ 400,000 in undrawn subsidy payments and Afghanistan's right to import arms without restrictions.[88]

The Amir was very cautious about British strategic manoeuvres. He declined to accord trade concessions to the British in Afghanistan as well as introduction of railways in his country.[89] Under the new treaty though the British failed to obtain the right to set up a diplomatic mission in Kabul yet they retained control of Afghanistan's foreign relations and considered the treaty as a renewal of the Durand Agreement.[90]

The Russians expressed apprehensions about the Anglo-Afghan agreement lest the British seek to alter the then existing pattern of Indo-Afghan relations by annexing or occupying Afghan territory. In this regard, the British Foreign Secretary, Lord Lansdowne, with a view to allay Russian misgivings, assured the Russian Ambassador in London, Count Benckendorff, that Britain would not interfere in the internal affairs of Afghanistan and maintain *status quo*.[91]

The British on their part sought a similar assurance from the Russian Government for maintaining *status quo* in their policy towards Afghanistan and regarding the latter "as wholly outside the sphere of their influence."[92] After having secured such an assurance from St. Petersburg, the British were willing to allow the Russians to have interchange of communications between the Russian and Afghan frontier officials on non-political matters of a local nature.[93] However the Russians refused to give a formal assurance in this regard.[94] However Russians expressed satisfaction over it.

Towards the Anglo-Russian Reapprochment (1907)

The Habibullah-Dane agreement was concluded at a time when Russia was entangled in hostilities with Japan. Russia was defeated at the hands of Japan. The renewal of Anglo-Japanese treaty of 1902 in 1905 made the Russians hesitant towards the British with regard to Afghanistan. For Russia, the treaty envisaged implications for the Afghan policy of the British Indian Government, and was, therefore, directed against it.[95] The Russians feared that the British Government had entertained some designs on the Russian possessions of Central Asia and "Special Russian interests" in Persia.[96] In October 1905, the Russian Foreign Minister, Count Lansdorff apprised the British Ambassador of the adverse effect caused in Russia about the Anglo-Japanese treaty.[97]

The year 1905 had brought changes in domestic political scenario both in Britain and Russia. The new set up of government in Russia with Alexander Isvalski as new Foreign Minister, sought friendly rather than competitive relationship with Britain. During the same year the Liberals came to power in London. The increasing influence of Germany had brought Britain and France close to each other under the immutable law of balance of power.[98] In the wake of Russia's close relations with France and French British *entente*, Russia also made efforts to forge close ties with London. Consequently, in May 1906 both countries started negotiations which lasted until August 1907, with the main purpose of resolving differences and forge cooperation on mutually agreed terms. Consequently on 31 August, 1907, Britain and Russia signed an agreement which came to be known as Aglo-Russian Convention of 1907. It comprised three agreements on each on Persia, Afghanistan and Tibet. The part pertaining to Afghanistan,[99] was on the whole more favourable to Britain.

The Russians conceded that Afghanistan was out of their sphere of influence and agreed to conduct their political relations with Afghanistan through the intermediary of the British Government.[100] The Russians gained only in terms of local question of a non-political nature which could be settled directly by the Afghan and Russian officials.

The British Government on its part declared its adherence to the provisions of the Anglo-Afghan treaty of 1905 and also declared not to interfere in the internal affairs of Afghanistan. In other words, British control over the conduct of Afghan foreign policy was conceded in the Convention.

However the Anglo-Russian Convention of 1907 came as a shock for Amir Habibullah and the people of Afghanistan. According to Vartan Gregorian, perhaps "no single event gave as much impetus to the growth of Afghan nationalism as the Anglo-Russian Convention of 1907".[101] The fifth article of the Convention provided that it would come into force only after the British Government had obtained the consent of the Amir of Afghanistan and notified the same to the Government of Russia. Though the convention required the approval of the Afghan Amir but he was not consulted by the British in this regard. The Afghan Government feared that the Convention posed a threat to Afghan independence.[102] Amir Habibullah was determined to keep Afghanistan completely independent and to that end he wanted to refrain from having any closer relations with either of the two great powers. Thus the Amir of Afghanistan expressed his reluctance to adhere to the Anglo-Russian Convention.

The British Indian Government offered several explanations that the Convention was in no way a slight on Afghan independence but all this failed to appease or allay the misgivings of Afghan Government.[103]

During Amir Habibullah's visit to India in 1908, the then Viceroy Lord Minto tried to convince the Amir: "I cannot but think that your Majesty will regard the conclusion of the Convention with lively satisfaction."[104] The Afghan Amir while acknowledging the receipt of Minto's message promised that he would send his reply. After keeping the British Government in suspense for about a year, Amir Habibullah in his fifty-four page reply stated that the Convention destroyed the independence of Afghanistan. It further added that "if they (the British) act in contravention of the principle laid down by them in the past, they will have to show a better principle to their own Government and to ours."[105] However, Afghanistan never signed the Convention.

Seeing that there was no change in Afghan attitude on Anglo-Russian Convention of 1907, the British Foreign Secretary, Sir Edward Grey and his Soviet counterpart, A.P. Isvolsky, agreed in late 1908 that consent of the Afghan Amir was not necessary. Consequently, the British Government declared that "as the Amir had raised no objection to Article 3, and was not prohibiting communication between his frontier officials and those of Russia, we saw no reason why the Convention should not continue to work well, for the Amir was in practice, acting upon it."[106]

Despite these differences, Anglo-Afghan relations remained normal in the years preceding the outbreak of First World War. The cautious and independent nature of foreign policy pursued by Amir Habibullah deterred both Britain and Russia from exerting any sort of pressure on Afghanistan.

On the home front, Amir further cosolidated his position by initiating reforms and projects of modeinization. The international developments occurring during that period had considerable impact in Kabul, Turkey's war with Italy and Balkan were "politicized Afghans and taught them the lesson of unity and Islamic solidarity."[107] Nationalists like Mahmud Tarzi played notable role in this regard. Tarzi's *Siraj-al-Akhbar*, a prominent newspaper, interpreted world affairs from the Pan-Islamic and Afghan perspective.[108]

Afghanistan and First World War

The outbreak of the First World War in the summer of 1914 forced both Britain and Russia not to force the Convention of 1907 on Afghanistan. On 7 August, 1914, Lord Hardinge informed Amir Habibullah about the outbreak of war in Europe between Russia, France and Britain on one side and Germany and Austria on the other and the Amir was urged to remain neutral. The Afghan Amir promptly replied pledging his continued adherence to the Anglo-Afghan trealy obligations and declared his determination to maintain neutrality in the war.[109]

Following Turkey joining the war, the British became apprehensive about the possibilities of misgivings between Britain and Afghanistan in the wake of Britain's war with the Ottoman Empire. Consequently on 5 November, 1915 Lord Hardinge informed Amir Habibullah "owing to the ill-advised. unprovoked and deliberate action of the Ottoman Government, war has broken out between Great Britain and Turkey."[110] The British Viceroy further added that Britain's war against Turkey was in no sense a religious war and Britain had the support of Muslim community in India and Persia. He finally urged the Amir: "I feel sure that Your Majesty will not waver from the attitude of neutrality...you have already guaranteed."[111] The Afghan Amir, Habibullah reiterated his country's continued commitment to the policy of neutrality. The British Government was satisfied with Amir's assurances.

However the British realized that the Afghan mood was sympathetic to the Turkey and not to Germany. An Englishman wrote to his relatives in Bombay from Kabul: "Almost everyone in Kabul was strongly anti-British and pro-Turkish, except the Amir, who speaks seldom in public...(but) occasionally remarks that the British were very powerful."[112] The Afghan public opinion was reflected by the popular newspaper *Siraj-al-Akhbar*. Mahmud Khan Tarzi writing in the issue of 16 April, 1915 of *Siraj-al-Akhbar* expressed his surprise that Allies and Axis powers were putting blame for the war on the shoulders of the other. While "the chief and the only cause of this general bloodshed is the commercial rivalry between England and Germany and their respective claims to supremacy based on their achievements in science, expansion of territory and naval strength.[113]

While pursuing the policy of strict neutrality, Amir Habibullah did not respond to German overtures. The British King George V sent a personal letter to Amir Habibullah commending the Afghan ruler for maintaining strict neutrality.[114] The British could not afford to disbelieve Amir Habibullah's commitment to the policy of strict neutrality during the war period. On 5 November, 1915, the Viceroy of India in his report sent to London observed: "The attitude of the Amir continues to be most satisfactory. He is one of the few statesmen in the East, and his conduct has really of all praise."[115] During 1915 and early 1916, the Germans tried to woo Amir Habibullah to sign a treaty with Germany.[116] But the Amir refused to respond to German overtures and reiterated his adherence to the principle of strict neutrality.

The collapse of the Ottoman Empire in the wake of Turkey's defeat in the First World War, the advent of the Bolshevik revolution in Russia in 1917 and the defeat of Axis Powers in the war had changed the international political scenario. The maintenance of strict neutrality by Afghanistan during the war period and rejection of German overtures by Amir Habibullah had made the British Government in India and London think how to reward Amir's loyalty. Amir Habibullah wanted his country's independence recognized by Britain including Afghanistan's freedom of maintaining political relations with other countries. Lord Chelmsford, the Viceroy of India, wrote to London, asserting that "the services of the Amir have been immense, and when the time comes to reward them, we must be generous".[117] According to Lord Chelmsford, the Afghan Amir could ask for the following concessions from Britain (i) complete political freedom, (ii) territorial aggrandizement, (iii) money, and (iv) representation in England.[118] On 2 February, 1919, Amir Habibullah wrote to the Indian Viceroy that his country be represented at the Peace Conference because Afghanistan was an independent country and had remained neutral during the war. The Amir further stipulated that if the Viceroy could bring a signed certificate of Afghan independence from the Conference he would be satisfied; otherwise an

Afghan representative must be allowed to attend the conference to obtain one . . .[119] The Viceroy's Council was willing to provide some concessions to Afghanistan. However Denys Brag, a number of Viceroy's Council remarked:

> . . . Our control of Afghanistan's foreign relations have been so long a fundamental principle of our Afghan policy that it requires an effort of mind to conceive of our willingly consenting to any diminution of it. Possibly it may prove essential that it should continue to dominate our policy. But the present is so different from the past, and the future seems likely to be so much more different still, that the time has come for us to scrutinize our traditional policy anew.[120]

Thus Brag opined that Britain should not alleviate its control over Afghan foreign relations and recommended the conclusion of a definite treaty between Afghanistan and the British India.

However, Viceroy's mood of "being generous" to Amir Habibullah was not shared by London which advised the Viceroy to stave off the Amir telling how that participation at the Peace Conference was open only to belligerents, and that international guarantee would be no good to Afghanistan, even if they could be secured, since they might lead to interference by other nations . . .[121]

(D) The Period of Defensive Neutrality (1919 to the End of Second World War)

Following the assassination of Amir Habibullah on 19 February, 1919, Amanullah succeeded the throne of Afghanistan on 21 February 1919. After assuming the power, the first thing Amir Amanullah did was that he wrote a letter on 3 March, 1919 to the British Viceroy in India, informing the latter of his father's death, reiterated his Government's policy:

> . . . Our independent and free Government of Afghanistan considers itself ready and prepared at every time and season

> to conclude, with due regards to every consideration of the requirements of friendship and the like, such arrangements and treaties with the mighty Government of England as may be useful and serviceable in the way of commercial gains and advantages to our Government and yours.[122]

Again on 13 April, 1919, Amir Amanullah announced in a durbar:

> . . . I have declared myself and my country entirely free, autonomous and independent, both internally and externally. My country will hereafter be as independent a state as the other states and powers of the world are. No foreign power will be allowed to have a hair's breadth of hight to interfere internally or externally. With the affairs of Afghanistan, and if any ever does I am ready to cut its throat with this sword.[123]

The Viceroy of India in his reply to the Afghan Amir remained non-committal and only thanked the latter for informing that he had become the Amir of Afghanistan. Amir Amanullah was proclaimed as King of Afghanistan in March 1919. However the British Government maintained complete silence to Amanullah's demand for recognition of his accession to the throne. The British silence conveyed an impression that Amanullah's rise to power was not favourably viewed by London . .[124]

Third Anglo-Afghan War

The proclaimation of Amir Amanullah as the King of Afghanistan was facilitated through a *firman* envisaging that he was proclaimed King by the people and that he accepted on condition that:

(i) Afghanistan should be internally and externally free;

(ii) the people should unite with him to avenge the assassination of Habibullah; and

(iii) the people should be free and no one be oppressed and government should be by law . .[125]

The dawn of the May month in 1919 marked the crossing of Indo-Afghan boundary by the regular Afghan force. On 1 May, 1919, Saleh Mohammad Khan, the Commander-in-Chief, moved to the Indian border, and reached at Dakka on 3 May, 1919 along with two companies of infantry "for the ostensible purpose of inspecting the border . . ."[126] In a couple of days, Mohammad Nadir Khan arrived in Khost with regular Afghan troops and Abdul Kuddus Khan proceeded to Kandhar. . .[127]

The *firman* issued by King Amanullah, which had begun to circulate among the tribesmen living on the Afghan side of the Indo-Afghan border, *inter alia*, stated in part:

> I send this order to all subjects of the Eastern circles who are sayyids, Shaikhs, Mullahs, Khans and Motabars and tell you that there is a great unrest in India. Hindus and Muhammedans have almost all remained faithful . . but it is a pity they have been rewarded by cruelty and all kinds of injustices in connection with their religion, their honour and their modesty.[128]

The *firman* further stated that the uprising occurring in India[129] also affected Afghanistan, therefore Saleh Mohammad was disputed with full power for the protection of Afghanistan's boundaries.[130] On 4 May, 1919, the Afghan troops cut the water supply to Landi Kotal once the British forces retaliated by closing the Khyber Pass. Two days later the Afghanistan forces in the region were increased and they occupied Tor Trappar and Spinatsuka.[131] The Afghans then moved three regiments from Jalalabad to Mohamand country, and Nadir Khan arrived at Khost with troops and several thousand tribesmen, most of them Ghilzais.[132]

The British retailed on 7 May, 1919 by dispatching a column to Landi Kotal and another to Parachinar. A Cavalry brigade was sent on 7 May to Shahgai on the Malagori Road.[132] In the beginning the hostilities were confined to the eastern front and the British registered some success. The tribal armies and the forces of Nadir Khan then opened up a new front and the British offensive moves were stopped. The British sent feelers to the Afghan King for ending the hostilities. On 24 May, 1919, King Amanullah responded to the British peace overtures and the British Government gladly accepted the end of hostilities in the wake of rapidly deteriorating situation in the North-West Frontier. Series of negotiations between the two countries led to the conclusion of the Anglo-Afghan Treaty on 8 August, 1919 at Rawalpindi under which Afghanistan was recognized as a fully sovereign country.[135] Amanullah paid a price for Afghan independence. "However, he was forced to recognize the Durand Line . . ."[136] It is worth mentioning here that it is Gregorian's version. Neither King Amanullah nor his predecessors of even successors to the Afghan throne ever recognized the validity of Durand Line. Hence the author does not agree with Gregorian's surmise.

Afghan-Russian Entente

When King Amanullah had assumed the reins of power in Afghanistan, the latter's confrontation with Britain was under way. Consequently, Amanullah's foreign policy followed three distinct paths—establishment of diplomatic relations with Russia, normalization of relations with Britain and forgign solidarity with the Muslim world and other free countries.

On 7 April, 1919, King Amanullah despatched two letters to Moscow. One letter sent in the name of Mahmud Tarzi, then named as Foreign Minister of Afghanistan informed the "Great President of the Russian Republic (Lenin)" of the enthronement of the benevolent Amir Amanullah Khan.[136] The second letter, a personal note from Amanullah to Lenin stressed the fact that Afghanistan was free and independent, and pointed out that the Afghan "psychology had always contained in it ideas of equality, humanity and liberty."[137] Lenin in his reply sent on 27 May, 1919, congratulated the Amir and the people of Afghanistan for their heroic defence of liberty and accepting the proposal to establish relations with Russia.[138]

In April 1919, an "Afghan Mission" headed by Maulvi Barakatullah arrived in Moscow. However, Maulvi Barakatullah, disowing any official status or relationship with Afghan Government, declared that he was neither a communist or socialist but an Asian nationalist interested in ousting the British from India.[139] In early June 1919, an Afghan mission led by Mohammad Wali Khan was cordially received in Tashkent and Russia granted permission to Afghanistan to open an Afghan consulate there. While opening the consulate, the Afghan envoy, Mohammad Aslam Khan, said: "We who have risen against the tyrannical British, and made friends with the Russian Soviet, have not done so merely to liberate ourselves or the oppressed Muhammadans of India alone. We strive for the salvation of Muhammadans all over the world".[140] The Afghan objective of establishing diplomatic relations with Russia was to make its northern borders secure and "to be able to conclude an alliance with the Soviets in case of a renewed outbreak of the Anglo-Afghan war."[141]

The Afghan Mission headed by Mohammad Wali Khan reached Moscow on 10 October, 1919 and welcomed by Narimanov, the representative of the Commissariat for Foreign Affairs and Sultan Galiev, the representative of the Revolutionary Council of the Soviet Republics. In his welcome address Narimanov, while referring to the visit of the mission as "first Ambassador" of Afghanistan further added that the "historic event proves that imperialism which aims at the enslavement and humiliation of large and small nations, has been given a death blow".[142] Sultan Daliev went further and frankly stated that Soviet Russia would render assistance to Afghanistan.[143] On 14 October, 1919, the Afghan envoy was received personally by Lenin who expressed the pleasure of his government at the presence of the Afghan Ambassador in the capital of Soviet Russia.[144] On this occasion the Afghan Ambassador handed over to Lenin, a letter from the Amir of Afghanistan and personally stressed the importance of military assistance to Afghanistan.[145] Lenin in his reply to Amir's letter on 27

November, 1919 wrote that Afghanistan was "the only independent Muslim state in the world, and the fate sends the Afghan people the great historict ask of uniting about itself enslaved Mohammedan people and leading them on the road to freedom and independence.[146] The desire of both Kabul and Moscow to normalize relations led to negotiations in Moscow in this regard.[147]

Afghan-Soviet Differences Over Bukhara

The negotiations regarding the normalization of relations between Afghanistan and the Soviet Union suffered a setback in the autumn of 1920 because of the rising differences between the two countries over the future of Bukhara. Prior to 1917, Bukhara was a protectorate of Russian Empire. In 1868, the Amir of Bukhara had acknowledged the sovereignty of the Russian Year and ceded to him the right to represent Bukhara with other powers.[148]

Following the advent of Bolshevik Revolution in Russia, the Russian leaders had made various declarations recognizing the secession of all states which had declared themselves independent from the Central Government in Moscow. However, the new Bolshevik Governments at the same time was awaiting a suitable opportunity to incorporate these states into Soviet Russia. The state of Bukhara was given tremendous revolutionary importance. The Soviet journal *Zhizn Natsionaenostei* wrote: "Bukhara represents a very important place for the development of revolution in central Asia. Either it will serve a bulwark of reaction led by Britain . . . or it will become the vanguard for a number of central Asian and Indian revolutionary movements."[149] Afghanistan also showed interest in Bukhara. King Amanullah in his pursuit of pan-Istamic policy, felt that he had a special responsibility to protect the interests of Islamic world. A Russian scholar, I.R. Reysner wrote: "The rular of Afghanistan appeared in the role of supreme protector of all Moslems, and was equally interested in the result of Greco-Turkish war, in the rising of Egypt and in the fate of

Bukhara."[150] Bukhara, besides being a Muslim country, was also of strategic importance for Afghanistan. According to Fraser-Tytler, Amanullah had dreams of a Central Asian confederacy under his own leadership of which neighbouring Bukhara would constitute an important part."[151] Most of the trade of Bukhara was conducted through Afghanistan. This flow of trade entitled Kabul to charge transit duties which, according to Reysner, constituted an important part of revenue of Afghanistan in 1920.[152] Thus in the wake of the conflicting nature of interests of Afghanistan and Russia, it was natural that any effort on the part of eithre of them to undermine the existing status of Bukhara would have been instrumental in straining their mutual relations.

In March 1918, when Kolesov, Chairman of the Turkestan Soviet Government, had moved with his troops to the capital of Bukhara, the Amir of Bukhara was openly assisted by Afghan volunteers, who undoubtedly played an important role in defeating the Soviet troops.[153] It was also reported that Afghan regular troops had crossed the frontier and for a few weeks had effectively occupied Merv and Eastern Bukhara.[154] Thus encouraged by this development, Kabul made efforts to establish even closer relations with the Amir of Bukhara, and to assist him in every possible way in order to make him strong enough to stop any further attack from Soviet territory, One of the first steps taken in this direction was the exchange of ambassadors by the two countries and making of public declarations of eternal friendship by the King of Afghanistan and Amir of Bukhara.[155]

While Afghanistan was helping Bukhara to strengthen it, the Russians were making attempts to launch another offensive against Bukhara. In August 1920, the Russian troops moved into Bukhara. The troops of the Amir of Bukhara gave a tough fight which lasted for over a week but finally on 2 September, 1920, the Red Army managed to capture the capital of Bukhara. The Amir of Bukhara fled to Afghanistan and a Soviet Government was established in Bukharan capital. On 15

September, 1920, the new Government of Bukhara, sent through the Russian envoy in Kabul, a cable to the Afghan Government requesting an exchange of diplomatic representatives between two countries and announcing firm intention to develop close relations between Bukhara and Afghanistan.[156]

However, Afghanistan continued rendering suppot to the oppositional elements in Bukhara to undermine the interest of pro-Russian elements. The Afghan activities came to the notice of Russians and on 21 September, 1920 Moscow instructed its Ambassador in Kabul to hand over to the Afghan Government a strong note containing a number of charges against Afghanistan and demanding an inquiry into the activities of the Afghan representative in Bukhara and the immediate withdrawal of the Afghan troops.[157] The future of Bukhara constituted an important issue during the negotiations between Afghanistan and Russia for concluding a friendship treaty between the two countries.

Afghan-Soviet Treaty of Friendship 1921

On 28 February, 1921, Afghanistan and Soviet Russia signed a Treaty of Friendship at Moscow which was ratified by Russia on 3 March, 1921 and by Afghanistan on 16 July, 1921.[158] The treaty was signed with the intention of "strengthening the friendly relations existing between Russia and Afghanistan and to protect the real independence of Afghanistan."[159] Article I of the treaty secured Russian recognition for independence of Afghanistan. It also enjoined upon the either side to undertake to respect it and enter into proper political relations with the other.[160] Article II provided that both countries would refrain from entering into any military or political agreement with a third party "that may be against the interests of the other party."[161] By obtaining the inclusion of such a provision in the treaty, Moscow had succeeded in forestalling in the area any military or political alliance which could have adverse effects on the Central Asian borders of Russia. Under Article IX, Russia agreed to return to Afghanistan all the lands situated in the frontier zone and which had belonged to Afghanistan in the past century.[162] Despite such a promise, Russia did not return any territory to Afghanistan.

Under Articles IV and V of the treaty, both countries agreed to open new consulates in each other's territory. Russia was to open five consulates in Afghan towns of Herat, Mezar-i-Sherif, Kandhar, Kaznein (Gazni) and Meimeneh and Afghanistan was to open seven consulates in Russia.

Under Article VII, both countries agreed to respect the freedom of the nations in the East on the basis of plebictly and self-government."[163] And as a corollary to this, Article VIII envisaged that both Russia and Afghanistan "recognise the independence and freedom of the government of Bukhara and Khiva under any form of government that may be desired by their nationals."[164] Despite such an explicit assertion in the treaty to recognise the freedom of Bukhara and Khiva by the Russians, they continued to prop up the "Bolshevik revolution" in those areas. The socalled popular revolution in Khiva in February 1920 and in Bukhara in September 1920 were "the result of subversive activities directed by Bolshevik agents in Tashkent."[165] Thus the open activities of the Bolsheviks in Bukhara and Khiva at the instance of Russians contradicted the spirit of Article VII and VIII of the Afghan-Soviet treaty of friendship as cited above. Under these circumstances, when having been faced with the open export of revolution and the breach of faith on the Russian side, the Afghan King, Amanullah considered himself entitled to accord the Amir of Bukhara all possible assistance. In March 1921, when the Amir of Bukhara was forced to leave his country in the wake of increased Bolshevik manoeuvres, the Afghan authorities welcomed him as a "guest of honour" without caring for the protests of the "government of the Bukhara People's Soviet Republic."[166]

In March 1885, the Russians occupid Panjdeh at a time when London and St. Petersburg were negotiating the precise demarcation of the new frontier between Russia and

Afghanistan.[167] During this period the Russian newspaper *Novosti* urged that Russia must press on to occupy the city of Herat and Panjdeh and so "pierce a window" looking south eastwards, a convenient halting place for a still further advance towards the Indian Ocean in fulfilment of Russia's "historic destiny."[168]

A supplementary article added to the treaty provided that within a year of coming into force of the treaty, a subsidy would be given by Russia to Afghanistan to the extent of one million rubles in gold or silver coin or bullion. It also provided for the construction of a telegraph line from Kushak through Herat and Kandhar to Kabul and place technical and other specialists at the disposal of the Afghan Government.[169] According to a news item published in London based *The Times*, Russia was also to establish a powerful radio station at Kabul and to supply engineers to improve Afghanistan's communications.[170]

Some writers have tried to interpret the conclusion of Afghan-Soviet friendship treaty of 28 February 1921 as a significant move towards Afghanistan's independence in international relations and as being "calculated to strengthen the hands of the Afghan Government in future dealings with Great Britain."[171]

However the present author does not ascribe to this view. The contemporary geo-political developments showed that despite having signed the friendship treaty, the Russians were eager to overthrow the legitimate government of King Amanullah. As Michael Valodarsky has also observed: "... point of conflict between Amanullah and Moscow was caused by evidence that the Bolsheviks were involved in the creation and activities of organizations and groups in Central Asia whose goal was to overthrow the Afghan monarchy and replace it by a pro-Soviet regime."[172] Towards the end of 1920, a group was formed under the name "The Committee of the Young Afghan Revolutionaries" in Bukhara. It declared its goal as to "overthrow the existing capitalist regime, to establish a Republican government in accordance with the people's will and thus to liberate the Afghan Nation from the despotism of the Amir and Beys and also to pave free roads for science and industry. . ."[173] The Soviet historian A. Kheifets who has traced out links between Moscow and the anti-Afghanistan organizations operating in Bukhara, and Turkestan during 1920-21, considers that the aims of these organizations "were close to the ideas of Marxism and Leninism."[174] Thus it was evident that despite its commitment to recognize the independence of Afghanistan and not to interfere in its internal affairs as envisaged in the Afghan-Soviet friendship treaty of 28 February, 1921, the Russians were busy in clandestine manoeuvres to overthrow the regime of King Amanullah.

In the backdrop of these developments, the then Foreign Minister of Afghanistan, Mahmud Tarzi, became skeptical about the outcome of the treaty and its implications for Afghanistan. He was convinced that "the obvious shift toward Moscow in Afghan foreign policy could be deterimental to Afghanistan and in the long run would not correspond to its interests."[175] Accordingly, Tarzi advised King Amanullah to exercise restraint and not to ratify the Afghan-Soviet treaty in haste.

Another apprehension that loomed large on Afghan minds was the fact of continued Russian annexation of Bukhara and Khiva and the continued presence of Russian troops in Persia (Iran) since May 1920. Besides, the Russian desire to open seven consulates in Afghan territory especially in strategic areas along the Afghan-Indian border had also alarmed the Afghan Government.

The Afghan-Soviet treaty had aroused British suspicions because only a couple of years back Britain had complete control over Afghan foreign relations and now Amanullah regime had proclaimed its independence which perhaps irritated the British. The British Government had become fearful and it voiced its concern in a note of March 1921 to Moscow that the major objective of Soviet policy in the region was to overthrow British rule in India.[176]

The Foreign Minister of Afghanistan, Mahmud Tarzi, though did not share fully the British misapprehensions yet he did admit the British anxiety over the increasing Russian influence in Afghanistan. Tarzi told the Russian Ambassador in Afghanistan, Surits, that the opening of Russian Consulates near the Afghan-Indian border, where Russia had no real interests, would be resisted by the Government of Afghanistan and could lead to deterioration in Anglo-Afghan relations. On 28 June, 1921, Surits informed Tarzi that he was prepared, "immediately after ratification of our treaty," to inform the Russian Government, "about all difficulties connected with the opening of consulates in Kandhar and Gazni and he expressed his confidence at the same time that the Soviet Government would in the meantime not open these consulates."[177] However the Afghan Government was not convinced by Surits's assurances. On 18 July, 1921, Russia again revived the question of the ratification of the treaty. The new Russian Ambassador in Kabul, Raskolmkov in a letter dated 24 July, 1921, while urging the Afghan Government to ratify the treaty reiterated the assurances given by Surits. However, there was no change in Afghan stand. Only a second letter of 30 July, 1921 from the Russian Ambassador, which hinted at the possibility of a deterioration of Soviet-Afghan relations and of a change in Moscow's position in the Anglo-Afghan conflict, produced an effect. Consequently on 13 August, 1921, the Afghan-Soviet treaty was ratified stipulating upon Moscow's refraining from opening consulates in Kandhar and Gazni. Finally on 21 November, 1921, Moscow categorically assured Afghanistan that it would not open consulates in areas specified by the latter.

It was in this background that decks were cleared for an Anglo-Afghan agreement which was signed on 22 November 1921. An official announcement made by the British authorities in India said that the British agreement with Afghanistan had been signed "after receiving assurances from the Afghan Government that Russian consulates would not be allowed in the regions of Jalalabad, Gazni and Kandhar."[178] Being provoked by the British statement, the Russian Embassy in Kabul lodged a protest with Kabul regime. This Russian move could be interpreted to mean that Moscow did not in principle relinquish the right to open these consulates and that Kabul's assurance to London had the same force as the annulment of Article V of the Afghan-Soviet treaty.[179] The Government of Afghanistan did not reply to the Russian Ambassador's protest. The pleasant aspect of the entire episode was that no Russian consulates were opend in areas objected to by Afghanistan.

King Amanullah was distrustful of both Great Britain and Russia, He did not trust either. Thus he laid emphasis on strict neutrality towards both contemporary great powers. Instead he fostered closer cooperation with Islamic countries especially Turkey and Iran. The symbol of growing friendship between Afghanistan and Turkey was best manifested in the conclusion of a Turko-Afghan friendship treaty on 1 March, 1921. Under Article I of the treaty, Afghanistan affirmed the Turkish independence and Turkey recognized Afghanistan "as independent in the most real and complete sense of the word."[180] Under Article II, both countries acknowledged the right of all Oriental Countries to absolute freedom and independence. Both countries also agreed not to enter into an agreement with a third nation, if either country objected, and to inform each other before concluding a treaty with any other country. Under Article VIII Turkey promised to send educational and military missions to Afghanistan for at least five years and to renew them thereafter at the request of Afghan Government.[181]

The two countries welcomed the awakening of the Orient as the handiwork of God, recognized the independence of Khiva and Bukhara and laid stress and acknowledged the need for establishing close contacts and relations with all the Muslim countries.[182] Turkey was recognized as the guide of Islam and upholders of the Caliphate. This treaty had tremendous geo-political significance for Afghanistan at a time when it was caught in the throes of big power rivalry. According to Gregorian Vartan: "This treaty was a most important one for Amanullah and the Afghan modernists, for Turkish military and cultural assistance was consonant with Islamic solidarity."[183]

Afghanistan, under the leadership of King Amanullah, concluded a Treaty of Friendship and Neutrality with Persia on 22 June, 1921.[184] Under Article I, both Afghanistan and Persia pledged to establish "sincere firiendship and a permanent and cardinal understanding between the two countries.[185] Articles II to VIII of the treaty referred to the mutual benefits and privileges to be accorded to the nations of each other and improvement of economic relations between the two countries. Under Article IX, both countries affirmed that the relations of cordial understanding between them would not be affected in the event of one party "becoming involved in a war with a third power. But in this case the other Party shall undertake, in accordance with the rules of neutrality, not to favour this third power in any respect."[186] The conclusion of Afghan-Persian treaty greatly strengthened Afghanistan's diplomatic position in the Middle East. Thus by concluding friendship treaties with Turkey and Persia, King Amanullah not only consolidated Afghanistan's position in the international arena but also won support for the independence of Khiva and Bukhara which had been annexed by Russia. These treaties were concluded at a time when Russia was trying to squeeze benefits from Kabul and hence it served as a deterrent to both Great Britain and Russia.

Despite King Amanullah's policy of strict neutrality, the British tended to regard him as a Soviet "Trojan Horse" but according to M.N. Roy, the Afghan made it clear that they had no intention of allowing any Soviet force to enter their territory and use it as a base of operations against India, nor did they desire to participate in such an operation.[187]

However, King Amanullah's primay concern was to steer Afghanistan by pursuing independent foreign policy without compromising the freedom and territorial integrity of Afghanistan in the presence of powerful Soviet Union and British India on its borders. He also followed the traditional policy of seeking a balance of power in the region. He signed a treaty with Britain on 22 November, 1921. The treaty provided for the establisment of legations in London and Kabul, and granted the exemption on materials destined to help modernize the country.[188] A major feature of the treaty was Afghanistan's agreement to keep the Soviet consulates out of eastern Afghanistan.[189]

The year 1922 witnessed the recrudescence of complications between Moscow and Kabul over Bukhara where the nationalists had again raised the banner of revolt against Moscow. The Russians, with a view to utilize the influence of Enver Pasha, a former, Turkish leader who had escaped to Russia after First World War, sent him to Bukhara to fight the nationalists. On the contrary, Enver Pasha joined hands with the Bukharan nationalists and managed to control important portions of Bukhara by May, 1922. King Amanullah, being encouraged by these developments, took the step of concentrating his armed forces on the northern borders and at the same time entered into correspondence with Enver Pasha.[190] However, the pro-Soviet Government of Bukhara, having "discovered Afghan complicity in the affairs," sent a formal note on 11 July, 1922 to the Afghan Foreign Ministry demanding the immediate withdrawal of Afghan aid to "rebels" in Bukhara, the extradition of all rebel leaders in Afghanistan to Soviet Russia and an assurance from the Afghan Government that Enver Pasha and his supporters would not be allowed to enter the Afghan territory.[191]

However, the Afghan Government declared that disturbances in Bukhara were "a kind of internal disorder…(and) Afghanistan remains neutral."[192] Moscow also expressed its displeasure to Kabul over these developments.[193] With a view to counter Soviet influence, King Amanullah wanted to secure support by enlisting the British support. Colonel Humphrys, the British Minister, who had arrived in Kabul on 6 March, 1922, was asked by the Afghan King to advise the London Government to publicly recognize the independence of Bukhara and Khiva to povide Afghanistan with a new lever in demanding the evacuation of Bolshevik troops.[194] Again in April, 1922 Mahmud Tarzi, the Afghan Foreign Minister requested Humphrys to supply *via* Afghanistan weapons and ammunition to the Bukhara forces but the British were reluctant to comply as they considered an eventual victory of the Soviets inevitable.[195]

Some Soviet leaders began to consider Amanullah as a puppet of the British and demanded the cancellation of the annual subsidy that Soviet Russia had been giving to Afghanistan under the treaty of 1921.[196] The death of Enver Pasha in August, 1922 and consolidation of power by Soviet Government in Bukhara and Khiva made King Amanullah to forsake his desire of consolidating Afghan power in Central Asia. In the meantime, the developments in the southern frontiers had also been taking dramatic turns. The Afghan King consequently focussed his attention on the Indo-Afghan border.

In the North-Western Frontier province (NWFP), the British followed the "forward policy" with a view to exert their administrative control in the region. King Amanullah saw British move as a slow advance towards Afghanistan. In early 1923 he visited the NWFP areas on the Afghan side and came to the conclusion that British policy was dangerous for Afghanistan as well as for the tribes living in the area,[197] The British reluctance to abandon the forward policy led to the revolt by the people in the NWFP.[198] Moscow tried to exploit the situation to its own advantage. The Russian Ambassador in Kabul, Raskalnikov, was alleged to have rceommended to Soviet authorities in Tashkent on 17 February, 1923 that the Afghan-British crisis be aggravated by the distribution of arms and money to the various tribal groups.[199] The British Government in an ultimatum sent to Moscow demanded among other things, the recall of Communist agents from India and the withdrawal of Raskolnikov from Kabul.[200] Though Moscow recalled its envoy from Kabul but the relations between Kabul and London remained estranged. In December 1923, the British Government sent an ultimatum to Kabul demanding the cessation of all Afghan support to the "rebels" in the NWFP area and severance of relstions between Kabul and Moscow.[201] The Soviet Russia denounced the British move and at the same time warned Kabul that the expulsion of Soviet ambassador from Kabul would in fact mean the end of an "independent Afghan state."[202]

King Amanullah, being a shrewd statesman, did not go by either British threats or Soviet advice. For him the national interest was supreme. Seeing the gravity of the situation, he ordered for the arrest of "rebels" who had sought asylum in Afghanistan.[203]

With a view to seize new opportunity, Moscow started negotiations for the construction of a telegraph line, a radio station, roads between the two countries and the agreement in July 1924 to commence talks at an early date for the conclusion of a commercial treaty.[204] During 1925 both countries again held negotiations to conclude a commercial agreement. The quantum of trade grew rapidly between the two countries in 1925-26. The question of the ownership of the areas of Darqad, situated in the Urta Tagai, also called Yangi Qala, an island covering about 160 square miles, in the Amu River became a bone of contention between Russia and Afghanistan. On 19 December, 1925, it was reported in the *Aman-i-Afghan*, a prestigious contemporary newspaper that Soviet troops had launched an attack on the "sacred soil of Afghanistan" resulting in Afghan casualities.[205] However, on 21 December, 1925, the same newspaper reported that the Soviet Minister Leonide Stark in his meeting with the then Afghan Foeign Minister Mahmud Tarzi, said that Russia had always would respect the integrity and sovereignty of independent Afghanistan "and that the occupation of Soviet troops of the areas of Darqad, Bustan,

Shaftalubuz and Qulabad—if it had actually occurred—must have been due to a misunderstanding."[206] The newspaper further added that about two decades prior to the occurrence of this incident, these areas had been taken over and administered by Afghanistan since then.[207] The island of Darqad is surrounded by branches of Amu River, the deeper of which was is south and formed the boundary of Afghanistan as defined by the Granville-Gortchakoff agreement of 1872 between Russia and Britain.[208] The thalweg line—the middle of the deep, was, accepted as the boundary. However by the turn of the nineteenth century, the River changed its course and the northern branch became the main river. While Afghanistan retained its hold over the area, the Russians also laid their claim over it. The issue was raised in 1906 and again in 1914. In the wake of the advent of Bolshevik Revolution in Russia in 1917, about one thousand Uzbeks refugees settled in the island which had also become a base of the Muslim freedom loving Basmachi refugees whom the Russians thought were raiding inside Soviet territory from that side.

Though Russia tried to under play its move of armed incursion into the Darqad Island but it aroused public indignation and rekindled fears of Russian aggression in Afghanistan. Between December 1925 till the end of January 1926, relations between Russia and Afghanistan remained tense over the issue. The negotiations between the two countries to solve the dispute commenced in early February 1926 and by the end of February Russian troops started evacuating from the Island. On 15 August, 1926, a Russian-Afghan protocol was signed under which Russia accepted Afghan ownership of the Island of Darqad.

Afghan-Soviet Treaty of Neutrality and Non-Aggression

On 31 August, 1926, both Kabul and Moscow signed the treaty of Neutrality and Non-Aggression.[209] Under the treaty, the two countries agreed to maintain neutrality in case either of them was involved in a military conflict with a third country.[210] It was also agreed not to take part in any alliance or agreement of a military or political character with another or several third powers which might be directed against the other contracting party. Both countries also agreed that they would abstain from interfering in the internal affairs of each other.[211] Despite the treaty, Afghanistan remained a base and a refuse for forces of resistance to the Soviets in Central Asia. "Nor did Kabul become right upto World War II, despite the agreement of 1921 and the later agreement of 1926, friendly to Russia."[212]

On 28 November, 1927, another agreement was signed between the two countries providing for the establishment of an airline between Kabul and Tashkent thus linking the two countries by air.[213] From December 1927 to July 1928, King Amanullah paid state visit to India, various countries in Europe and the Middle East. While in India, King Amanullah spoke of Islamic solidarity and in turn was hailed as the King of Islam.[214] He then visited Egypt, Italy, France and Germany. During his visit to England, he was presented the Collar of the Royal Victorian Order by King George. The visit was marked by Amanullah's visit to the various places in England.[215] During his visit to the Soviet Union, Amanullah delayed three days in Warsaw *enroute*, judiciously avoiding the May Day Celebrations in order to spare his host's embarrassment and in order to molify the British.[216] Before his return to Afghanistan, the King also visited Turkey and Iran.

King Amanullah was greatly influenced by the progress made by Europe and he now recognized the enormity of the task of modernizing Afghanistan. His western ways and radical reforms were opposed by the orthodox forces in Afghanistan. His opponents said that the King "had turned against Allah and Islam."[217] He reduced the autonomy of the tribes and the influence of the religious leaders, opposed polygamy and the veil, established schools for girls and extended the military draft to the whole country. Though these were progressive measures undertaken by King Amanullah but the vested interests were opposed to any change and preferred the *status quo*. The resultant impact was the outbreak of a revolt against King Amanullah in January which forced him to flee from Kabul to Kandhar. The leader of the rebellion was an illiterate person called Bacha-i-Saqao who proclaimed himself as the King.[218]

This new development in Afghanistan divided the leadership in Moscow on the question of rendering support to Bacha-i-Saqao. According to Agabekov, a former officer of OGPU,[219] the OGPU was in favour of aiding Bacha in the hope that he would carry out a radical revolution in Afghanistan and that through him, the country would gradually be Sovietized.[220] Consequently, he received the help of OGPU to come into power.

Soviet Invasion of Afghanistan

In view of the fluid situation in Afghanistan after Bacha-i-Saqao had proclaimed himself as the King of Afghanistan, Moscow decided to avail the situation to its own advantage. According to Agabekov "It was decided to form an expeditionary force of red soldiers disguised as Afghans who would secretly cross the frontier and march against Kabul."[221] The Soviets provided forty airplanes as well as horsemen especially equipped with machineguns.[222] Thus Soviet army entered Afghanistan and after crossing the Amu River captured the town of Mazar-i-Sharif on 30 April, 1929. There occured a fierce battle between the Russian army and the supporters of Bacha-i-Saqao near Khulm and after defeating the latter they marched toward Kabul. In the meanwhile two Basmachi leaners also conducted raids inside Soviet Union from Afghanistan, though unsuccessful. The Soviet media claimed that those attacks were instigated either by Bacha or the British.[223]

While Ghulam Nabi's army was marching toward Kabul, word came that Amanullah had abdicated and fled to India. This created a panic in the Ghulam Nabi's army of whom many had deserted.[224] The Russians promptly withdrew their troops, the last of them leaving in June 1929.[225] Another reason for Soviet Union to abandon the Afghan invasion was that Moscow did not want to alarm the British at a time when it was hoping to restore diplomatic relations with the newly elected Labour Government in London.[226] Thus by launching a well concerted attack on Afghanistan, Moscow had demonstrated that "like its Tsarist predecessor, it had ambitions regarding Afghanistan and was willing to use military force to back them up."[227] It is Worth mentioning here that Amir Amanullah neither interested nor acquired any body's help to capture power. The Amir had asked Nabi to go back.

Afghan Foreign Policy under Nadir Khan (1929-1933)

Following the defeat of Bacha-i-Saqao in October 1929, Nadir Shah became the King of Afghanistan. The new Afghan King pursued a cautions modernization programme at home and followed the traditional policy of neutrality. While giving the opening speech in the Afghan National Consultative Assembly, Nadir Shah said:

> In my opinion the best and more useful policy that one can imagine for Afghanistan is a policy of neutrality. Afghanistan must always entertain good relations with its neighbours as well as all the friendly powers who are not opposed to the national interests of the country. Afghanistan must give its neighbours assurances of its friendly attitude while safeguarding the rights of reciprocity. Such a line of conduct is the best one for the interest of Afghanistan.[228]

Nadir Shah was really faced with an uphill task which was to make Afghan neutrality a reality and to convince among others Moscow and the Islamic world—that he was not a tool of British imperialism. While refuting the charge that he had received British assistance in overthrowing Bacha, he said: "It was only through the exclusive help of the Almighty God, and thanks to the sacrifices of the people of Afghanistan, unassisted by any foreign power, that I took Kabul."[229]

He adhered to a policy of non-involvement both in India and in Central Asia seeing in "positive neutralism" the best means of securing internal stability and external independence. In May 1930, Afghanistan confirmed the Anglo-Afghan treaty of 1921 and the Trade Convention of 1923 which had envisaged the tacit understanding that no Soviet trade agencies were to be opened in the eastern provinces of the Afghan Kingdom adjacent to India. At the same time Nadir Shah |tried to put a stop to anti-British revolutionary activity in Afghanistan. He discouraged the activities of the Red Shirt Movement and the Afridi and Mohmand tribal struggles on Indo-Afghan border by making clear to them that the "whole frontier policy of the Afghan government would be actuated by a desire for peace on both sides of the frontier and a spirit of frue friendship towards His Majesty's Government."[230]

King Nadir Shah also took steps to further normalize relations with the Soviet Union, While welcoming the enthronement of Nadir Shah the Soviet Foreign Minister, Maxim Litvinov, said that Moscow intended to continue to be a good neighbour to Afghanistan and hoped to develop relations with it on the basis of existing agreements.[231] Afghanistan concluded a non-agrression pact with the Soviet Union in 1931 which was in fact the reiteration of the Afghan-Soviet treaty of 1926. The new treaty also gave Afghan commitment againt the use of Afghan territory as a base for subversive activities against the Soviet Union. Following the combined blow of Russian Army Central Asia and the suddenly effective Afghan border patrols, Basmachi activities were on the decline. The relations between Kabul and Moscow were further improved by the signing of a Soviet-Afghan agreement on the defintion of aggression.[232]

This *entente* in Afghan-Soviet relations was accompanied by an expansion of trade between the two countries. Between 1928 and 1932 Moscow gained a greater share of the Afghan market and in Herat and northern Afghanistan, goods made in Bukhara and Tashkent dominated.[233]

However, the policy of Nadir Shah with regard to forging close relations with Moscow could in no way be interpreted that he was pro-Soviet. He was scrupulous in his adherence to the Afghanistan's traditional policy of neutrality. He denied a Soviet request for establishing a commercial mission in Afghanistan.[234] In place of departing Soviet advisers, Afghanistan acquired the services of expects from Germany, Italy, Japan and India.[235] Nadir Shah wanted "foreign advisers only those who were unlikely to be supported by neighbouring armed forces in case of any disagreement."[236]

Besides, Nadir Shah also made attempts to have cordial relations with Islamic countries, especially Turkey and Iran. He also took steps in forging Afghan relations with Italy, France, Germany, United States and Japan.[237] The activities of the British and the Russians within Afghanistan were curtailed during Nadir Shah's reign.

Post-Nadir Shah Period

The Charkhi brothers especially Ghulam Nabi and other supporters of Amanullah were opposed to the regime of Nadir Shah. The execution of Ghulam Nabi in November 1932 ushered in a brief spell of political violence in Afghanistan which culminated in the assassination of Nadir Shah on 8 November, 1933. On the same day, Zahir Shah, the nineteen year old son of Nadir Shah, was proclaimed as the new King of Afghanistan. The young Zahir Shah was assisted by his paternal uncle Shah Mahmud Khan, Shah wali Khan and Mohammad Hashim Khan, the latter being the Prime Minister and being in full control of Afghanistan's domestic and foreign policies.[238]

King Zahir Shah in a speech in 1934, said that the general foreign policy aims of Afghanistan were "shaped by the desire of the King and his government for world peace so that Afghaniston could continue to combat its socio-economic retardatian and catch up with progress.[239] The King laid emphasis on three points: his desire to maittain friendly relations with all countries; his hope to live in peace and friendship with neighbouring countries, and his intention not to raise political difficulties or obstacles for other governments, a policy he anticipated other governments to adopt for Afghanistan.[240]

Strict adherence to the traditional policy of neutrality remained the main hallmark of Afghanistan foreign policy during the post-Nadir Shah period. Kabul assured the Soviet Government that the Basmachis and other emigre elements from Turkistan would not be allowed to indulge in anti-Soviet activities from its territory. Despite British protests, the Afghan Government continued to render political and moral support to the Indian freedom fighters like Raja Mahandra Pratap who had formed provisional government in Afghanistan during the reign of King Amanullah. The Afghan tribes also indulged in acts hostile to British India.[241]

Afghanistan became the member of the League of Nations in 1934 and during the same year Soviet Union also joined the League. In May 1935, Kabul and Moscow signed an agreement on an antilocust campaign and this agreement paved the way for mutual cooperation and pretext for the covening of annual meetings.[242] In 1936, Kabul renewed the Soviet-Afghan mutual pact of 1931, which was extended upto 29 May, 1946.[243] This was followed by a commercial agreement in May, 1936 which envisaged transit facilities for Afghans through Soviet Union and a financial agreement between the Soviet Commissariat for external commerce and the Bank-i-Milli.[244] Kabul and Moscow also decided to close their respective consulates in Tashkent and Mazar-i-Sharif with an avowed objective of non-interference in each other's affairs.[245] This move was welcomed by Great Britain which had campaigned since 1921 against the establishment of Soviet consulate in the strategic regions of Afghanistan.

Afghanistan During the Second World War

By the time the Second World War broke out in Europe with Japanese involvement in East Asia, Afghanistan had become heavily dependent on the financial and technical assistance of the Axis powers, especially Germany, Italy and Japan. The best way for the Allies "to have ended to dominance of the Axis in this strategic country was for the United States and Great Britain themselves to have extended technical assistance and long term credits to the Afghan Kingdom but neither chose to do so."[246] However, the only alternative before Afghanistan was to turn to the Soviet Union instead of Axis powers. But such a move was not keeping in tune with the Afghanistan's tradional policy of neutrality and it would have been highly unwelcome for the British as well. Afghanistan was opposed to both Russian and British influence in the country.

Thus, when the Second World War broke out in the early 1939, it posed a big challenge to Afghanistan's foreign and economic policies. As Vartan Gregorian has aptly observed: "The possibility that Afghanistan independence might be jeopardized or that the country might become a battleground of European diplomacy—even a theater of war—seemed very real."[247] Consequently, King Zahir Shah after consulting the Afghan Parliament, issued a decree on 6 September, 1939, proclaiming the neutrality of Afghanistan.[248] This proclamation was made with a view to keep Afghanistan away from the flames of Second World War and safeguard its independence and territorial integrity.

The decree of neutrality restricted the activities of nationals of the belligerent powers; no propaganda activities were to be tolerated and the dissemination of news was restricted to official press releases by the government of the belligerent in the Kabul daily *Islah*.[249]

In the wake of the Nazi-Soviet non-aggression pact concluded in 1939, Moscow did not pressurize Kabul to sever its relations with the Axis powers until 1941. And the British being deeply involved in the war in Europe also did not raise any eyebrow in this regard.

During 1939-41 period, Germany made further efforts to woo Afghans, including the supporters of Amanullah, to create troubles among the tribesmen of the NWFP to weaken the position of the British but King Zahir Shah's Government refused to comply with German overtures and reiterated its commitment to the policy of strict neutrality.[250] W.K. Fraser-Tytler, who during that period was a British envoy to Kabul, described the situation as one in which "the Afghans figuratively buttoned their coats and turned their backs to the blast, couching behind the frail shelter of their international frontiers, and their proclaimed neutrality. . . hoping that the whirlwind would pass them by. . .'"[251]

The events had taken decisive turn during the close of 1941 and following the German invasion of the Soviet Union, the latter had joined the Allies. There were hundreds of Axis powers' nationals in Afghanistan during that period and the changed war scenario was bound to give worries to Kabul. Both Iran and Afghanistan were of strategic significance for the Allies. The presence of Axis subjects in Afghanistan was bound to attract the attention of the Allies. In October 1941, Moscow and London sent similar notes to the Afghan Government demanding the ouster of German and Italian citizens.[252] This demand by the powerful neighbours of Afghanistan had created misapprehensions among the minds of many Afghans. Finally the Zahir Shah's Government after consulting the *Loya Jirga*, decided to comply with the demand and at the same time reiterated Afghanistan's will and determination to preserve its strict neutrality, independence and territorial integrity.[253] With a view to induce the Afghan Government in order to free some of its troops on the NWFP area for use in European battlefields, the British reportedly offered Afghanistan a free port on the Indian Ocean and the construction of a railroad from Chaman to Kandhar to provide Afghanistan with a link to the sea.[254] However Afghaistan in pursuance of its declared policy of strict neutrality declined the British offer.

Accordingly, Kabul was placed under strict surveillance and gasoline rationing was imposed in July 1941. During the same month, the Afghan border guards shot two German Agents on their way to the camp of the Fakir of Ipi resulting in the death of one and other was wounded. The then Afghan Prime Minister, Hashim Khan, conveyed his regrets to the Germans over the incident.[255] Following the British and Soviet invasion of Iran during the last week of August 1941, the Germans were trapped in Afghanistan. Both Moscow and London exerted pressure on Kabul for the expulsion of Axis nationals from Afghanistan. The German legation in Kabul was not satisfied with the British promise of safe passage for the Axis nationals trapped in Afghanistan. However, on 15 October, 1941, Najibullah Khan, the Director-General of the Political Department of the Afghan Foreign Ministry, explained Afghanistan's actions in yielding to Allied pressures as being prompted by his Government's desire for peace.[256] The British propaganda and reports in the Indian press continued reporting about the dangers inherent in the continued presence of Axis in Afghanistan.[258]

During this perod of crisis, the Afghan Government reiterated its policy of peace and neutrality and expressed surpise over the excess propaganda over the presence of Axis nationals in Afghanistan. The *Loya Jirga* met during 5-6 November, 1941 to approve the dismissal of the Germans and at the same time it confirmed Afghanistan's neutrality and as a warning issued a declaration that no further fight or interference would be tolerated.[258]

Following the departure of the Axis nationals from Afghanistan there was no more further pressure from Great Britain or Soviet Union in this regard and perhaps both London and Moscow were convinced of Afghanistan's adherence to strict neutrality.

The Durand Agreement

The Durand Line Agreement was signed between Afghanistan and British India in November, 1893.[259] Under this agreement,

Afghanistan agree to relinquish its control over all districts to the north of the Upper Oxus in exchange for all districts, not held by Afghanistan in the south of the Oxus river.[260] Afghanistan was also allowed to retain Asmar Kunar and Birmal Valley. Afghanistan in return promised not to advance or interfere in Chitral, Bajaur and Swat and relinquished its claim to Chagai, Dawa and Waziristan.[261] The conclusion of the agreement was facilitated by Sir Mortimer Durand on behalf of the British Government and it came to be known after him. The line demarcating the frontier between Afghanistan and British India came to be known as Durand Line.

The task of demarcation of frontier between British India and Afghanistan, as envisaged in the Durand agreement, was carried out for the most part by joint commission of the two countries during 1894-1896, except a small portion remaining undemarcated in the vicinity of Mohmand and Khyber.[262] The Durand agreement instead of solving the border problem, envisaged more complications for Afghanistan. The tribes inhabiting the areas which had come under British rule after the demarcation, were opposed to the very idea of delimitation of the boundary and regarded it as an interference with their independence.[263] When the map demarcating the boundary-line was sent by the British to Abdur Rahman, then the Afghan King, the latter protested against it by pointing out many discrepancies but the British insisted that the frontier drawn on the map was final and Kabul was bound to follow it. The intransigence shown by the British led to large scale uprising on the frontier areas in 1897.[264] Under these circumstances the Durand agreement came under severe criticism. According to Fraser-Tytler, the Durand agreement presented the concrete symbol of compromise, "the manifestation of a policy which, whatever its merit, was not carried out to its logical conclusion."[265] He regarded it illogical from the standpoint of ethnography, strategy and geography as it cut across the people split the nation into two and even divided the tribes.[266] According to C.C. Davies, the Durand agreement was forced on

Afghanistan and the new boundary line was not based on sound topographical data "for during the process of demarcation it was discovered that certain places marked on the Durand map, did not exist on the actual ground. Many ethnic absurdities were perpetrated... the worst blunder of all was the arrangement by which the boundary cut the Mohmand tribal area into two separate parts."[267] King Abdur Rahman refused to accept the agreement and permanent cession of any Afghan territory to the British under this agreement.[268] In 1901, the British created the North West Frontier Province (NWFP) in which included Baluch and Pakhtoon inhabited areas "grabbed" by the British from Afghanistan after the Durand agreement. The British Government used every opportunity to impose the validity of Durand Line on Afghanistan. The Treaty of Peace between the British Government and the Government of Afghanistan concluded at Rawalpini on 8 August, 1919 contained Article V which *inter alia* stated: "The Afghan Government accepts the Indo-Afghan frontier accepted by the late Amir."[269] At this stage, the Afghan Government could not succeed in getting the Durand Line agreement abrogated largely due to the fact that it was a temporary treaty. But this could not be interpreted as shift in Afghan stand on the issue. Soon after the conclusion of the treaty, a British Commission, on the basis of a proviso in the treaty, unilaterally demarcated a portion of the yet undemarcated section of the Durand Line west of the Khyber in August and September 1919, resulting in the addition to British territory of an area claimed by the Afghans.[270]

The Afghan Government utilized every opportunity to impress upon the British the urgency of undoing the Durand agreement and return of Pushtun areas under British occupation to Afghanistan as a precondition for establishing durable friendship between the two countries, In April 1920, when negotiations between the British and Afghan Governments commenced for concluding a friendship treaty, the then Afghan Foreign Minister. Mahmud Tarzi in his talks with his British counterpart insisted that the settlement of the tribal matters between the two countries could be reached by Britain's either ceding the tribal areas to Afghanistan or granting them independence. According to Abdul Samad Ghaus, it was for the first time that Afghanistan invoked the principle of self-determination in the search for a solution to the problem of Pashtun areas under British domination.[271] However the British showed intransigence to the Afghan proposal.

So serious was the Afghan concern and attachment with the Pushtun tribes living on British Indian side of the Durand Line that King Amanullah, even on the occasion of signing 1921 treaty with the British told the British representative that the treaty could not be one of friendship but only of neighbourly relations so long as Britain oppressed Muslims, especially the Pushtun tribes.[272] Even during the negotiation stage, between the British delegation and Afgan delegation to conclude the treaty in January 1921, the question of Pushtuns again cropped up. The Afghan delegation basing its position on the principle of self-determination, wanted the return of territories lost to Britain or the complete independence of trans-Durand Pashtuns. However, the British rejected this. The Pushtun question was so difficult to deak with that it "threatened several times to lead to rupture in the negotiation and according to Debbs, a breakdown was averted only when Britain signed a trade agreement with Russia on 17 March, 1921."[273]

Afganistan's concern for the Pushtuns in trans-Durand area was dealt with only vaguely in Article XI of the Anglo-Afghan Treaty signed on 22 November, 1921 which referred to the parties "goodwill" and "benevolent intention towards the tribes residing close to their respective boundaries. Both parties were obligated to inform the other of any military operations of major importance that were contemplated for the maintenance of order in their respective spheres.

Even after the conclusion of Anglo-Afghan Treaty of November 1922, the Afghan concern for Pushtuns had not susbsided. During the regime of King Amanullah, the Afghan support to Pushtun continued. The British had forced the Durand Line Agreement on Afghanistan. However the British writ did not run upto the Durand Line. It stopped at the administrative frontier just outside the settled areas protected by British military cantonments.[274] The Pushtun inhabited areas were quite autonomous for all intents and purposes.

The Afghan Kings who succeeded Amir Amanullah also continued voicing concern at the forced Durand Line Agreement and expressed Afghan solidarity with the trans-Durand Pushtuns. In September 1931, King Nadir Shah in his speech to *Loya Jirgah* made it clear that the fate of the Pushtun tribes in what he called the *Sarhad-i-Azad* (Free Frontier), were of special concern to the Afghan Government.[275]

Until the British withdrawal from the Indian subcontinent and the subsequent partitioning of it into India and Pakistan, the differences over Pushtun issue and Durand Line remained between Afghanistan and British authorities in undivided India. Following the emergence of Pakistan as a free and independent geographic and political entity, the Pushtun areas of trans-Durand Line in the North West Frontier Provinces were ceded to Pakistan by the British, contrary to the hopes of Afghanistan. According to Abdul Samad Ghaus, as far back as in 1944, when the Allies victory in the Second World War had been ensured and the developments in the Indian subcontinent indicated that the British might transfer power to the native people, the Government of Afghanistan had informed the British Government that the former hoped to be consulted should a change occur affecting the fate of the Pushtuns living east and south of the Durand Line.[276] The British authorities did not respond favourably to Afghan request. However, "certain statements made later by Lord Mountbatten, the last viceroy of India, were construed by the Afghans as implying that their views with regard to the future status of the Pushtun areas would be sought when independence was granted to India.[277] On 3 June, 1947, when the Independence of India Act was approved by the British Parliament, "with the provision that a plebiscite in British India (but not the princely states) should give the population the choice of joining Hindu India or Muslim Pakistan",[278] then the princely or native states had three options: (i) joint India, or (ii) join Pakistan; or (iii) remain independent for a specified period until a decision could be made to join India or Pakistan.[279] The case of North-West Frontier Province (NWFP) was to be determined by a plebiscite enabling it to join one of the new states. The Government of Afghanistan in a prompt protest to British Government asked that "two additional choices be offered to the North-West Frontier Province—Union with Afghanistan or the establishment of a separate Pushtun nation. Their request brought a curt refusal; a second request was met with silence.[280]

In view of the partitioning of the Indian subcontinent, the communal violence had assumed unprecedented proportions. The Congress controlled government of the NWFP wanted its union with India while the local Pushtun and other tribes wanted independence. However the departing British authorities hurriedly conducted a plebiscite in the late July 1947 in the NWFP without consulting Afghanistan. The Pushtun leaders asked their followers to boycott the plebiscite. The outcome of the stage-managed plebiscite held under the aegis of the British authorities, as summed up by Arnold Fletcher, was:

> . . 289,244 votes for union with Pakistan and 2,074 for union with India. The Afghans, however, were unimpressed by the seeming one sidedness of the result. They pointed out that only 55.5 per cent of the eligible voters cast ballots in the plebiscite, whereas 68 per cent had voted in the provincial elections of the previous year--an indication that a considerable number had boycotted the polls. The Afghans maintained, furthermore, that any other result would have been impossible in a land that was 98 per cent Muslim. . .[281]

The result of the plebiscite was also rejected by the nationalist Pashtun leaders. Following the emergence of

Pakistan as an independent country in August 1947, the area of NWFP was ceded to Pakistan on the basis of the plebiscite. The British who were still in control of affairs played another mischief. They held a series of Jirgas within the tribal elders of the Tribal Agencies in November 1947 to discern their wishes as to the future political status of the tribal helt. These Jirgas were held at a time when trouble in Kashmir had started. Undoubtedly, "these developments had stimulated pro-Pakistan sentiments in the tribal areas".[282] It is worth mentioning here that the tribal elders having opted for attachment of the Tribal Agencies to Pakistan, had, however, in their written statements, expressed the wish that the tribes "preserve the same relations with Pakistan as they had with the British.[283]

Afghanistan declared the plebiscite in NWFP and the tribal jirgas null and void on the ground that the colonial British masters had imposed these against the wishes of the majority of the native people without giving them an opportunity to properly decide their own future. Subsequently Afghanistan demanded the right of self-determination for the Pushtuns east and south of the Durand Line. Thus the Durand Line agreement which had been the bone of contention between Afghanistan and the British India, now emerged as the major area of disagreement between Afghanistan and Pakistan. This controversy inherited by Pakistan as a colonial legacy from the British and its reluctance to accede to Afghan demand for right of self-determination for the Pashtuns remained a major obstacle in the normalization of relations between Kabul and Islamabad in subsequent years. The potential of Pushtun issue as a pawn in super powers' rivalry in Afghanistan has been analysed in appropriate places in the present study.

It is evident from the above analysis that Afghanistan preserved its freedom, independence, sovereignty and territorial integrity throughout the ages by pursuing on independent and neutral policy. By the time Afghanistan consolidated itself politically under the leadership of Ahmad Shah Abdali by the middle of eighteenth century, the British power in India and

Russian power in Central Asia had gained foothold. The subsequent period witnessed Afghanistan being in the midst of severe Anglo-Russian rivalry. However, the Afghans paid price by laying down their lives in three Anglo-Afghan wars and confrontations with Russia to preserve their independence and territorial integrity. It was Amir Amanullah who secured Afghan independence both from Russia and Britain by getting it recognized in respective treaties. He laid the foundations of a modern and strong Afghanistan which in the post-war period were further consolidated by Sardar Mohammad Daoud Khan.

The conclusion of the Second World War in 1945 changed the international political scenario which left its mark on Afghanistan as well. The war-time allies—United States and Soviet Union emerged as the main rivals for dominating the world scenes. The traditional great power—United Kingdom had lost its "Sun never sets in the British empire" status, and its withdrawal from the Indian subcontinent in 1947 changed the geopolitical power configuarations. The traditional Anglo-Russian rivalry was replaced by Soviet-US rivalry which unleashed an era of cold war. The impact of super power rivalry on Afghanistan and its response to it in the post-war period forms the subject of subsequent analysis.

REFERENCES

1. A.H. Habibi, "Afghans and Afghanistan", *Afghanistan* (Kabul). Vol. XXII, No. 2, Summer 1969, p. 1.
2. Hasan Kawun Kakar, *Government and Society in Afghanistan: The Reign of Amir Abdul-Rahman Khan* (Austin: University of Texas Press, 1979), p. xv.
3. *Ibid.*, p. xvi.
4. For details see, Ghulam Muhammad Ghobar, *Khurasan* (Kabul: History Association, 1946).
5. Mountstuart Elphinstone, *An Accouut of the Kingdom of Caubul* (London: Richard Bentley, 1839), p. 200.
6. Kakar, No. 2, p. xvi.

7. *Ibid.*
8. A.R. Pazhwak, *Aryana: Ancient Afghanistan* (London: Royal Embassy of Afghanistan, 1957), p. 7.
9. Saifi Herawi, *Risala-i-Tariqi-i-Qismat-i-Ab-i-Qalb* (The Irrigation of Herat), edited by Magil T. Herawi (Tehran, 1968), p. 77.
10. Louis Dupree, *Afghanistan* (New Jersey: Princeton University Press, 1978), p. xviii.
11. A. Foucher, *The Ancient Way of India and Bactee to Taxila* (Paris, 1947), pp. 235-52.
12. For details see, Pazhwak, No. 8, pp. 77-91.
13. T.W. Arnold and A. Guillaume, *The Legacy of Islam* (Oxford, 1936), p. 79.
14. Vartan Gregorian, *The Emergence of Modern Afghanistan* (Stanford, Calif.: Stanford University Press, 1969), p. 14.
15. G.N. Molesworth, *Afghanistan 1919* (Bombay: Asia Publishing House, 1962), p. 3.
16. Gregorian, No. 14, p. 15.
17. Molesworth, No. 15, p. 4.
18. Gregorian, No. 14, p. 43.
19. *Ibid.*, p. 45.
20. Ludwig W. Adamec. *Afghanistan's Foreign Affairs to the Mid-Twentieth Century* (Tucson: Arizona: The University of Arizona Press, 1974), p. 2.
21. G.P. Tate, *The Kingdom of Afghanistaa* (Bombay: Times of India Press, 1911), p. 71.
22. Sultan Mohammad Khan, *Tarikh-i-Afghanistan* (n.d.), p. 27.
23. Asghar H. Bilgrami, *Afghanistan and British India, 1793-1907* (New Delhi: Sterling Publishers, 1972), p. 13.
24. Gregorian, No. 14, p. 51.
25. For full text of the treaty see, C.U. Aitchison, *A Collection of Treaties, Engagements and Sanads Relating to India and the Neighbouring Countries* (Calcutta: Government Printing Press, 1909), Vol. VIII, p. 44.
26. Bilgrami, No. 23, p. 35.
27. Aitchison, No. 25, Vol. XI, p. 309.
28. *Ibid.*

29. For text of the Treaty, see *ibid.*, Vol. XIII, pp. 53-55.

30. The name Persia is used for Iran here because the official use of name "Iran" was started only in 1937. Hence prior to that reference is made to Persia in the present study.

31. For text of the treaty of 1809, see Aitchison, No. 25, Vol. XIII, (Calcutta: Government of India Publication Branch, 1933), pp. 53-55.

32. *Ibid.*

33. For text of Anglo-Persian treaty of 1814, see *ibid.*, p. 54. Also see J.C. Hurewitz, *Diplomacy in the Near and the Middle East: A Documentary Survey 1535-1914* (New York, 1956), Vol. I, pp. 86-88.

34. Philip E. Mosley, *Russian Diplomacy and the Opening of the Eastern Question 1838-39* (Cambridge, Mass., 1934), pp. 3-4.

35. H.W.C. Davis, "The Great Game in Asia: 1800-1844", *Proceedings of the British Academy* (Oxford, 1926), p. 230.

36. Vincent A. Smith, ed., *Oxford History of India* (Third edn.) (Oxford, 1958), p. 591.

37. *Ibid.*, p. 603.

38. John William Kaye, *History of the War in Afghanistan* (London, 1851), Vol. I, p. 273.

39. Text of the Treaty given in Sir Edward Hertslet, ed., *Commercial Treaties, 1827-1925* (London, 1936), Vol. VIII, p. 719, cited in Gregorian, No. 14, p. 100.

40. Smith, No. 36, p. 591.

41. For details see, Kaye, No. 38, pp. 355-59. Also see, Sir Percy Sykes, *A History of Afghanistan* (London: Macmillan, 1940), Vol. II, pp. 3-6.

42. For details see, Kaye, No. 38, Vol. II, pp. 218-46.

43. For details see, Munawar Khan, *Anglo-Afghan Relations: 1798-1878* (Peshawar, 1963).

44 Bilgrami, No. 23, p. 109.

45. Percy Sykes, *A History of Afghanistan*, Vol. I (London; Macmillian and Co., 1940), pp. 407-408.

46. For the text of the treaty, see Bilgrami, No. 23, pp. 313-15.

47. NAI, Diary of H.B. Lumsden, entry for 18 April, 1857.

48. Demetrius C. Boulger, *Central Asian Question, Essays on Afghanistan, China and Central Asia* (London, 1885), p. 62. Also see, Anupchand Kapur, "Disraeli's Forward Policy in the North-west Frontier of India, 1874-1877," *The Research Bulletin of the Punjab University* (Lahore), No. 1, 1951, pp. 4-6.

49. H.C. Rawlinson, *England and Russia in the East* (London, 1875), p. 14.

50. For details regarding "Forward Policy", see W.K. Fraser-Tytler, *Afghanistan* (London: Oxford University Press, 1950), pp. 137-47.

51. Sirdar Ikbal Ali Shah, *Modern Afghanistan* (London: Sampson Low, 1938), p. 21.

52. Betty Balfour, *Lord Lytton's Indian Administration* (London: Longmans, 1899), pp. 247-48.

53. Shah, No. 51, p. 22.

54. For text of the Treaty of Gandamak, see Aitchison, No. 24, Vol. XI (Calcutta, 1909), pp. 344-47.

55. Ludwig W. Adamec, *Afghanistan, 1900-1923: A Diplomatic History* (Berkeley, Calif. University of California Press, 1967), p. 14.

56. National Archives of India (NAI, New Delhi), Foreign and Political Department, Secret F, Nos. 243-50, June 1880, No. 244A.

57. *Ibid.*, Nos. 143-44, August 1905, No. 143.

58. Adamec, No. 55, p. 17.

59. NAI, No. 56, Nos. 34-40, August 1889, No. 34.

60. *Ibid.*, Nos. 256-80, July 1880, No. 261, p. 8.

61. For the full text of this Proclamation, see Stephen Wheeler, *The Ameer Abdur Rahman* (London, 1895), pp. 248-50.

62. NAI, No. 56, Nos. 213-239, August 1882, K.W. I, p. 4.

63. *Ibid.*, Nos. 475-88, June 1892, No. 475.

64. Adamec, No. 55, p. 23.

65. NAI, No. 56, Nos. 76-83, August 1899, No. 81A, pp. 6-7.

66. *Ibid.*, Nos. 573-77, August 1892, No. 575, p. 5.

67. Adamec, No. 55, p. 24.

68. Mir Munshi Sultan Mahomed Khan, ed., *The Life of Abdur Rahman* (London, 1900), Vol. II, p. 260.

69. *Ibid.*

70. *Ibid*, p. 272.

71. *Ibid.*, p. 266.

72. *Ibid.*, p. 171.

73. Adamec, No. 20, p. 9.

74. NAI, No. 56, Nos. 1-129, November 1901, Nos. 9, 22, 36.

75. *Ibid.*, Nos. 8-48, December 1901, No. 37.

76. *Ibid.*

77. *Ibid.*, No. 106-108, May 1899, No. 108.

78. *Ibid.*, Nos. 145-47, May 1900, Note No. 147, Encl. 1, p. 55.

79. Quoted in Adamec, No. 55, p. 33.

80. *Ibid.*

81. NAI, No. 55, Nos. 145-46, May 1900, No. 147, Encl. 1, p. 59.

82. *Ibid.*, Nos. 42-183, February 1904. Encl. 1, No. 147.

83. *Ibid.*, Nos. 83-162, August 1903, No. 155, Notes.

84. Adamec, No. 20, p, 10.

85. NAI, Foreign Section F, No. 34-136, January 1905, No. 125, Notes.

86. For text of the Treaty see Aitchison, No. 25, Vol. XIII, pp. 282-83.

87. Ibid.

88. Augus Hamilton, *Problems of the Middle East* (London, 1909), p. 268.

89. *Ibid.*, Also see, Mohammad Ali, *Afghanistan: The Mohammedzai Period* (Kabul, 1959), p. 148.

90. C. Colin Davies, *The Problem of the North-West Frontier* (Cambridge, U.K., 1932), p. 167.

91. Lansdowne to Benckendorff, 17 February, 1907, *British Documents on the Origin of War, 1898-1917* (London, 1929), Vol. IV, pp. 520-21.

92. *Ibid.*

93. Lansdowne to Hardinge, 8 March, 1905, *ibid.*, p. 521.

94. *Ibid.*

95. *Ibid.*, pp. 203-7.

96. *Ibid.*

97. *Ibid.*, pp. 203-4, Enclosure in No. 193.

98. For details about British policy towards France and Germany see, *ibid.*, Vol. III, pp. 379-440.

99. For the text of the Convention dealing with Afghanistan, see C.H. Phillips, *The Evolution of India and Pakistan 1858-1947* (London, 1962), pp. 485-86.

100. British Documents, No 91, Vol. IV, p. 535.

101. Gregorian, No. 14, p. 211.

102. Percy Sykes, *History of Afghanistan* (London, 1940), Vol. II, p. 47.

103. NAI, Foreign Section F, No. 111, 14 August 1908.

104. *Ibid.*, No. 94-128, October 1908, No. 98.

105. *Ibid.*, No. 99.

106. *Ibid.*, E. Grey to A. Nicolson, 13 October 1908, Nos. 51-65, December 1908, No. 61.

107. *Ibid.*

108. Hardinge to Habibullah, 7 August, 1914, *British Documents*, No. 91, Vol. 4, pp. 528-29,

109. Habibullah to Hardinge, 18 August, 1914, *ibid.*, pp. 540-42.

110. India Office (London), PS Papers 4741 (1914), Memo, No. 373.

111. *Ibid.*

112. NAI, FPS War, Nos, 1-202, December 1915, No. 12.

113. *Ibid.*, March 1916, No. 16, p. 7.

114. *Ibid.*, Frontier B, May 1916, Nos. 1-288, No. 280.

115. India Office, N. 110, Memo A-173a.

116. For details see Adamec, No. 55, pp. 28-40.

117. NAI, Foreign Secret F. Nos, 705-806, October 1920, No. 705, Notes.

118. *Ibid.*

119. *Ibid.*

120. *Ibid.*, No. 706, Notes.

121. *Ibid.*, No. 705, Notes.

122. NAI, Foreign Secret B, Nos. 92-101, September 1919, No. 98.

123. *Ibid.*, Foreign Secret F, Nos. 705-806, October 1920, No. 720.

124. Harish Kapur, *Soviet Russia and Asia, 1917-27* (Geneva: Victor Chevalier, 1965), p. 216.

125. NAI, Foreign Secret B, Nos. 18-191, September 1919, No. 121.

126. Adamec, N. 54, p. 111.

127. NAI, Foreign Secret F, Nos. 1-235, July 1919, No. 1.

128. *Ibid.*, Nos. 1-200B, August 1919, Appendix to Notes.

129. During that period, the Khalifat movement was launched in India which called upon the British Government that Indian Muslims could cooperate with the British during the war the latter did not launch was against Turkey, the seat of Khilafat.

130. NAI, Foreign Secret F, Nos. 1-230B, August 1919, Appendix to Notes.

131. India Office Library (London), Memoranda Nos. A 177, A 183.

132. *Ibid.*

133. *Ibid.*

134. For text of the Treaty see, Aitchison, No. 25, Vol. XIII, pp. 286-88.

135. Gregorian, No. 14, p. 231.

136. For the text of the letter, see *Ministerctvo Innostranikh del SSSR*, Vol. II, p. 175 as cited in Kapur, No. 124, p. 217.

137. *Ibid*,

138. *The Times* (London), 13 June, 1919.

139. Xenia J. Eudin and Robert C. North, eds., *Soviet Russia and the East 1920-1927* (Stanford: Stanford University Press, 1957), p. 83.

140. Adamec, No. 20, p. 53.

141. *The Times* (London), 28 October, 1919.

142. *Ibid.*

143. *Ibid.*

144. *Ibid* , 15 October, 1919.

145. Louis Fischer, *The Soviets in World Affairs: 1917-1929* (London: Jonathan Cape, 1930), Vol. 1, p. 286.

146. Kapur, No. 124, p. 221.

147. *Ibid*

148. For background details, see, Joshua Kunitz, *Dawn Over Samarkand, The Rebutt of Central Asia* (New York, 1955).

149. *Zhizn Natsionalnostei* (Moscow), No. 6 (14), 23 February, 1919, cited in Kapur, No. 124, p. 223.

150. I.R. Reysner, *Afghanistan* (Moscow, 1946), p. 205.

151. W.K. Fraser-Tytler, *Afghauistan: A Study of Political Developments in Central and Southern Asia* (London: Oxford University Press, 1953), p. 203.

152. Reysner, No. 150, pp. 205-207.

153. Sir George MaCartney, "Bolshevism as I saw it in Tashkent in 1918", *Journal of Central Asian Society* (London), Vol. VII, Parts 2-3, 1920, p. 44.

154. *L'Asie Francaise* (Paris), May 1923, p. 500, cited in Kapur, No. 124, p. 224.

155. Kunitz, No. 148, p. 118.

156. *Ministerctvo Innostranikh del SSR*, Vol. III, p. 183, cited in Kapur, No. 124, p. 224.

157. *Ibid.*, p. 225.

158. For full text of the Treaty see L. Shapiro, *Soviet Treaty Series* (Washington, D.C.: The Georgetown University Press, 1950), Vol. I, pp. 96-97.

159. *Ibid.*, p. 96.

160. *Ibid.*

161. *Ibid.*

162. *Ibid.*, p. 97.

163. *Ibid.*

164. *Ibid.*

165. Michael Volodarsky, "First Steps in Soviet Diplomacy Towards Afghanistan, 1917-1921", in Yaacov Ro'i (ed.), *The USSR and the Muslim World* (London, 1984), p. 220.

166. *Ibid.*

167. John C. Griffiths, *Afghanistan* (New York: Praeger, 1967), p. 24.

168. *Ibid.*

169. Gregorian, No. 14, p. 232.

170. *The Times* (London), 21 September, 1921.

171. Kapur, No. 120, p. 229.

172. Volodarsky, No. 161, p. 229.

173. A. Kheifets, "Uzy dobrososedstvaibratva nerastorzhimy", *Azia i Afrika segodnia*, No. 2. (1981), pp. 17-18, as cited in, *Ibid.*, p. 221.

174. *Ibid.*

175. *Ibid.*, pp. 221-29.

176. *British Command Papers*, No. 1869 (London, 1921), p. 7.

177. Cited in Volodarsky, No. 161, p. 222.

178. *Ibid.*, p. 223.
179. Cited in, US Congress, House of Representatives, *An Assessment of the Afghanistan Sanctions: Implications for Trade and Diplomacy in the 1980s* (Washington, 1981), p. 4.
180. For the text of Turko-Afghan treaty, see A.J. Toynbee (ed.), *Survey of Internatianal Affairs 1925*, Vol. I (London, 1927), pp. 385-87
181. *Ibid.*, p. 387.
182. Gregorian, No. 14, p. 234.
183. *Ibid.*
184. For full text of Afghan-Persian Treaty, see League of Nations, *Treaty Series*, Vol. XXXIII, pp. 295-301.
185. *Ibid.*, p. 295.
186. *Ibid.*, p. 297.
187. M.N. Roy, *Memoirs* (New Delhi, 1964), pp. 492-93.
188. See Aitchison, No. 24, pp. 288-96.
189. *Ibid.*
190. Fraser Tytler, No. 147, p. 203.
191. Kapur, No. 120, pp. 234-35.
192. Adamec, No. 19, p. 71.
193. Kapur, No. 120. p. 235.
194. Adamec, No. 19, p. 70.
195. *Ibid.*
196. Fischer, No. 141, Vol. II, p. 786.
197. Fraser-Tytler, No. 151, p.
198. For details see, Toynbee, No. 178, p. 563.
199. Great Britain, *Command Papers*, No. 1869, p. 7.
200. *Ibid.*, p. 13.
201. Kapur, No. 124, p. 237.
202. *Ibid.*, p. 238.
203. Toynbee, No. 178, p. 564.
204. *Ministerctvo Innostranikh del SSR*, Vol. VII, p. 395, cited in Kapur, No. 124, p. 239.
205. *Aman-i-Afghan* (Kabul), 19 December, 1925. Also see, National Archives of India, File No. 33-F, 1926, Nos. 1-59, Affairs of Badakhshan.

206. Cited in Adamec, No. 20, p. 109.

207. See *Aman-i-Afghan*, 21 December, 1925.

208. Adamec, No. 20, p. 109.

209. For full text see Shapiro, No. 158, pp. 322-23.

210. *Ibid.*, p. 322.

2.11 *Ibid.*

212. A. Michael Volodarsky, "First Steps in Soviet Diplomacy towards Afghanistan, 1917-21", in Yaacov Roi (ed.), *The USSR and the Muslim World: Issues in Domestic and Foreign Policy* (London: George Allan and Unwin, 1984), p. 223.

213. For full text, see *ibid.*, pp. 356-57.

214. *Muslim Outlook* (Lahore), 24 July, 1928.

215 *Ibid.*

216. Dupree, No. 10, p. 450.

217. *Ibid.*

218. Nancy P. Newell and Richard S. Newell, *The Struggle for Afghauistan* (.thaca, N.Y.: Cornell University Press, 1981), pp. 37-38.

219. The Russian name for the then secret service, predecessor of the present K.G.B.

220. Georges Agabekov, *OGPU, The Russian Secret Terror* (New York: Brentano's 1931), p. 164.

221. *Ibid.*, pp, 166-67.

222. India Office Library (London), LPS/10/1203, p. 135/1927.

223. Adamec, N.

224. Leon B. Poullada, *Reform and Rebellion in Afghanistan, 1919-1929* (Ithaca, N.Y : Cornell University Press, 1973), p. 186.

225. Agabekov, No. 215, p. 168.

226. Fischer, No. 145, Vol. II, p. 817.

227. Thomas T. Hammond, *Red Flag Over Afghanistan* (Boulder, Col.: West View Press, 1984), p. 18.

228. *Islah* (Kabul), 8 July, 19 1.

229. *Ibid.*

230. Fraser-Tytler, No. 151, p. 236.

231. Jane Degras, ed., *Soviet Documents on Foreign Policy* (Oxford, 1952), Vol. II, pp. 430-31.

232. On this Soviet-Afghan Agreement, see *Islah*, 13 July, 1933.

233. Abdul Qadir Khan, "The Outlook in Afghanistan", *Journal of the Royal Central Asian Society* (London), July, 1932, pp.

234. Louis Dudree, "Afghanistan's Big Gamble, Part I", *American Universities Field Staff Reports (AUFSR)*, Vol. 4, No. IV, 1960, p. 14.

235. *Ibid*

236. Anthony Arnold, *Afghanistan: The Soviet Invasion in Perspective* (Stanford, Cali.: Stanford University Press, 1985), p. 21.

237. For details see, Gregorian No. 14, pp. 335-37.

238. Fraser-Tytler, No. 151, p. 243.

239. For full text of King Zahir Shah's speech, see *Kabul Alamanach* 1933.

240. *Ibid*.

241. Joseph Castagne, "Soviet Imperialism in Afghanistan", *Foreign Affairs* (New York), July 1935, p. 703.

242. Percy Sykes, "Afghanistan: The Present Position", *Journal of Royal Central Asian Society* (London), April 1940, p. 161.

243. For the text of the agreement, see Jane Degras, ed., *Calendar of Soviet Documents on Foreign Policy* (London, 1948), p. 152.

244. *Islah*, 23 May, 1936.

245. *Ibid*., 25 April, 1938.

246. Gregorian, No. 14, p. 382

247. *Ibid*., p. 383.

248. *Salnama-ye-Kabul* (Kabul, 1940), pp. 46-47.

249. Adamec, No. 20, p. 243.

250. Gregorian, No. 14, pp. 385-87.

251. Fraser-Tytler, No. 151, p. 253.

252. *The Times* (London), 21 October, 1941.

253. *Kabul Almanach 1941-42*, pp. 280-85.

254. Adamec, No. 20, p. 255.

255. Gregorian, No. 14, p. 389.

256. Adamec, No. 20, p. 257.

257. *Islah*, 18 October, 1941.

258. *Anis* (Kabul), 8 November, 1941.

259. For full text of the agreement, see Aitchison, No. 25, pp. 255-57.

260. *Ibid.*, p. 218.

261. *Ibid.*, p. 219.

262. *Ibid.*

263. For details see, C.C. Davies, *The Problem of the North-West Frontier, 1890-1908* (London: Cambridge Universty Press, 1932), p. 98. Also see, J.W. Spain, *The Pathan Borderlands* (The Hague: Mouton and Co., 1963), pp. 177-80.

264. Adamec, No. 20, p. 79.

265. Graser-Tytler, No. 151, p. 188.

266. *Ibid.*

267. Davies, No. 259, pp. 161-62.

268. Mir Munshi, No. 69, p. 158.

269. For full text of the treaty see, C.U. Aitchinson, *Treaties, Engagements and Sanads, Vol. XIII* (Calcutta, 1933), pp.

270. Abdul Samad Ghaus, *The Fall of Afghanistan: An Insider's Account* (Washington, D.C.: Pergamon-Brassey's, 1988), p. 35.

271. *Ibid.*, p. 37.

272. Cited in Leon B. Poullada, "Pushtunistan Afghan Domestic Politics and Relations with Pakistan", in A.T. Embree, (ed.), *Pakistan's Western Borderlands* (New Delhi: Vikas Publishing House, 1976), p. 128.

273. Adamec, No. 20, p. 161.

274. Louis Dupree, "The Durand Line of 1893: A Case Study of Artificial Boundaries and Cultural Areas", [as cited in Poullada, No. 268, p. 132.

275. *Ibid.*, p. 128.

276. Ghaus, No. 266, p. 66.

277. *Ibid.*

278. Arnold Fletcher, *Afghanistan, Highway of Conquest* (Ithaca, N.Y., 1965), p. 249.

279. Dupree, No. 270, p. 319.

280. Fletcher, No. 274, p. 252.

281. *Ibid.*, p. 251.

282. Ghaus, No. 266, p. 68.

283. George Cunningham, "The North West Frontier and the Tribes", *Sunday Statesman* (Delhi), 29 May, 1949.

CHAPTER II

BASIC POSTULATES OF AFGHAN FOREIGN POLICY

Foreign policy is the most significant component of a country's political system. It defines "the needs and wants (the interests) of a state and the means by which they are to be pursued."[1] The foreign policy also reflects an image of a future state of affairs and future set of conditions which governments through individual policy makers aspire to bring about by wielding influence abroad and by changing or sustaining the behaviour of other countries.[2]

It is now a well established fact that the foreign policy of a country is more than simply a series of responses to international stumuli and it also takes into account the forces at work within a society which contribute to the quality and contents of its external behaviour. Thus the foreign policy of a country is closely linked to and dependent on its domestic policy.[3]

The foreign policy pursued by a country is the manifestation of the sum total of domestic and external factors like national interest, geo-political situation of the region or strategic significance of the country, its response to regional and global problems etc. While analysing the basic postulates of the foreign policy of Afghanistan all these aspects coupled with the ethno-cultural characteristics of Afghanistan which have wielded a tremendous impact in the shaping and evolution of that country's foreign policy. have also to be examined. This analysis of the basic postulates of Afghan foreign policy pertains to the period prior to the advent of Soviet-backed communist *coup* of April, 1978 in Kabul. Under the present circumstances, especially after the Russian invasion, the Kabul regime has not been pursuing an independent foreign policy as it used to be in the past. Afghanistan has become just like other satellite countries of Russia and a dependent of Russian policy. According to Abdul Rahman Pazhwak, a veteran Afghan diplomat, now in the United States, the basic ingredients or essentials of Afghan foreign policy, prior to the communist *coup d'etat* of April, 1978, could be summarized as follows:

(i) Non-alignment in the political and military affairs;

(ii) Independent judgement on international issues on the basis of the merits of the issue;

(iii) Mutual respect on the basis of equality among the nations whether large or small;

(iv) Respect for the principles of peaceful coexistence;

(v) Coordination and cooperation between the countries without any conditions;

(vi) Good and friendly relations with all the countries, especially with the neighbouring countries and region;

(vii) Respect for the principles of the Charter of the United Nations, principles of Bandung Conference, and principles of the Non-aligned Movement (NAM);

(viii) Struggle against colonialism, neo-colonialism, and exploitation in all its manifestation, struggle for the attainment and preservation of political and economic, social and cultural rights of the nations, especially the right to self-determination by the free will of the people of each country; and fundamental human freedom;

(ix) Respect for the international law.[4]

The succeeding pages provide an indepth analytical assessment of the basic postulates of Afghan foreign policy.

(i) Strategic Significance of Afghanistan

The concept of strategic significance embraces an overall view of strategy. Strategy being an integral component of foreign policy has emerged as an amalgamation of military and political policy areas. There is no denying the fact that the analysis of national security entails the study fields of strategic studies and foreign policy since it constitutes an integral part of the both. As J. Baylis and others have opined, "If anything, they reflect differences of emphasis rather than differences in subject matter."[5]

The term "strategy" acquires added significance by providing an option for action aimed at the maximization of own values including interests, based on an indepth assessment of all potential gains and losses as well as the identification of hostile action which is also called "threat perception". This concept of threat perception includes the whole threat spectrum. Thus the concept of "strategic significance" which is a derivative from the term "strategy" is prone to be closely linked to perception.[6]

Raymond Aron is of the view that the concept of strategic significance is viewed historically in the same light as strategy, that is, in terms of military superiority and the ability to wage war.[7] Broadly speaking, there are three determinants of strategic significance. In the first place, strategic significance is linked to the sum total of a country's capabilities. As Lerche and Said have observed: "It is the general strategic role played by a state in world politics that raises issues of capability in the first place."[8]

Besides, the role perception of a country in the global and regional context is another determinant. "A second manifestation of the impact of the state's international strategic position upon capability is derived from its interpretation of the position it occupies in the world."[9] Thirdly, the perception of other states in the international political system is also important because this perception determines the strategic significance of a country. According to Padleford and Lincoln: "The relations of states are partly the interaction of the way the people and leaders of one state view the world situation and respond to it, as contrasted with the ways other people and leaders view the same situation and factors.[10]

Thus the strategic significance is perceived as the interaction between a country's capabilities,, its geo-perception and the perception on the part of the external environment. Thus, the concept of strategic significance is perception oriented.

The strategic significance of a country is dependent on its own national power and capabilities in comparison to those of other countries, which "indicate a relative power relationship and influences the strategic significance of that country."[11]

In essence, the relative strategic significance of a country is defined within the scope of a dynamic international system. It is subject to comprehensive security interests and shifting configurations and is based on the particular role perceptions of the countries in terms of national capabilities, as well as the perception of the same factors by other countries in the external environment at a given time.

While applying this thesis of strategic significance to Afghanistan, it is essential to analyse the geographical situation of Afghanistan. Many geographers have called Afghanistan as the heart of Asia.[12] It is a mountaineous landlocked country bounded on the north by "the Soviet Republics of Uzbekistan, Tajikistan and Turkmenistan; on the west by Iran and the south-east by Pakistan."[13] It also shares a short boundary with the Sinkiang province of people's Republic of China.

The Afghan boundary with Russia starts at the eastern end in the Pamirs, south of a small village called Qizie Robat where Soviet Union, China and India meet. Then it passes through Lake Victoria, then folloows the course the Amu Darya or Oxus River until Khamap.[14] The Russian railroad terminus of Kushk Post is but a few kilometres from the border.

The Afghan border with Iran runs south from Zulfiqar crosses the swamp and the desert regions of Persian Baluchistan and western Afghanistan to the top of the Siah-Kuh. Thence it turns sharply east across the marshes and lake Hamum of the Helmand River, follows the latter a short distance, and runs south-west to the Kuh-i-Malik Siah thus dividing the Sistan.

Afghanistan's border with Pakistan begins from Kuh-i-Malik Siah along with Pakistan's Baluchistan, at first running east through the Chaghai Hills and the southern end of the Registan desert, then due north to the Khwaja Amran range to a point near New Chaman, the terminus of the railroad from Quetta.

Thus the strategic significance of Afghanistan assumes tremendous geo-political importance. In this regard Poet Iqbal said:

"Asia Yak Pakiar aab-o-gil ast;
Millat-e-Afghan daran paikar die ast"

(It means Asia is a body made up of water and earth and Afghan nation is the heart of this body)

Sardar Mohammad Daoud then President of Afghanistan quoted this couplet of Iqbal on 7 March, 1978 during his visit to Pakistan and said: "This heart (Afghanistan) has always been throbbing for Asia. . ."[15]

Afghanistan has had a strategic position throughout history. First in distant centuries it was the crossroads of Asia, as the main east-west trade routes passed through its northern and southern plains and over its mountain passes during the period when waterborne trade was negligible between European and Asia. Later on it assumed added significance as a highway of conquest for powers to the east and west, and for the Mongols and Turks from the north. According toDonald N. Wilber, "it became a prize sought by the expanding Russian and British empires during the nineteenth century.[16]

In the post-Second World War period when cold war rivalry between Soviet Union and United States exacerbated, Afghanistan assumed tremendous strategic significance in the geo-politics of South West Asia. Its geo-political location has been of tremendous importance for enhencing its strategic significance. The various forces, especially the contemporary great powers during the different intervals of the history had been infiuenced by Afghanistan's strategic location. This aspect has been dealt in details in the first chapter.

(ii) Preservation of National Interest

The people of Afghanistan have a strong sense of nationalism. The Afghan national character is reflected in the literature and culture of that country. Throughout its history, there has always prevailed a cohensive national unity in Afghanistan. It is because of their love for motherland that Afghanistan has never been subject to alien rule. Even in the wake of Russian invasion of Afghanistan in December 1979 and the continued presence of Russian troops, the majority of Afghans have since been fighting for the liberation of their homeland.

Since the emergence of Afghanistan as a national entity under the leadership of Ahamad Shah Durrani[17] in 1747, Afghanistan consolidated its inner strength to become a force to reckon with. The subsequent Afghan rulers followed a genuinely non-aligned and independent foreign policy even in the midst of Anglo-Russian rivalry, during the two world wars, cold war and subsequent period in the post-Second World War. All the rulers of Afghanistan have kept the national interest as uppermost while pursuing the foreign policy.

Thus it emerges, from the above analysis, that sense of nationalism has been a great determinant of Afghan foreign policy.

(iii) Opposition to Colonialism and Neo-Colonialism

Opposition to all forms of colonialism and neo-colonialism in all manifestations has been one of the main basis of Afghan foreign policy. Its chequered history as an independent nation having never been subject to be colonized, has been instrumental in Afghan opposition to all form of colonialism and neo-colonialism. "Afghanistan was the first country to support the countries of Central Asia against Russian hegemony and expansionism during the hineteenth century and early years of the twentieth century".[18]

Following the conclusion of the Second World War which also inaugurated the process of decolonization, many a countries in Asia aud Africa attained their independence from the colonial rule during late 194)s and 1950s. In December 1960, the UN General Assembly adopted a declaration on Decolonization. While welcoming the UN Declaration, the head of the Afghan delegation, A.R. Pazhwak said that a declaration on the abolition of colonialism should have been one of the first jobs of the United Nations and he regretted it had been delayed so long.[19]

Besides the points covered in the UN Declaration, the Afghan delegate made further suggestions:

(a) . . . immediate abolition of the system of domination of any people by any alien people in all its forms and manifestations;

(b) independence from domination should apply not only to those peoples and territories which are usually called colonies but to all dependent peoples;

(c) abolition of domination by giving independence should be completed;

(d) independence should not mean only political independence but should mean economic and cultural independence, free from any direct or indirect influence or exercise of pressure of any kind on peoples and nations in any form and under any pretence;

(e) the implementation of the provisions of the declaration on decolonization should be universal and should apply to all peoples and territories.[20]

These suggestions reflected Afghan concern for colonialism. While echoing similar sentiments, the then Prime Minister of Afghanistan, Sardar Mohammad Daoud told the first non-aligned summit held at Belgrade in September 1961 that although colonialism was being forced to withdraw, it still sought through "intrigue and deception to retain its self-interests in other forms and shapes".[21]

Afghanistan, because of its strong opposition to colonialism and active support for the UN efforts in the processes of decolonization was made a member of the Special Committee with Regard to the Implementation of the Declaration on the Granting of Independence to Colonial Countries and Peoples. It has played an active role in this regard both in the UN and at other international fora.

While addressing the twenty-sixth session of the General Assembly, the Afghan Foreign Minister, Mohammad Mousa Shafiq, who later became Prime Minister, said: "We have always supported the struggle of majority of the peoples of Southern Rhodesia [now Zimbabwe] peoples of Namibia, Angola, Mozambique and other territories still under domination.''[22]

Commending the work done by the UN Committee on Decolonization, Afghanistan reiterated its support to the Committee and "our sympathy and our backing for all nations and peoples ftill struggling for the recognition of their rights".[23]

Since the advent of United Nations till April 1978 when Afghanistan was pushed into rhe Soviet orbit, the legitimate regimes in Kabul always rendered unqualified support to the people subject to colonial rule. During 1975-77 countries like Angola, Mozambique and Seychelles had attained independence and joined the United Nations. While welcoming these nations, the Afghan delegate told the General Assembly on 7 December, 1977 that it was a matter of satisfaction that a number of small territories had been "able to exercise their right to self-determination and some of whom had reached complete internal self-government and on the threshold of independence."[24] The Afghan delegate said that it was another achievement of the UN in the field of decolonization.

It is evident from the above analysis that Afghanistan has been consistently opposing colonialism and always espoused the cause of decolonization.

(iv) Support for National Liberation Movements

Another cornerstone of Afghan foreign policy has been its full support for the national liberation movements and struggles for the attainment of independence from the colonial domination. Afghanistan was the first country to recognize the freedom fighters of Algeria, when the latter was struggling for independence.[25] Even at the first NAM summit held at Belgrade in September 1961, Sardar Mohammad Daoud, Prime Minister of Afghanistan, announced his country's support for the Algerian struggle. While addressing the General Assembly on the Algerian question, Afghanistan's chief delegate to the UN, A.R. Pazhwak said: "Afghanistan is convinced that its support for the cause of the Algerian people. . . is right and just."[26] Afghanistan also welcomed the admission of Algeria into the UN: "It is a great privilege. . . to welcome the admission of Algeria to the United Nations, on behalf of the Afghan Government and the people of Afghanistan."[27]

Besides, Afghanistan has also rendered support for liberation movements in South Africa, Namibia, Zimbabwe, Angola and expressed solidarity with the people of Palestine in their struggle against Zionism. These aspects are analysed in succeeding pages.

(v) Opposition to Racist and Apartheid Regime of South Africa

Strong opposition to the racial and apartheid policies pursued by the white minority regime of South Africa has been another bulwark of Afghan foreign policy. Be it the General Assembly or other international forum, Afghanistan always espoused the cause of the people of South Africa and severely condemned the apartheid regime.

Zalmai Mahmud-Ghazi, a member of the Afghan delegation to the UN, told the *Ad hoc* Political Committee of the General Assembly in April 1961 that Afghanistan was shocked to note the blatant violation of basic principles of freedom and equal opportunity by the racist regime of South Africa.[28] While reiterating the Afghan opposition to recialism and apartheid, Afghan Foreign Minister, M.M. Shafiq, told the twentysixth session of the General Assembly: "We have never failed to condemn apartheid and all forms of racial discrimination as flagrant violation of principles and purposes of the Charter of the United Nations"[29]

Afghanistan keenly watched the developments within South Africa and the steps taken by international community in that direction. While addressing the thirtyfirst session of the General Assembly, the Afghan Deputy Foreign Minister, Wahed Abdullah, said:

> As a staunch supporter of the principles of freedom, nationalism, and respect for the rights of nations, Afghanistan hopes that these efforts will eventually enable the people of Southern Africa, who have suffered under the oppression of the privileged classes to attain their ideals and aspirations.[30]

In 1976. when the racist regime of South Africa resorted to massacres and massive repression against the innocent people, Afghanistan not only condemned them but expressed its wholehearted support to the "legitimate struggle of the people of South Africa for self-determination and the eradication of the inhuman policy of the apartheid".[31]

The United Nations had taken certain measures against racist regime of South Africa but these measures could not dissuade the latter to abandon the policy of apartheid. While addressing the thirtysecond session of the General Assembly, the Afghan delegation noted that though certain measures had been initiated by the world community to reverse this trend but regretted that "the nefarious doctrine of apartheid and social discrimination still prevails".[32]

(vi) Support for Namibia

Afghanistan has consistently supported the people of South-West Africa, known as Namibia, for their struggle to attain independence from the racial regime of South Africa. The Union of South Africa was given the mandate over Namibia by the League of Nations with specific responsibilities to ensure the welfare of the local population.[33]

However, after the Second World War, South Africa annexed the territory and the people of Namibia were not only denied independence but subjected to repression. In May 1961, Dr. A.H. Tabibi, Councillor to the Afghan Permanent Mission to the UN, said that the situation in South-West Africa was tragic because South Africa had violated all the political, legal and moral obligations embodied in the UN Charter.[34] Keeping in view the fact that efforts of the United Nations had borne no fruits until 1962, Afghanistan regretted that the endeavours or the UN to solve the problem of South-West Africa by peaceful means had failed because of the unrelenting obstinacy of the South African racist regime.[35]

With the passage of time, there was no change in South African policy of repression towards the people of Namibia. Afghanistan's reaction to it become more vehement and strong. While addressing the thirtysecond session of the General Assembly, the Afghan delegation said: "We believe that apartheid in Namibia means not only racial discrimination, segregation in homelands, and slave labour but also the fragmentation and brutalization of the Namibians. . ."[36]

Thus, Afghan support for the people of Namibia was keeping in consonance with its foreign policy which was consistently pursued.

(vii) Support for Palestine

Afghanistan has been the ardent supporter for the people of Palestine in their struggle against Zionism and has reiterated its support for the inalienable rigats of Palestinians to return to their homeland. The problem of Palestine arose in 1947 when the UN General Assembly recommended the partition of Palestine into two territories—One for the Palestinians and the other for the Jews. However, the Zionists unilaterally declared the establishment of a Zionist State of Israel in May 1948 and usurped other areas by force.[37]

Since then, the Palestinians are struggling to regain their motherland. The Arab-Israel Wars of 1948, 1956, 1967 and 1973 and continued hostilities have further added to the miseries of the Palestinians. The formation of the Palestine Liberation Organization (PLO) and its recognition by the international community in 1974, as the sole representative of the Palestinians have been welcomed by Afghanistan. While voicing Afghanistan's concern, Malikyar, the Afghan representative told the thirty-first session of the General Assembly:

> The position of Afghanistan on Palestine is clear. The question of Palestine, the essence of which is the restoration and exercise of the inalienable rights of the Palestinian people forms the core of the solution. . . It is obvious that this purpose cannot be achieved unless Israel withdraws from all the occupied territories.[38]

Afghanistan continuously insisted that the total and complete withdrawal of Israel from all the occupicd Arab territories and the restoration of the inalienable rights of the Palestinian people including the right of self-determination and the establishment of a Palestinian State would only solve the problem.[39]

Thus, Afghan support for the Palestine people has been keeping in tune with its objectives of foreign policy.

(viii) Support for the Right to Self-Determination

Afghanistan has attached tremenedous significance to the right for self-determination whether in the UN General Assembly or other international forum, Afghanistan has consistently and ardently espoused the cause of exercising right to self-determination by the people still under domination.

The UN Charter recognizes the right to self-determination. Article 1(2) envisages that one of the purposes of the United Nations is: "to develp friendly relations among nations based on respect for the principle of equal rights and self-determination of peoples, and to take other appropriate measures to strengthen universal peace."[40] It was Afghanistan which suggested for the first time that the right to self-determination which prior to that was incorporated as a political principle in the UN Charter and Universal Declaration on Human Rights to be treated as a fundamental right.[41] Afghanistan's vigorous espousal in this regard resulted in the incorporation of right to self-determination in the first Article both in the UN Charter and both the UN Covenants on Human Rights.[42]

Afghanistan's vigorous espousal for the right to self-determination forms the cornerstone of its foreign policy and opposition to colonialism; racialism, apartheid and support for the national liberation movements, all these stem from Afghan support for right to self-determination. This point was made clear by A.R. Pazhwak in his address to the nineteenth session of the General Assembly when he said:

> Afghanistan reaffirmed its belief in the principles of coexistence and asked for a clearer understanding of these principles through their codification and declaration to the world as principles which would include mutual respect for all; support of the right of all nations to choose their own political, economic and social system; respect for the

> undeniable and inherent right of all peoples to self-determination. . .[43]

Elaborating further the Afghan stand on right to self-determination. Pazhwak told the twentieth session of the General Assembly:

> In all cases, we have believed and expressed our belief that peace and stability depend solely on the respect for and observance of self-determination. The sincerity of those who uphold this right can be fully tested only by observing whether they adhere to it in all cases and in all places.[44]

Afghanistan has continuously championed the cause of dependent people throughout the world and pleaded for the exercise of right to self-determination. The Afghan delegate while addressing the twenty-seventh session of the General Assembly, said on 20 October, 1972:

> . . .In view of the prevailing situation, our delegation most strongly demands the implementation of the right of the dependent territories to self-determination and independence on the basis of the undeniable conviction held by the majority of the members of the international community.[45]

This is evident from the above analysis that Afghanistan has been vocal enough in championing the cause of dependent people and territories with a view to enable them to exercise the right to self-determination.

(ix) Support for Universal Human Rights

Afghanistan has played a key role in the framing and then adoption by the General Assembly of Universal Declaration on Human Rights. It has not only actively participated but made positive contribution in improving the working of the UN Commission on Human Rights. In April 1961, Abdul Rahman Pazhwak, the then chief Afghan delegate to the United Nations, suggested that the Commission should transmit without delay a general recommendation to all the governments on the preparation of periodic reports.[46] The Afghan suggestion was adopted unanimously

In April 1963, A.R. Pazhwak was unanimously elected as the chairman of the Human Rights Commission. Speaking on the occasion, Pazhwak said that his unanimous election was a honour for his country and his person and his impartiality had been the consequence of Afghanistan's basic policy in the interest of international cooperation and peace among mankind.[47]

Afghanistan was opposed to the encroachment upon individual's basic rights. While speaking on the occasion of the fifteenth anniversary of Declaration of Human Rights, A.R. Pazhwak emphasized that though the collective rights of peoples to dignity and equality within the United Nations were an accepted fact, the world would better prosper if forces of resistance against the rights of individuals and peoples did not persist in most parts of the world.[48]

(x) Support for New International Economic Order (NIEO)

The call for New International Economic Order (NIEO) was given by the Algerian non-aligned summit in 1973, which was later adopted as a Declaration and Programme of Action on the Establishment of New International Economic Order by the General Assembly at its sixth special session held in April 1974.[49]

The Declaration adopted by the General Assembly, proclaimed the determination of the Member States to work urgently for the establishment of a new international economic order based on equity, sovereign equality, interdependence, common interest and cooperation among all countries which would correct inequalities and redress existing injustices, make it possible to eliminate the widening gap between the developed and developing countries.

It was but natural for less developed and landlocked country like Afghanistan to spport the speedy implementation of new international economic order. A close analysis of the pronouncements made by Afghan statesmen, especially by A.R. Pazhwak, reveals that Afghanistan had been pressing for NIEO even prior to its being adopted by the General Assembly. While making a statement before the Economic and Social Council (ECOSOC) on 12 July, 1960, Pazhwak said: "As a representative of a less developed country, I should think that it is in favour of both of underdeveloped countries and also the lessening of tension if more emphasis is put on the necessity of international cooperation."[50] He also called for the liberalization of trade and stabilization of commodity prices. Being a landloked country, Afganistan has no direct access to the sea. Hence it is faced with numerous problems like transit facilities from the neighbouring countries. The resultant impact is increased burden on Afghanistan in foreign exchange.

A conference on International Economic Cooperation was held in Paris in 1977 to discuss the developments made in implementing the NIEO.[51] However the least developed countries idcluding Afghanistan were not represented in this conference. Afghanistan's concern about this was expressed by the Deputy Foreign Minister, Wahed Abdullah, in his statement before the Thirtysecond session of the General Assemly:

> How can a meeting which ignored the existence of such an important section of the international community and its problems, safeguard the interests of the least developed landlocked countries and consequently reach decisions benefiting the whole mankind including those countries. . .I propose that in future that factor should be taken into considerationn.[52]

Apart from voicing its own problems, Afghanistan took up the case of other least developed and landlocked countries with a view to get their problems solved.

(xi) Support for Disarmament

Unqualified support for general and complete disarmament forms the bedrock of Afghan foreign policy. Be it in General Assembly or Disarmament Commission or in non-aligned conferences, Afghanistan has called for the halt to arms race, liquidation or destruction of nuclear weapons and vigorously espoused for the attainment of complete disarmament in the larger interest of mankind. Reiterating Afghan stand on disarmament, the permanent Afghan delegate to the UN, A.R. Pazhwak, told the First Committee of the General Assembly in December 1960:

> We agree that no time should be wasted and situation should not be allowed to develop in a manner which would make the efforts sor disarmament more difficult. We share the grave concern that any delay in the solution of the disarmament problem will result in more serious situation and grave consequences.[53]

Along with other non-nuclear weapon countries, Afghanistan has also expressed its opposition to nuclear tests from time to time. In December 1961, A.R. Pazhwak told the General Assembly that his country was against nuclear weapons of any size by any country.[54] He further added that Afghanistan felt that it was imperative that the concern of the General Assembly should be expressed regarding the tension which had been caused by the nuclear powers to resume nuclear testing.[55]

The Partial Test Ban Treaty (PTBT) was signed in 1963. Afghanistan while welcoming the PTBT urged the General Assembly to work out a comprehensive test ban treaty. In October 1963, A.R. Pazhwak told the General Assembly that though the PTBT had no practical effect on Afghanistan but his country adhered to it in the larger interest of world peack.[56] He further added that the climate of the agreement between the big powers could be extended through a comprehensive treaty covering underground tests. Afghanistan was convinced that durable peace could only be attained if general and complete disarmament under effective control was achieved.[57]

Policy of Non-alignment

Commitment and strict adherence to the principles of non-alignment forms the cornerstone of Afghan foreign policy. Afghanistan is one of the oldest nonaligned countries. The present analysis of Afghan commitment to the policy of non-alignment pertains to the period prior to the advent of Soviet-backed communist *coup* in April 1978 in Kabul. According to Abdul Rahman Pazhwak, Afghanistan has been the first non-aligned country in Asia and one of the forerunners of the NAM.[58]

Afghanistan throughout its history has essentially remained a free country and in case it was invaded or some of its territory was under alien occupation, the people of Afghanistan fought tooth and nail against the invaders and liberated their territory. The three Angola-Afghan wars are testimony to it. This Afghan tradition of resistance to alien occupation continued until the period of Abdul Rahman when the Afghan foreign policy had come under the British influence. But in its internal affairs Afghanistan was totally free.[59]

At a time when the Anglo-Russian rivalry was at its zenith, Afghanistan pursued a policy of genuine non-alignment. This aspect is analysed in detail in the first chapter. Afghanistan maintained strict neutrality during he First World War, between First World War and till the outbreak of the Second World War and even during the World War II period.

"Following the advent of the NAM, it was natural that those countries which wanted to bring this movement into life, found in Afghanistan a country which had traditionally followed the policy of strict neutrality in the past and which now formed the basis of non-alignment".[60] In early 1950s when the idea for launching NAM was mooted by Yugoslavia, Egypt,

India, Indonesia and others, the Afghan leaders were also consulted in this regard. President Nasser of Egypt paid a visit to Afghanistan after the Bandung Conference to elicit Afghan support for the NAM.[61]

Afghanistan had never been subject to alien rule and the principles of non-alignment as understood in the current connotation of the term have formed the very basis of Afghan foreign policy even before the concept of NAM gained currency. While addressing the first NAM summit held at Belgrade, the Afghan Premier, Sardar Mohammad Daoud said that "nonalignment has been the traditional basis of Afghan foreign policy which it has followed under the name impartial judgement."[62]

Afghanistan not only pursued the policy of non-alignment vigorously but also played a pivotal role in the NAM summits. The term "non-alignment" gained currency only in late 1950s and prior to that Afghan foreign policy was called "neutral policy". The Afghan leaders criticized those who regarded neutralism as an escapist policy and reiterated that "our neutrality is not a passive but an active one and we reserve our freedom of judgement in all question of world importance".[63]

While further elaborating the Afghan concept of "neutralism", the then Primk Minister of Afghanistan, Sardar Mohammad Daoud, said on 24 August, 1959 the Afghan neutralism should "never be interpreted as lack of interest. For even though we take a neutral stand in the differences of views and struggles. . . we cannot remain aloof and disinterested in the problems which affect humanity at large."[64]

The change of leadership or government in Kabul had never affected Afghanistan's steadfast commitment and adherence to the principles of NAM. A.R. Pazhwak, the Permanent Afghan Representative to the United Nations, while addressing the eighteenth session of the UN General Assembly in October 1963 said that Afghanistan's traditional policy of non-alignment had remained unchanged.[65] He further pointed out that the policy of non-alignment had enabled Afghanistan in the past and still enabled it to maintain impartiality towards all peoples and to remain absolutely independent of all international situations.[66]

A strong and stable United Nations, in Afghanistan's view, was essential for maintaining peace and security in the world. As Sardar Mohammad Naim told the seventeenth session of the General Assembly : "It is a strong United Nations that comes first as an international instrument in which we can place our hope for the solution of all major and minor problems confronting the world".[67]

Being an ardent supporter of a strong UN, Afghanistan rendered its fullest cooperation in strengthening the world body. It had been of the view that the UN could become strong only if its member countries extended full cooperation. This point was stressed by the Afghan delegate to the General Assembly in his address to the thirtyfirst session of the General Assembly:

> The success or failure of the UN in carrying out its responsibilities under the Charter for the maintenance of international peace and security and for the realization of the right to self-determination and independence depends upon the amount of support which Member States extend to this organization; and to the extent of their compliance with the principles of the Charter and the resolutions of this organization.[68]

In Afghanistan's view, if all Member countries of the UN rendered full cooperation to the world body it could certainly be strengthened. As Abdullah, the Deputy Foreign Minister, told the thirtysecond session of the General Assembly :". . . what must be wrong, therefore, is the lack of political willingness on the part of Member States to bring into being a more effective United Nations and our reluctance to accept to be guided in international gatherings by the norms of reason and justice."[69]

Thus it is evident from the analysis *supra* that Afghanistan since its induction into the UN as a fullfledged member had played a constructive role in strengthening the world body. At the same time it also urged the other member countries to render full support and cooperation to the UN. It was through mutual cooperation and support that the United Nations could be strengthened.

The above-mentioned points highlight the main postulates of Afghan foreign policy. It is in the light of these basic postulates that the relations of Afghanistan with Super Powers in the post-Second World War would be analysed in the succeeding chapters.

REFERENCES

1. Werner Levi, *International Politics: Foundations of the System* (Minneapolis: University of Minnesota Press, 1974), p. 88.
2. Paul Seaburg, *Power. Freedom and Diplomacy* (New York: Random House, 1963), p. 86.
3. For details see, James N. Rosenau, ed., *Domestic Sources of Foreign Policy* (New York: The Free Press, 1967). Also see, Hans J. Morganthau, *Politics Among Nations* (New York: Alfred J. Knop, 1956), pp. 136-37. Also see, Henry A. Kissiner, "Domestic Structure and Foreign Policy", *Daedalus* (Boston), Vol. XCV, No. 2, Spring 1966, pp. 503-29.
4. Author's interview wiih Abdul Rahman Pazhwak, 6 February, 1986. Mr. Pazhwak is a seasoned Afghan diplomat and statesman. He has served as Afghan Ambassador to India, West Germany and United Kingdom. He had been Afghanistan's Permanent Representative to United Nations for many years. His expertise was utilized by UN many times. He served as President of the UN General Assembly. He was member of the UN Peace Mission for Vietnam andOman crisis. He also represented his country in the Non-aligned Summit Conferences, Islamic Conference and other international agencies. At the time of Communist *coup* in Kabul in April, 1978, Mr. Pazhwak was Afghan Ambassador in UK from which he resigned as a mark of protest against the Communist takeover. He was kept under house arrest and in 1982 he left Kabul. During this

period he visited many European countries and United States and then went to Pakistan. During 1983, he was kept under house arrest by the Pakistani authorities who later asked him to leave Pakistan without any reason. He left Pakistan because he was not prepared to compromise on the national interests of Afghanistan. He has also been critical of so-called Geneva talks. Presently he is staying in Washington D.C.

5. J. Baylis *et. al*, *Contemporary Strategy: Theories and Palicies* (Reprint) (London: Croom Helm, 1976), p. 4.
6. N.J. Padleford and G.A. Lincoln. *The Dynamics of International Politics* (Second edn.) (New York: The Macmillan, 1967), p. 52.
7. Raymond Aron, *Peace and War* (Translated by D.R. Howard) (London: Weidenfeld and Nicolson, 1966), p. 52.
8. C.O. Lerche and A.A. Said, *Concepts of International Politics* (Englewood Cliffs, New Jersey: Prentice Hall, (1963), p. 67.
9. *Ibid.*, p. 68.
10. Padleford and Lincoln, No. 6, p. 52.
11. R.S. Clive, *World Power Assessment: A Calculus of Strategic Drift* (Washington, D.C.: Georgetown University, 1975), p. 8.
12. George B. Cressey, *Asia's Lands and Peoples* (Third edn.) (New York: McGraw-Hill, 1963), p. 77. Also see, Louis Dupree, "Afghanistan" in Donald N. Wilder, ed., *The Nations of Asia* (New York; Hart Publishing Co., 1964), pp. 35-36.
13. M.A. Sohail, "Contemporary Afghanistan", *Afghanistan News* (London), Vol. 4, No. 4, August 1960, p. 11.
14. Donald N. Wilder (ed.), *Afghanistan* (New Haven: Human Relations Area Files, 1956), p. 24.
15. For full text of Daoud's speech see, *Pakistan Horizon*, Vol. XXXI, Nos. 2-3, 1978, p. 247.
16. Wilber, No. 14, p. 22.
17. He is also known as Ahamad Shah Abdali.
18. Interview with Abdul Rahman Pazhwak, No. 4.
19. *Afghanistan News* (London), Vol. 4, No. 42, February 1961, p. 15.
20. *Ibid.*
21. *The Conference of Heads of State of Government of Non-aligned Countries, 5-11 September 1961* (Belgrade, 1961), p. 83.
22. *Official Records of General Assembly* (hereafter *GAOR*), Twenty-sixth session, Plen. Meeting 1961, 11 October, 1971, p. 9.

23. *Ibid.*, Twentyseventh session, Plen. Meeting 2060, 10 October, 1972, p. 2.
24. *Ibid.*, Thirtysecond session, Plen. Meeting 96, 7, December, 1977, p. 1590.
25. Interview with A.R. Pazhwak, No. 4.
26. *Afghanistan News*, Vol. 5, No. 54, February 1962, p. 16.
27. *Ibid.*, Vol. 5, No. 64, December 1962, p. 19.
28. *Ibid.*, Vol. 4, No. 45, May 1961, p. 21.
29. *GAOR*, Twentysixth session. Plen. Meeting 1961, 11 October, 1971, p. 10.
30 *Ibid.*, Thirtyfirst session, Plen. Meeting 10, 29 September, 1976, p. 161.
31. *Ibid.*, Plen. Meeting 52, 2 November, 1976, p. 876.
32. *Ibid.*, Thirty-second session, Plen. Meeting 96, 7 December, 1977, p. 1591.
33. UN, *The United Nations At Forty* (New York, 1985), p. 71.
34. *Afghanistan News*, Vol. 4, No. 45, May 1961, p. 21.
35. F.A. Zikria, Afghan representative's statement before the Fourth Committee of the General Assembly. *Ibid.*, Vol. 6, No. 65, January 1963, p. 17.
36. *GAOR*, Thirtysecond session, Plen. Meeting 96, 7 December, 1977, p. 1591.
37. For a detailed background see Pamela Ann Smith, *Palestine and the Palestinians 1876-1983* (London: Croom Helm, 1984).
38. *GAOR*, Thirtyfirst session, Plen. Meeting 32, 19 November, 1976) p. 1122.
39. Statement of Wahed Abdullah, Afghan representative. *Ibid* , Thirty-second session, Plen. Meeting 79, 4 October, 1977, p. 340.
40. UN, *Everyone's United Nations* (Ninth edn.) (New York, 1979), p. 382.
41. Interview with A.R. Pazhwak, No. 4.
42. *Ibid.*, Also see, *GAOR*, Fifth session, December 1950, UN Doc. A/C. 3/L. 88.

43. *GAOR*, Nineteenth session, Plen. Meeting 1323, 15 December, 1964, p. 8.
44. *Ibid.*, Twentieth session, Plen. Meeting 1362, 21 September, 1965, p. 7.
45. *Ibid.*, Twentyseventh session, Plen. Meeting 2069, 20 October, 1972, p. 14.
46. *Afghanistan News*, Vol. 4, No. 45, May 1961, p. 21.
47. *Ibid.*, Vol. 6, No. 69, May 1963, p. 10.
48. *Ibid.*, Vol. 7, No. 78, February 1969, p. 16.
49. *Everyone's UN*, No. 44, p. 122.
50. *Afghanistan News*, Vol. 4, No. 34, September 1960, p. 15.
51. For details see UN Doc. A/31/478/Add. 1.
52. *GAOR*, Thirty-second session, Plen. Meeting 19, 4 October, 1977, p. 349.
53. *Afghanlstan News*, Vol. 4, No. 41, January 1961, p. 20.
54. *Ibid.*, Vol. 5, No. 53; January 1962, p. 8.
55. *Ibid.*
56. *Ibid.*, Vol. 6, No. 75, November 1963, p. 15.
57. *GAGR*, Thirty-second session, Plan. Meeting 19, 4 October, 1977, p. 349.
58. Interview with A.R. Pazhwak, No. 4.
59. *Ibid.*
60. *Ibid.*
61. *Ibid.*
62. Speech of Afghan Prime Minister Sardar Mohammad Daoud at the Belgrade Summit, *The Conference of Heads of State or Governments of Non-Aligned Countries*, No. 25, p. 80.
63. Statement by an Afghan Foreign Minister cited in H.C. Taussing, "Afghan Neutralism", *Eastern World*, Vol. 15, No. 12, December 1961, p. 11.
64. *Afghanistan News*, Vol. 3, No. 26, October 1959, p. 7.
65. *Ibid.*, Vol. 6, No. 75, November 1963, p. 15.
66. *Ibid.*

67. *Ibid.*, p. 11.

68. *GAOR*, Thirtyfirst session, Plen. Meeting 85, 1 December, 1976, p. 1307.

69. *Ibid.*, Thirtysecond session, Plen. Meeting 19, 19 October, 1977, p 348.

CHAPTER III

AFGHAN-SOVIET RELATIONS: THE POST-WAR PERIOD

Afghanistan maintained a policy of strict neutrality throughout the course of the Second World War and ending of the hostilities had least effect on the internal and external situation of Afghanistan. However, the global geopolitics underwent a tremendous change immediately after the war. The status of the United Kingdom (UK) as a great power had been relegated to the oblivion paving way for the United States. However the Soviet Union retained its great power status. Rather it emerged as much more stronger. The period of entente between the members of the anti-Axis coalition proved to be short-lived. The immediate post-war period very soon degenerated into the cold war, dividing the Allies into two antagonistic camps—one led by the United States and other by the Soviet Union. Advent of Communist regime in China also brought it into Soviet camp.

Despite the onset of the cold war in late 1945, Afghanistan was not faced with any immediate threat either from British India or Soviet Union. Thus, as a traditional adherent to the policy of strict and positive non-alignment, Afghanistan kept aloof from the manoeuvres of both the Super Powers. The then Afghan rulers addressed themselves to envisage an allround development of Afghanistan. In the early months of 1946, Shah Mahmud took over as Prime Minister of Afghanistan. In May 1946, Shah Mahmud declared that the principle of establishing friendly relations with all countries, especially with the neighbouring countries formed the bedrock of Afghan foreign policy.[1] On 13 June, 1946, Kabul and Moscow signed an agreement to define the Amu river border, thus settling the ownership of some 1,191 islands.[2] However prior to signing this treaty, the Russians always claimed without justification that the Amu river's boundary lay on the southern bank—on Soviet side.[3] Signing of this treaty showed a relatively benign post-war Soviet attitude to Afghanistan which was because "perhaps Afghanistan seemed too unimportant, too unthreatening to be worth the trouble and outcry of a territorial grab".[4] Besides Moscow also wanted to get the sympathy of Afghanistan.

The Afghan Government was addressing itself for promoting the economic development of Afghanistan. As the then Prime Minister Shah Mahmud said: ". . . for the first time in our history, we are free of the threat of great powers' using our mountain passes as pathways to empire. Now we can concentrate on talents and resources in bettering the living conditions of our people".[5]

Consequent upon the British departure from India and initial US indifference, Afghanistan started reviewing its attitude toward Moscow. The imperatives of large-scale economic development and the need to strengthen the armed forces, in view of a dispute between Afghanistan and the newly created State of Pakistan "over the trans-Durand Pushtun lands and their inhabitants, drew the Afghans closer to Russia".[6]

Partition of Indian Subcontinent and Afghanistan

The partition of the Indian subcontinent in August 1947 resulted in the emergence of India and Pakistan as two independent sovereign countries. Pakistan emerged as the immediate neighbour of Afghanistan. A major area of Pushtunistan, as a sequal to Durand Line demarcation of 1893, had been inherited by Pakistan after the partition. "The Afghans saw perhaps their last chance to retrieve by negotiation their lost territories in the NWFP"[7] which was originally annexed by the British. At the time of partition, the question of North-West Frontier Provinces (NWFP) was to be decided whether it should go to India or Pakistan. The Afghan case was that since it was the aggrieved party, it should have been involved.

The British had spread their imperialistic tentacles by pursuing the policy of divide and rule. Even while leaving the Indian subcontinent, they did not hesitate to do their best to erect perennial or permanent source of irritations between the neighbouring countries. The plebiscite stagemanaged by the British ignored the requested addition of independence as an option for the Pashtuns. The Pushtun leaders asked their followers to boycott the plebiscite. The result of the plebiscite was not accepted by the Pushtuns as being arbitrary.[8]

The plebiscite conducted under the aegis of the British awarded NWFP to Pakistan. It was claimed that 99 per cent of those who voted in the plebiscite opted union with Pakistan. However only 55.5 per cent of the enfranchised electorate turned out to vote.[9] The Afghan Government rejected the "plebiscite" and thus the issue of "Pushtunistan" became the major irritant in Afghan-Pakistan relations. The detailed analysis on this aspect is beyond the scope of present study. The issue is analyzed in light of Afghan-Soviet relations.

On 26 July, 1949, a *Loyah Jirgah* in Kabul formally and specifically abrogated all of its international treaties which supported the Durand Line as a border or which referred to the status of the Pushtuns.[10]

The Soviet Union after the Amu river agreement was gradually increasing its influence in Afghanistan. On 14 June, 1946, the *New York Times* reported that the Soviet Embassy in Kabul had about 600 personnel and Soviet officers were imparting training to the Afghan Air Force personnel.[11]

On the Pushtun issue, the Soviet Union supported Afghan stand. The Soviet scholar A. Dyakov commented that the British and Americans were planning to establish military bases in the Pushtun region.[12] Another Soviet scholar, E. Atramonov while supporting the Afghan stand on Pushtunistan, wrote that UK and United States were determined to create instability in the region by inciting Pakistan and Afghanistan.[13]

In 1947, there was an agreement to establish a telegraph link between Kabul and Tashkent. In the wake of its strained relations with Pakistan over Pushtun issue, and a Super Power as its neighbour, the Afghan Government sought military and economic assistance from the United States in 1948-49. However it got only economic assistance and military aid was denied because US preference was for Pakistan. This aspect is discussed in details in Chapter IV. It is suffice here to say that the US refusal to accede to Afghan request for supply of arms was one of the main blunders which made Kabul dependent on Moscow for arms supplies

Beginning of Soviet Opportunities

The Soviet ventures in Afghanistan during the post-war period commenced with economic aid. In July 1950, Moscow and Kabul signed a four year trade agreement which envisaged Soviet petroleum products, cotton, cloth, sugar and other commodities in exchange for Afghan goods—wool, fur, raw cotton, fruits and nuts at a higher currency exchange rates and duty free exchange.[14]

Pakistan's joining of US sponsored military alliances—South-east Asia Treaty Organization (SEATO) in September 1954 and Central Treaty Organization (CENTO) in 1955, further heightened Afghan apprehensions of Pak military might. The US refusal to provide military assistance to Afghanistan in October 1954 made Afghanistan feel dejected. In the meanwhile, Sardar Mohammad Daoud took over as Prime Minister of Afghanistan in 1953 and he wanted to make Afghanistan a strong and prosperous country.

In January 1954, Kabul and Moscow signed a major agreement in terms of which the Soviet lent $ 3.5 million for the construction of grain elevators at Kabul and Pul-i-Khumri and a flour mill and bakery at Kabul.[15] Until the death of Stalin on 5 March, 1953, Moscow had not favoured the policy of forging close relations with the Third World countries. When Khruschev succeeded Stalin, the official policy towards Third World began to change quickly. According to Rubinstein, Moscow began to represent itself abroad as the champion of developing countries, helping the latter to establish economic as well as political independence.[16] The Soviet leader, Khrushchev in 1953 told visiting US Congressmen that "We value trade least for economic and most for political reasons".[17] Thus it becomes evident that after 1953, Moscow adopted the strategy of using economic aid as a bait to hoodwink the developing countries into its orbit of influence. In pursuance of this policy, Moscow augmented its economic assistance to Kabul. In July 1954 an agreement worth $ 1.2 million was signed between the two countries for the construction of a gasoline pipeline across the Amu river.[18] In August 1954, another agreement worth $ 2 million was signed between the two countries for road building equipment.[19] Again in October 1954, Soviet Union advanced another loan worth $ 2.1 million which provided for an asphalt factory and equipment.[20] According to Bradsher: "These were early examples of a Soviet talent for getting maximum propaganda value from aid projects. . . ."[21] On 28 June, 1955, Afghanistan negotiated a new agreement on duty-free transit of Afghan goods through Soviet territory based on Article 6 of the 1921 treaty between the two countries.[22]

Despite procuring economic assistance from Moscow, in early 1950s, the Afghan rulers were quite conscious of not leaning towards Soviet Union. Since May 1946 when Shah Mahmud became Prime Minister and his close associates, reared in the traditional suspicion about Kremlin, shied away from taking steps that would bring Afghanistan close to Soviet Union.[23]

The Soviet diplomats in Kabul were engaging in clandestine campaign to proke Afghans to take over Pushtun areas. A Soviet journal hinted in 1951 that Moscow had suggested Afghanistan to take over Pushtun areas of Pakistan while the Soviets would take over the Tajik, Uzbek and Turkman areas of Afghanistan "thus tidging up the ethnically massy nineteenth-century boundaries".[24] However, this information could not be corroborated from other printed sources. But keeping in view the Soviet manoeuvres in Afghanistan, it cannot be dismissed as well. But as regards to Afghanistan, it had on many occasions made it clear that it had no territories designs on Pakistan or any other country. What Afghanistan insisted on was that the Pushtuns living in the NWFP should be given the right to self-determination. When in September 1947, Pakistan applied for the membership of the United Nations, Afghanistan was the only country to cast a negative vote. While explaining his vote, the Afghan representative, Abdul Hussain Khan Aziz stated that:

> . . . The Afghanistan delegation does not wish to oppose the membership of Pakistan in this great organization, but it is with the deepest regret that we are unable to vote for Pakistan. This unhappy circumstance is due to the fact that we cannot recognize the North west Frontier as a part of Pakistan so long as the people of the North West Frontier have not been given an opportunity free from any kind of influence,—and I repeat, free from any kind of influence to determine for themselves whether they wish to be independent or to become part of Afghanistan.[25]

Thus Afghanistan had no territorial designs on Pakistan and what it asked for was the right of self-determination to be exercised by the people of NWFP. At the same time, Afghanistan which had maintained policy of strict neutrality could not be expected to compromise with the Soviets on territorial issue or cede its areas to Moscow just for nothing.

It is also worth mentioning here that during the first half of 1950s, Afghanistan having launched ambitious programmes of economic development, needed external financial assistance very badly. The US reluctance to meet Afghan requirements had left no options for Kabul but to look towards Moscow. At the same time majority of Afghans were aware of the dangers of Russian involvement in their economic development, but Afghanistan had reached a "stage in its history when meaningful progress could no longer be delayed".[26] Arnold Fletcher also observed in this regard:

> They [the Afghan rulers] were aware that failure to do so [bring progress to their country], might prove more dangerous than any agent of the Kremlin. The 'revolution of rising expectations' has come to Afghanistan at last; and no people so volatile and energetic could be expected to remain contented if their country lagged behind while its neighbours forged ahead.[27]

The Soviet economic assistance to Afghanistan during the heydays of the cold war was viewed seriously in Washington. John Foster Dulles, the US Secretary of State observed on 12 April, 1955 that the closer economic relations between Afghanistan and Soviet Union "have facilitated the Soviet Union's penetration of Afghanistan and the US has observed Soviet penetration elsewhere has proved conducive to a variety of difficulties and in some instances has led to loss of independence."[28]

In view of the prevailing tension between Pakistan and Afghanistan over the Pushtun issue and growing Soviet-Afghan relations, the United States feared exacerbation in Pak-Afghan tension and increased Afghan dependence on Moscow. In this regard, Armstrong, Special Assistant for Intelligence in a note sent to the US Secretary of State on 15 April, 1955 wrote that though there was no positive information that the Soviet Union was prompting Afghanistan to step up anti-Pakistan campaign:

> While it is not clear that the USSR would actually intervene in the event of a. . . coup, it can certainly be expected to

exploit the situation to the fullest in the UN and before the world public opinion to the detreiment of the US and might even threaten to invoke the Afghan-Soviet Treaty or June 1931 under which the USSR has the legal obligation not "to tolerate on the part of anybody whatsoever any act which might inflict political or military damage" on the Kabul Government.[29]

Thus by 1955, while Soviet-Afghan relations had become closer, the United States though seemed worried about the Soviet penetration in Afghanistan, did little to wean it away from Moscow.

Khrushchev and Bulganin's Visit to Afghanistan

On 15 December, 1955, the First Secretary of the Soviet Communist Party, Nikita S. Khrushchev and Soviet Premier, Nikolai A. Bulganin, paid an official visit to Afghanistan. The Soviet dignitaries were given a rousing welcome at the Kabul airport by King Zahir Shah and Prime Minister, Sardar Mohammad Daoud,[30] and other Government officials. While thabking the Afghan people, Bulganin hoped that the visit would help in forging closer relations between the two countries.[31]

The visiting Soviet leaders being aware of the Afghan sentiments over Pushtunistan said: "We sympathise with Afghanistan's policy on the question of Pushtunistan. The Soviet Union stands for an equitable solution of this problem which cannot be settled correctly without taking into account the vital interests of the people inhabiting Pushtunistan".[32] The Afghan Prime Minister, Sardar Mohammad Daoud in his welcome address said that Afghanistan was the staunch adherent of the principles of non-alignment; "Afghanistan will accept economic assistance with gratitude but it should not be linked with political strings."[33]

Both the Soviet leaders also announced the gift of 100-bed hospital to be built in Kabul with Russian aid. It was also promised that Soviet Union will give a credit worth $ 100 million repayable in thirty years at two per cent interest.[34] The Soviet leaders also visited the military training school at Kabul and thereafter Bulganin said that his country fully appreciated the Afghan desire for modernizing their armed forces.[35] After paying a five day visit to Afghanistan, the Soviet leaders returned to Moscow.

While recounting the Soviet thinking during this period on Afghanistan, Khrushchev later in his memoirs said:

> American was courting Afghanistan, appearing to give that country economic aid but actually being much more interested in carrying political favour. . . At the time of our visit it was clear to us that the Americans were penetrating Afghanistan with the obvious purpose of setting up military base. . . The capital which we've invested in Afghanistan hasn't been wasted. We have earned the Afghan's trust and friendship, and it has not fallen into the American trap. . . The amount of money we spent in gratuitous assistance to Afghanistan is a drop in the ocean compared to the price we would have had to pay in order to counter the threat of an American military base on Afghan territory.[36]

The Soviet leaders extended an invitation to the Afghan leaders to visit Soviet Union and Prime Minister Daoud accepted the invitation.[37]

On 18 December, 1955, both the countries concluded a treaty under which the Article 8 of the Treaty of June 1931 ensuring the neutrality and non-aggression was amended and the treaty was extended for further ten years. It also contained a provision that either side could abrogate the treaty by giving an advance notice of six months.[38] It marked a new phase in Russo-Afghan friendship and Afghanistan tunered this phase cautiously hopeful that its new constructive relationship with the Soviet Union would act as a deterrent to Kremlin's compulsion to intervene in Afghanistan's internal affairs.[39]

The massive Soviet economic aid and the visit of top Soviet leaders to Afghanistan made the Western specialists think that

Afghanistan was lost to communism and the *Time* magazine called Sardar Daoud as Red Prince.[40] However nothing of this sort happened and as the months passed by, it became clear that there was no change in Afghanistan's traditional policy of neutrality. Even prior to the visit of Soviet leaders to Kabul, the Afghan Foreign Minister, Naim had told the US Ambassador in Kabul that "during forthcoming talks with Russians, Government of Afghanistan will not accept any conditions which will prejudice the independence of Afghanistan".[41] When the US Ambassador Ward asked Naim that an arms deal with Soviet Union during the visit of Soviet leaders would be construed by whole world as clear evidence Afghanistan was becoming Soviet satellite, the Afghan Foreign Minister replied that arms were merely for self-defence and as for satellite status, "Afghan leaders would never concur".[42]

Following the conclusion of Bulganin and Khrushchev's Afahan visit, the US Ambassador in Kabul in a telegram to the US state Department on 21 December, 1955 observed: "For all intents and purposes Afghanistan has become a complete economic satellite of USSR and due to this economic enslavement, the Afghans will also be subject to Soviet whims and wishes political—despite Daoud and Naim's protestations that no political conditions or implications exist."[43]

In its National Intelligence Estimate on Afghanistan the US State Department observed on 10 January, 1956 that Afghan Prime Minister Daoud's acceptance of extensive Soviet aid was motivated by his desire to strengthen Afghanistan in its controversy with Pakistan over Pushtunistan issue and also to develop Afghanistan economically.[44] It further added that as long as Daoud continued dedicated to the Pushtunistan issue, the Soviet Union would have a means, not available to the West, of making itself useful as even indispensable to him.[45]

Following the visit of the Soviet leaders to Afghanistan, the Kremlin started evincing keen interest in Kabul. In March 1956, the projects selected by a joint Afghan-Soviet survey team, though excluding railroads, were linked to a large extent with creating and modernizing other transportation facilities. These included two airport projects, one major highway linking Kabul with the strategic Soviet border, one river port facility, construction of bridge, auto repair workshops etc.[46]

In March, 1956, both countries signed an agreement that provided for regular flights between Tashkent and Kabul.[47] The Article VI of this agreement provided a curious fact of Soviet strategic concerns in Afghanistan: "Each side has the right to refuse or amend flight permission to the other if it does not have proof that the majority ownership or actual control of that enterprise is being realized by citizens or organs of that country".[48] This provision makes it evident that Moscow did not want any other country to challenge the Soviet monopoly in Afghanistan. At that period, 49 per cent of the Ariana Afghan Airlines, the only airlines of Afghanistan, with which the Soviets had concluded the said agreement, was owned by one Peter Baldwin, an American businessman who had sported that airlines in April 1955.[49] At this juncture the inclusion of such a provision in the agreement insisted by Moscow aimed at alleviating the American influence. However, in 1957, the Pan American Airways bought out Baldwin's share in the Ariana Airway for $ 400 thousand and actively helped the Ariana with its operation and maintenance problems for more than to decades thereafter.[50]

During March, 1956, another agreement was signed between Kabul and Moscow under which the Soviet specialists were to be stationed in Afghanistan for the purpose of establishing, maintaining and training the Afghan personnel regarding various projects to be jointly set up.[51] These Soviet specialists were also supposed to oversee the Afghan construction activities according to the approved project plans.

In January 1956, the Soviet Vice-President A. Mikoyan visited Afghanistan during which the earlier mentioned agreement worth $ 100 million credit was signed.[52] In February 1956, the Soviet leaders sent messages of greetings to mark the twenty-fifth anniversary of Soviet-Afghan Friendship Treaty of

1931.[53] Soviet media and scholars tried to project a rosy picture of "friendly relations" between Moscow and Kabul and emphasised that Soviet economic assistance to Afghanistan was without any "political strings".[54]

Prime Minister Daoud's Visit to Russia

On 17 October, 1956, Sardar Mohammad Daoud reached Moscow on an official visit. He was given a warm welcome on his arrival.[55] The leading Soviet daily *Pravda* in its issue of 18 October, 1956 while welcoming the visit of Afghan Prime Minister commented that Afghan-Soviet friendship had stood the test of time.[56]

Concluding his fortnight's visit to the Soviet Union, the Afghan Prime Minister said that his visit had been very fruitful because there had been a frank exchange of views between the leaders of the two countries.[57] However, Sardar Mohammad Daoud remained very cautious about his views on global issues. He stressed emphasis on Afghanistan's traditional policy of neutrality.

King Zahir Shah's Visit to Soviet Union

In July 1957, the King of Afghanistan, Zahir Shah, along with Deputy Prime Minister and Foreign Minister Mohammad Naim and other ministers visited Soviet Union. They were given warm welcome on their arrival in Moscow.[58] In his welcome address the Soviet President Varashilov said that the visit of Afghan King was of tremendous significance because it was symbolic of the growing friendship between the two countries professing different political systems.[59]

In his reply the Afghan King referred to the growing friendly relations between the two countries. On 30 July, 1957, at the conclusion of the visit of King Zahir Shah, a joint communique was issued. Both the countries expressed their faith in the principles of peaceful coexistence and Afghanistan was praised for pursuing the policy of strict neutrality.[60]

According to a report published in *Pravda* or 31 July, 1957, the Foreign Ministers of both countries agreed in principle to conclude an agreement regarding the demarcation of border areas between the two countries.[61] The Soviet Union attached great importance to this visit because since King Amanullah's visit, it was the second visit by any Afghan King to the Soviet Union. Moscow promised Kabul to advance a credit worth $15 million for the development of natural gas exports to the Soviet Union.[62]

Augmentation of Soviet Military Influence

The beginning of 1950s had witnessed the inau uration of the penetration of Soviet military influence in Afghanistan. According to Bradsher, Afghanistan was first in the Third World to receive Soviet economic aid and second to receive military aid.[63] In August 1955, Afghanistan negotiated a cash deal worth $ 3 million for Czechoslovak weapons.[64] According to Anthony Arnold, "Afghanistan signed an agreement with the Soviet Union in August 1956 on re-equipping Afghanistan's armed forces with Soviet materials." Of necessity, given the complexity of modern armaments, this agreement involved the training of Afghan officers in Soviet military schools and the stationing of Soviet experts at Afghan military bases. This gave the USSR an opportunity for assessing and recruiting individual officers to serve Soviet political aims is self-evident, and it was not ignored.[65]

In the wake of these developments, many observers on Afghanistan apprehended that Daoud was pushing his country into Soviet vassalage. Others perceived his actions as a high-risk gamble to improve his country's lot by playing off the great powers against each other.[66] However Louis Dupree is optimistic of Daoud's policies during 1950s. According to him, Afghanistan had become an "economic Korea where the competition between the East and the West benefited a local population without endangering its independence."[67] During 1956-58, Afghanistan got substantial economic assistance from Moscow as well as Washington. Between 1950 to 1959, the

US assistance to Afghanistan totalled to $143 million, while the Soviet assistance amounted to $ 246.2 million. The bulk of the US assistance comprised in the form of outright grants, the Soviet provided long-term loans.[68] The US objective in augmenting its Afghan share of aid aimed at securing "maximum internal political stability, promoting friendly economic relations with her ['fghanistan's] Free World neighbours; and minimizing any possibility that Afghanistan might either be a victim of, or a pathway for, Soviet domination in South Asia."[69]

However, a close analysis of the Soviet strategy of extending economic assistance and trade facilities to Afghanistan reveals that beween 1950 and 1960, Kabul's dependence on Moscow for arms had become almost hundred per cent, for petroleum products from 10 per cent to 90 per cent and in case of foreign trade from 17 per cent to almost 50 per cent.[70]

Under the cover of providing economic assistance for transportation and road construction, the Soviet Union was also concentrating on strategic areas. The Soviet highway project that ran from the Soviet border at Kushka to Herat and Kandahar, linked up there with the other highway to Kabul being constructed by the US assistance. Thus the Kremlin was building up strategic highway linking its border with important parts of Afghanistan which it could use one day for exerting its control over that country, as happened in December 1979. Moscow had stipulated such clauses in its agreements with Kabul which it could exploit at short notice. Article 21 of the border agreement between the two countries signed on 18 January, 1958 envisaged that at 48-hour notice either side could examine those parts of international bridges linking the two countries that were situated on the other side's territory.[71]

In May 1959, Moscow and Kabul signed another agreement on building the Kushka-Kandhar road. In July 1959 both countries signed another agreement regarding the construction of three new bridges across the Besud, Kamesh and Asmar Rivers. The construction of the bridges was to be carried out by the Afghan workers under the supervision of Soviet Union.[72]

Khrushchev's Visit to Kabul

On 2 March, 1960, the Soviet Premier N. Khrushchev visited Afghanistan. King Zahir Shah while welcoming the visit of Soviet Prime Minister, hoped that the relations between the two countries would improve further.[73] Khrushchev lauded Afghan foreign policy of non-alignment, international peace and economic development. He also referred to the growing political, economic and cultural relations between Soviet Union and Afghanistan.[74]

Just a couple of months ago, prior to Khrushchev's visit to Afghanistan, Soviet Union and Afghanistan had signed an agreement in Janauary 1960 in which Moscow promised to give economic assistance worth $ 22.4 million during the five year development plan for 1960-65.[75] Even during his visit in March 1960, Khrushchev offered to finance the entire Afghan five year plan for 1960-65 on the condition that Soviet advisers be placed at the highest levels in all Afghan ministries. But Prime Minister of Afghanistan, Sardar Mohammad Daoud, was cautiously skeptical and he reportedly turned down the Soviet offer.[76]

The visiting Soviet Premier visited various projects launched with the Soviet help. In dinner hosted by Soviet leader Khrushchev in favour of Afghan Prime Minister, Mohammad Daoud on 4 March, 1960, the Soviet Premier repeatedly emphasized the fact that it was Soviet leader, Lenin, who first recognized the independence of Afghanistan.[77] The Prime Minister of Afghanistan, Sardar Mohammad Daoud, in his reply, said that Soviet Union under the leadership of Lenin recognized independence of Afghanistan and the latter also took no time in according recognition to the new Government which assumed power after October Revolution.[78] This was characteristic of Daoud to tell the Soviets that Afghanistan did not lag behind in repaying the gratitude it owed to others.

On 4 March, 1960, both countries signed a cultural agreement to promote and cooperate in the fields of science, art and culture.[79] The joint communique issued on 5 March, 1960 at the conclusion of Soviet Premier's visit to Kabul, reiterated the desire of both countries to further improve their relations.[80]

The above analysis makes it evident that Afghan leadership while accepting Soviet economic and technical assistance, did not compromise the foreign policy of Afghanistan but rather secured Sovied endorsement of Afghanistan's independent and non-aligned policy. In early 1963, Sardar Daoud Khan resigned as Prime Minister of Afghanistan. Some Western exports on Afghanistan are of the view that Sardar Daoud during his premiership (1953-63) allowed Soviet influence to increase in Afghanistan unhindered. According to Leon B. Polluda, during Daoud's rule of a decade "the USSR had established a firm base of operation in Afghanistan."[81]

However Prime Minister Sardar Mohammad Daoud until 1963 had remained cautiously skpetical about the Soviet motives in Afghanistan. In reply to a question about Soviet subversion in 1956, Daoud had, while referring to the 1948 Communist takeover in that country, replied: "Does anyone think we have not heard of Czechoslovakia?"[82]

Poullada cities another example to prove his dictum that Daoud dismissed in 1956 a warning from an American Ambassador the Soviet economic aid was laying a logistical infrastructure for invasion and the Soviet training of Afghan military officers could create a fifth column in the armed forces.[83] Such misgivings about Daoud's foreign policy might have been prompted in the light of the fact that he ignored such "warnings" or "advices."

Despite heavy US arms and economic assistance to Pakistan during 1953-63, with which Afghanistan had strained relations over the issue of Pushtunistan, Daoud neither criticised the United States nor sought massive arms aid from the Soviet Union; rather he pursued a policy of genuine non-alignment.

Daoud had declared sometime in 1960: "Our whole life, our whole existence, revolves around one single focal point—freedom. Should we ever get the feeling that our freedom is in the slightest danger, from whatever quarter, then we should prefer to live on dry bread, or even starve, sooner than accept help that would restrict our freedom."[84] By the early 1960s, the people of Afghanistan had realized that:

> . . . Soviet actions were always motivated by their own interests and by those alone. But [the Afghans] reasoned assuming Soviet planners to be reasonable men, those interests could only be augmented by an attack on Afghanistan. The country would be an economic liability to the USSR, to control it would be difficult and costly; and most important, any such as aggression would have disastrous repercussions among the neutralist nations in Asia and Africa.[85]

Thus on the basis of above analysis, it is clear that though during the period 1953-63, Soviet Union did render considerable economic assistance to woo Afghanistan to its fold, the latter did not fall a prey to Soviet overtures and pursued an independent and genuinely non-aligned foreign policy.

Following the ouster of Sardar Mohammad Daoud in 1963, Dr. Mohammad Yusuf became the new Prime Minister of Afghanistan. He could remain in office for a short time and in October 1965, Mohammad Hashim Maiwandwal was appointed as the new Prime Minister of Afghanistan.

Mohammad Zahir Shah, the King of Afghanistan paid an official visit to the USSR from 3 to 16 August, 1965. The King's encourage was accompanied by other ministers and officials of Afghanistan.[86] During the visit the Afghan King had meetings with Leonid Brezhnev, A.N. Kosygin and other Soviet leaders. The talks between the leaders of the two countries proceeded in an atmosphere of friendship, sincerity and mutual understanding.[87]

The two sides expressed full satisfaction with the continuous development of friendship which had a traditional basis and mutual confidence, and comprehensive cooperation between the two countries. Both sides reaffirmed that they would not permit any damage to be done to these relations.[88]

The Joint communique issued at the end of Afghan King's visit to Soviet Union also noted the conviction of both countries that "the friendship and cooperation between the peoples of their countries is a brilliant example of the realization of the principles of peaceful co-existence of states with different economic, social and political systems and that there is an important factor in the consolidation of peace in this part of the world and corresponds to the sincere designs of all the peoples of the world."[89] It was further acknowledged that the Soviet economic assistance had played important role in implementing the first and second five year plans for the development of Afghanistan and that the "continuation of this assistance towards the realization of the third five year plan will have a great and positive effect on the economic development of Afghanistan."[90]

The Afghanistan side emphasised and reaffirmed its policy of neutrality and non-alignment which was in the interest of the people of Afghanistan and of peace throughout the world. The Seviet side reaffirmed that "this policy of Afghanistan is an important contribution to the cause of relaxation of international tension and the strengthening of peace and friendship among the people."[91] Thus the visit of Afghan King to Moscow proved instrumental in procuring Soviet endorsement of Afghan foreign policy.

Between 1963-73 the Soviet-Afghan relations continued on the friendly pattern. There was no major point of departure in the traditionally friendly relationship. Between 1967-70, the value of Russian assistance approximated 70 per cent of the total aid received by Afghanistan from all sources.[92] On 6 February, 1968, both Afghanistan and Soviet Union signed an agreement for economic and technical assistance. Under this and earlier agreements, Afghanistan was bound to export 2.5 billion cubic metres of natural gas, on average, to the Soviet Union upto the year 1985.[93] Though under the agreement of 1968, it was envisaged that the prices of the natural gas would be "determined by the two sides" but in practice the Soviet Union unilaterally determined the price it would pay and controlled all information regarding the quantum of gas it imported. "In fact, the Soviet Union never paid Afghanistan more than twenty per cent of the going world market price for natural gas."[94]

Afghanistan and Brezhnev Doctrine

In the wake of growing schism between Soviet Union and People's Republic of China (PRC) in the late 1960s, Moscow sought to isolate China from the world Communist movement and in Asia. In late May 1969. the then Soviet Prime Minister A. Kosygin during his visit to Kabul, proposed regional economic co-operation among Afghanistan, Pakistan and India as a step toward creating peaceful environment in the region.[95] On 7 June, 1969, the Soviet leader Leonid Brezhnev, while addressing the International Conference of Communist and Workers' Parties held in Moscow, declared: "We are of the opinion that the course of events is putting on the agenda the task of creating a system of collective security in Asia."[96] This concept of collective security in Asia came to be known as "Brezhnev Doctrine." The Soviet leader Brezhnev did not elaborate his doctrine in 1969. However, it was on 30 March, 1972, that Brezhnev stated:

> Collective security in Asia must, in our view, be based on such principles as renunciation of use of force in relations between states, respect for sovereignty and the inviolability of borders, non-interference in internal affairs and the broad development of economic and other co-operation on the basis of full equality and mutual development.[97]

In pursuance of Brezhnev Doctrine, the Soviet Union wooed Afghanistan to endorse the plan for Asian collective security.

However, Afghanistan kept cool towards this plan and reiterated its commitment to the policy of non-alignment. During May 1973, the Soviet President, Podgorny visited Kabul. The joint communique issued after his visit spoke of the great importance which the Soviet Union attached to "Afghanistan's policy of positive neutrality and non-alignment." It further noted:

> Considering that observance of the principles of peaceful coexistence of states with differing social and political systems is an effective way toward establishing lasting peace both in Asia and other parts of the world, the USSR and Afghanistan again declare that in order to guarantee security in Asia it is essential for all countries of the area to make joint efforts in that direction.[98]

However this could not be considered as Afghan endorsement of the Brezhnev Doctrine.

Afghan-Soviet Relations During Daoud Period (July 1973—April 1978)

Sardar Mohammad Daoud who had resigned in 1963, seized power in Kabuly in July 1973 in a bloodless *coup* by overthrowing the monarchy. On 26 July, 1973, the Soviet leadership in a congratulatory message to Sardar Daoud expressed its confidence that "the genuinely good neigbourly relations of friendship and all-round cooperation existing between the Soviet Union and Afghanistan will further develop."[99] Thinking that the leftists had played significant role in Daoud's return to power and the latter being surrounded by a solid corps of pro-Moscow leftists, Soviets deemed it a significant step in the furtherance of their interests in South West Asia. "It was therefore necessary not only to actively support the new 'leftist' regime in Kabul but also to strive to increase Afghanistan's dependence on the Soviet Union, to extract maximum benefit from the unexpectedly fortuitous new conditions."[100]

After about a year of his assumption of power, President Daoud paid an official visit to Soviet Union from 4 to 7 June, 1974. Prior to his departure for Moscow, Daoud had dissociated himself from most of the leftists members of his cabinet. Thus during the Soviet visit of President Daoud, the Afghans were keenly watching for any sign of Soviet annoyaance with the change of outlook in Kabul but could not detcet any, either prior to Daoud's visit to Moscow or during his stay there. One passage of Soviet President Podgorny's speech during the State luncheon hosted in Kremlin in honour of President Daoud was retrospectively interpreted by some analysts as asking the Afghan President to continue to work closely with the PDPA.[101] President Podgorny said:

> Great and complex tasks (of renovating political, economic and cultural life) will have to be tackled. . . But as experience shows, they can be solved successfully when the course chartered is pursued firmly, when broad popular masses are drawn into the work of building a new life and when forces which are sincerely interested in strengthening the new system, act vigorously and in close unity.[102]

Such a statement, however, could not be construed as an expression of Soviet disappointment over Daoud's purging of the leftists. Rather Soviet leader reiterated Soviet desire to strengthen relations with Afghanistan. President Podgorny said that following the establishment of the Republican system in Afghanistan in July 1973, the Soviet-Afghan relations had risen to a still higher level: "The Soviet Union was the first to recognize the new Republic and immediately after it was proclaimed it declared its readiness to develop relations of friendship and fruitful cooperation with it."[103] The Soviet laeders in their public statements and private talks with President Daoud expressed Soviet readiness to participate substantiaally in Afghanistan's forthcoming Seven Year Development Plan. Both sides also agreed to set up a joint commission for economic and technical co-operation whose task would be to identify those projects to be implemedted with Soviet co-operation. Moscow also agreed to open a $ 600 million line of credit for financing various Afghan projects within the proposed Seven Year Plan.[104]

Some analysts believe that during his visit to Soviet Union in June 1974, President Daoud "accepted Soviet-drafted language in joint communique endorsing the Brezhnev Doctrine."[105] However, it was no easy a task to procure blank Afghan endorsement of the Brezhnev Doctrine. During the delegation level when the text of the Joint communique was being finalized, Moscow insisted that the reference to Brezhnevs proposal be rendered more explicitly and concise. However Afghanistan insisted that establishment of a security system in Asia would entail the fulfilment of certain conditions. According to Abdul Samad Ghaus, of senior Afghan diplomat who was intimately ivolved in foreign policy formulations during Republican period under President Daoud, Afghanistan proposed that "that objections to the colonial frontiers and their adherence to peaceful settlement of disputes be reflected in an appropriate fashion in the relevant part of the communique related to Asian security if the Kabul formulations were to be altered.'[106] Subsequently the following paragraph was in corporated in the joint communique:

> The Republic of Afghanistan and the Soviet Union are deeply interested in securing peace and co-operation in Asia and consider that the creation of a security system by joint efforts of all the States of Asia would meet the interests of the Asian peoples. This would require the settlement of disputable issues through peaceful means and elimination of the remnants of colonialism.[107]

While at the farewell ceremony, after the conclusion of Daoud's Soviet visit, President Podgorny stated that the idea of collective security in Asia was gaining increasing support from the Asian countries that the conditions were being created for the "translation of the idea into life."[108] President Daoud again quipped instantly by saying that the collectives security in Asia was a commendable idea, "but Afghanistan is of the opinion that real peace is achieved only when the lawful rights of human masses are respected by all states, and colonialistic attitudes are condemned on the basis of the principles of the United Nations Charter."[109]

A few month after Daoud's visit to Moscow, Soviet Union started showing interest in Afghanistan's Seven Year Development Plan. Apart from evincing general interest in irrigation agricultural projects, urea fertilizer plant, thermal plant, the Soviet Union showed keen interest in am ambitious joint venture aimed at locating Afghanistan's natural resources and the Haji Gak iron ore development project in the Central Hindu Kush. The Soviets committed financial assistance for the Haji Gak iron ore, which after the exploitation was to be trasported to the Soviet Union where the production of iron and steel would take place.[110] According to an observer it was typical Kremlin strategy to keep Afghanistan as a supplier of raw material and the receiver of Soviet manufactured goods-a classic example of colonial exploitation.[111]

During the second week of September 1974, two senior Afghan leaders Mohammad Naim and Waheed Abdullah visited Soviet Union. During their meeting Soviet leaders—Brezhnev and Kosygin, the Afghan leaders exchanged views on bilateral and multilateral issues. Deteriorating Afghan-Pakistan relations and the dangers that the situation presented for the region formed the main substance of their talks. According to Ghaus, Mohammad Naim emphasized upon the need for Soviet financial help to develop the Ainak and Haji Gak projects "but the Russians were vague and non-commital in their project."[112]

In October 1974, Marshal Maskolenko, Deputy Defence Minister of Soviet Union, paid an official visit to Kabul. It was a routine visit forming part of periodic exchanges of military exchanges between the two countries. Since the visit took place in the wake of deteriorating Afghan-Pakistan relations, it gave rise to the speculation that Kabul was preparing for launching an attack on Pakistan.[113] However, as latter developments proved, it was totally unfounded.

By the beginning of 1975, Daoud's domestic and external policy had embarked on a more independent path with minmum dependence on pro-Moscow leftists in Kabul and lesser economic and military dependence on Moscow. He had started taking measures to phase out communist influence in the government and in the Army. This aspect is analysed in detail in the fifth chapter. With a view to reduce its economic dependence on Soviet Union, it was inevitable for Afghanistan to broaden its economic and political base. Accordingly, Daoud administration started making friendly overtures to Islamic, Arab and other non-aligned countries.

Besides, Daoud was also unhappy over the enhancing Soviet influence in the non-aligned movement in Africa and Latin America mainly through Cuba. According to Samad Ghaus, Daoud did not approve of Cuba's membership of NAM because of its being subservient to Soviet policies.[114] Daoud even refused Rumanian request for Afghanistan's support to the former's efforts to become an observer at the ensuing Colombo summit meeting of the non-aligned countries.

Though these broadbased developments had no direct and immediate impact on Afghan-Soviet relations, but it did reflect Daoud's desire to lead Afghanistan to an independent and truly non-aligned path with minimum Soviet or American influence.

It was in this background that Soviet President Podgorny paid two-day state visit on 9-10 December, 1975 to Kabul. Talks between the visiting Soviet leader and president Daoud were of routine and uneventful nature. Unlike earlier visits, this visit lacked enthusiasm both in Kabul and Moscow. The official Soviet reports spoke coolly of Podgorny's visit to Afghanistan and made reference to Soviet-Afghan relations in a sterotyped fashion.[115] Divergent interests seemed to have overshadowed the talks on regional issues. While Daoud laid stress on the deteriorating Afghan-Pakistan relations, Podgorny was curious to know the role played by the then Shah of Iran helping Afghanistan and Pakistan in overcoming their differences. Podgorny made frequent references to Asian collective security system in his banquet speech while Daoud "glossed over it"[116] in his statements.

The joint communique issued after Podgorny's visit to Kabul expressed the firm determination of both sides "to do everything possible to develop still further Soviet-Afghan relations and fruitful co-operation between the two countries in political, trade, economic and other spheres".[117] On this occasion a protocol was also signed between Daoud and Podgorny extending the 1931 Soviet-Afghan friendship and non-aggression treaty for a period of ten years. One could notice the "cool-off" stage in Afghan-Soviet relations which had started surfacing by the end of 1975.

Such turn of events showed that by that time Daoud had realized that the growing Soviet influence was contrary to Afghanistan's traditional policy of genuine non-alignment. Thus with a view to alleviate Afghan economic dependence on Soviet Union and keeping in consonance with the principles of non-alignment, President Daoud took positive measures to improve Afghanistan's relations with Pakistan, Iran and other Islamic countries. In October, 1974. Iran promised Afghanistan to provide $ 2 billion in economic aid over a period of ten years, and a part of this aid was to be spent on the construction of a railroad from Kabul to Iran, which eventually would have provided Afghanistan with a trade route through Iranian ports, thereby decreasing Afgha dependence on Soviet trade.[118] This shows that President Daoud was following an independent and non-aligned policy by developing close relations with non-aligned and Islamic countries.

By 1976, Soviet Union had started evincing keen interest in the Parcham and Khalq factions of the people's Democratic Party of Afghanistan (PDPA) with a view to unite them.

President Daoud was aware of the Soviet overtures to PDPA's leaders. Samad Ghaus has claimed that during the second half of 1976, intelligence reports were continuously pouring in Kabul about the Soviet subversive activities aimed at organizaing and revitalizing the Afghan communist elements.[119] He further claims that Daoud was aware of Soviet tactis but adopted a "wait-and-see" attitude with a view not to embarass the Soviets prematurely and to take action against the local communists whenever enough hard evidence of their anti-regime activities became available.[120]

Afghanistan's growing economic and political interaction with the neighbouring Islamic countries, especially Iran was irritating for Moscow. In November 1976, Soviet Ambassador in Kabul, Puzanov, enquired from Samad Ghaus, then a senior Afghan official in Afghan Foreign Ministry whether Afghan Government was confident that Iran would honour its pledge of economic assistance. To this, Ghaus replied that there was no reason to doubt the sincerity of Iran's pledges of assistance.[121]

Consequently Moscow stepped up its economic assistance to Kabul with an avowed objective of keeping the latter under its sphere of influence and also to reduce its dependence on neighbouring Iran. During 1975, Moscow provided a credit of $ 437 million to Afghanistan. In 1977, the two countries signed a trade agreement calling for a 65 per cent increase by 1980. According to Alfred Monks, by September 1977, the Soviet presence in Afghanistan overnumbered that of any other foreign power.[122]

According to Samad Ghaus, in February 1977, President Daoud mentioned to Waheed Abdullah and Ghaus that the time had come when Afghan government should ask "highest authority in Soviet State—Leonid Brezhnev, whether the Soviet subversive activities in Afghanistan were being conducted with his approval. Daoud said that "Brezhnev could have to tell him frankly what the Soviet intended to achieve by pursuing this course".[123]

It was in the wake of these developments that President Daoud paid an official visit to Moscow from 12 to 15 April, 1977. Before proceeding to Moscow, Daoud had undertaken certain measures in his own country which included the removal of Soviet military advisers from the lower levels of the Afghan Armed forces.[124] While on his way to Moscow, Daoud had asked Waheed Abdullah, to arrange an exclusive private meeting with Brezhnev in Moscow, Consequently, on his arrival in Moscow on 12 April, 1977, President Daoud had meeting with Soviet leaders including Brezhnev, Podgorny and Kosygin.

During the talks, the Soviet and Afghan leaders exchanged views on bilateral political and economic issues. President Daoud said that Afghanistan "had embarked on the construction of a new, and, it was to be hoped, prosperous society that demanded considerable efforts by the people and the government of Afghanistan. In this undertaking. . . Afghanistan needed the disinterested help of all friendly countries and was actively seeking that help.[125]

At a banquet given in honour of Afghan President, the Soviet President Podgorny said that "the role of the Republic of Afghanistan which is situated in the heart of Asia, and its favourable contribution are very important. The Soviet Union and Afghanistan have a common approach to many urgent problems related to the contemporary situation in Asia and the rest of the world."[126] According to Samad Ghaus, some of the Afghans present at the banquet regarded Podgorny's remarks about Afghanistan's geopolitical importance as a reminder "to the Afghans that their country's geographical closeness to Russia did not allow it diversions from a common approach by both countries. . . ."[127]

Sardar Daoud in his reply laid stress on Afghanistan's steadfast commitment to the policy of non-alignment which was based on "the strong foundations of peaceful coexistence, mutual respect, non-interference in each other's domestic affairs [and], non-participation in political groupings and war blocs".[128]

On 14 April, 1977, Sardar Daoud had a meeting with Soviet leader Brezhnev. During the talks, Brezhnev expressed displeasure over the increase in presence of experts from the NATO countries working in Afghanistan in bilateral ventures as well as on the UN and other multilateral aid projects. Brezhnev further added that Soviet Union "took a grim view of these developments and wanted the Afghan government to get rid of those experts, who were nothing more than spies bent on promoting the cause of imperialism".[129] To this Sardar Daoud immediately reacted by saying that such a statement was a flagrant interference in the internal affairs of Afghanistan. According to Samad Ghaus, Daoud instantly reacted by saying: "We will never allow you to dictate to us how to run our country and whom to employ in Afghanistan. How and where we employ the foreign experts will remain the exclusive prerogative of the Afghan State. Afghanistan shall remain poor, if necessary, but free in its acts and decisions".[130] According to Thomas T. Hammond, who has interviewed many Afghans, President Daoud reportedly told Brezhnev, "I want to remain you that you are speaking to the President of an independent country, not one of your East European satellites. You are trying to interfere in the internal affairs of Afghanistan and this I will not permit".[131] Henry Bradsher, who interview various Afghan officials In Kabul, has also confirmed this.[132] It is evident that Sardar Mohammed Daoud behaved in a true Afghan spirit and was not cowed down or bullied by the Soviet leaders.

This incident is generally interpreted as the beginning of the fall of Daoud's regime. However, Daoud completed his visit and the joint communique issued after the visit did not contain any reference or even linking of any rupture in Afghan-Soviet relations. The language of the joint communique was familiar, speaking about cordial bilateral relations.[133] On his return to Kabul, from Moscow, President Daoud expressed his confidence that the relations between Afghanistan and

Soviet Union were based on "good neighbourliness, mutual respect and non-interference in domestic affairs".[134]

After Daoud's visit to Moscow in April, 1977, there was no visible change in the overall relationship of pattern between Moscow and Kabul. However, the simmer differences had started surfacing on occasions providing an indication of growin Soviet disenchantment with Daoud regime.

The seizure of power by the communists on 27 April, 1978 in Kabul under the banner of PEPA marked the end of Daoud's regime and emergence of pro-Moscow government. Since the end of Second World War and until the fall of Daoud's regime, the overall pattern of Afghan-Soviet relations remained cordial. Afghanistan, in pursuit of its policy of non-alignment, maintained cordial and friendly relations with Moscow. However, the assumption of power by Sardar Mohammad Daoud in 1973 made Afghanistan's commitment to the principles of non-alignment as more steadfast, Daoud did not want Afghanistan to be solely dependent on Moscow for economic and political support. Thus during Daoud's period, Afghanistan improved its relations with neighbouring Islamic and other non-aligned countries. Daoud wanted Afghanistan genuinely non-aligned country and a friend of Soviet Union but not latter's dependent. The fall of Daoud's regime marked the end of a glorious period in Afghan history. It was for the cause of his nation that Sardar Daoud laid down his life. The Russians were perhaps convinced that they could not succeed in Sovietizing Afghanistan so far Sardar Daoud and like of him were alive. Thus he was physically eliminated. Though Sardar Daoud died but the path shown by him kept the Afghan spirit and morale aloft.

REFERENCES

1. *Islah* (Kabul), 15 May, 1946.
2. For text of the Treaty see, United Nations (UN), *Treaty Series*, Vol. 31 (New York, 1949), pp. 147-68.
3. Roman T. Akhramovich, *Outline History of Afghanistan After the Second World War* (Moscow, 1966), p. 69.
4. Henry S. Bradsher, *Afghanistan and the Soviet Union* (Durham, N.C.: Duke Press, 1983), p. 16.
5. *New York Times*, 9 August, 1946.
6. Abdul Samad Ghaus, *The Fall of Afghanistan: A Insider's Account* (Washington, D.C.: Pergamon-Brassey's, 1988), p. 66.
7. Anthony Arnold, *Afghanistan: The Soviet Invasion in Perspective* (Revised edn.) (Stanford, Calif: Stanford University), p. 26.
8. Arnold Fleteher, *Afghanistan: Highway of Conquent* (Ithaca: N.Y.: Cornell University Press, 1965), p. 251.
9. Louis Dupree, "Afghanistan's Big Gample: Part II, Economic and Strategic Aspects of Soviet Aid", *American University Field Staff Report* (*AUFS*), Vol. 4, No. 4, May 1960, p. 6.
10. Louis Dupree, *Afghanistan* (Princeton, N.J.: Princeton University Press, 1973), p. 492.
11. *New York Times*, 14 June, 1946.
12. For details see, A. Dyakov, "A Partitioned India", *New Times* (Moscow), 14 January, 1948.
13. E. Atramonov, "How the British and American Imperialists are Interfering in the Afghan-Pakistan Dispute", ibid., 22 June, 1949.
14. Dupree, No. 9, p. 3.
15. Marshal I. Goldman, *Soviet Foreign Aid* (New York, 1967), p. 115. Also see Peter G. Franck, *Afghanistan between East and West* (Washington, 1960), p. 55.
16. Alvin Z. Rubinstein, *The Foreign Policy of Soviet Union* (New York, 1960), pp. 395-97.
17. *Ibid.*, p. 383.
18. Goldman, No. 15, pp. 56-58.
19. Franck, No. 15, p. 115.
20. *Ibid.*

21. Bradsher, No. 4, p. 24.
22. Arnold, No. 7, p. 35.
23. Ghaus, No. 6, p. 74.
24. United States, *Foreign Relations of the United States 1951. Vol. VI, Asia and the Pacific, Part II* (Washington, 1977), p. 2.
25. UN, *Official Records of General Assembly (GAOR)*, Second Session, Plen. Meeting 92, 30 September, 1947.
26. Ghaus, No. 6; p. 82.
27. Fletcher, No. 8, p. 269.
28. US, *Foreign Relations of the United States, 1955-57, Vol. VIII, South Asia* (Washington, D.C., 1987), p. 171.
29. "Memorandum from the Secretary of State's Special Assistant for Intelligence (Armstrong) to the Secretary of State, 15 April, 1955", *ibid.*, pp. 172-73.
30. *Aslah*, 16 December, 955.
31. N.A. Bulganin and N.S. Khrushchev, *Speeches During Sojourn in India, Burma and Afghanistan, November-December 1955* (New Delhi, 1956), p. 173.
32. *Ibid.*, p. 175.
33. *Ibid.*
34. Goldman, 15, p. 115. Also see Dupree, No. 10, pp. 508-9.
35. Bulganin and Khrushchev, No. 31, p. 176.
36. Nikita S. Khrushchev, *Khrushchev Remembers* (Boston, 1971), pp. 560-2.
37. *Islah*, 19 December, 1955.
38. For details of the Treaty see, Bulganin and Khrushchev, no. 31, pp. 188-92.
39. Ghaus, No. 6, p. 86.
40. Cited in Fletcher, No. 8, p. 285.
41. *Foreign Relations 1955-57*, No. 28, p. 206.
42. *Ibid.*
43. *Ibid.*, p. 212.
44. *Ibid.*, p. 218.
45. *Ibid.*
46. Franck, No. 15, p. 57.

47. Y.M. Vinogradov, *et. al*, eds., *Sovetsko-Afghanskive Otnosheniya 1919-1969* (Moscow, 1971), pp. 129-34 as cited in Arnold. No. 7, p. 36.

48. *Ibid.*

49. Louis Dupree, "American Private Enterprise in Afghanistan: The Investment Climate as it Relates to One Company", *AUFS*, Vol. 4 No. 9, December 1960, p. 4.

50. Franck, No. 15, p. 461.

51. Arnold, No. 7, p. 38.

52. *Islah*, 29 January, 1956.

53. *Moscow News* (Moscow), 29 February, 1956.

54. For details see S. Ineutin and V. Peterkhov, "The Consolidation of Soviet-Afghan Friendship and Cooperation", *International Affairs* (Moscow), No. 1, January, 1956, pp. 41-49.

55. *Islah* 18, October, 1956.

56. *Moscow News*, 20 October, 1956.

57. *Ibid.*, 30 October, 1956.

58. *Pravda* (Moscow), 18 July, 1957, cited in *New Times* (Moscow) July 1957.

59. *Ibid.*

60. *Ibid.*, 31 July, 1957.

61. *Ibid.*

62. Franck, No. 15, p. 57.

63. Bradsher, No. 4, p. 27.

64. "Soviet Bloc Economic Activities in the Near East and Asia as of November 25, 1955" in the *Declassified Documents Retrospective Collective* (Washington, 1976), 3F.

65. Arnold, No. 7, p. 38.

66. *Ibid.*

67. Dupree, No. 10.

68. Richard S. Newell, *Politics of Afghanistan* (Ithaca, New Yark: Cornell University Press, 1972), pp. 1282-29.

69. Franck, No. 15, p. 72.

70. Dupree, No. 9, p. 3.

71. Vinogradov, *et. al.*, No. 47, p. 156, as cited in Arnold, No. 7, p. 39.
72. *Ibid.*, pp. 179-82.
73. *Happiness And Peace for the Peoples: N.S. Khrushchev's Visit to India, Burma, Indonesia and Afghanistan February 11 –March 5, 1960* (Moscow, 1960), p. 266.
74. *Ibid.*, pp. 266-67.
75. *New York Times*, 21 January, 1960.
76. Louis Dupree, "The Mountains Go to Mohammad Zahir," *AUFSR* Vol. 4, No. 6.
77. *Khrushchev's Visits*, No. 73, pp. 288-90.
78. *Ibid.*, p. 291.
79. *Ibid.*, pp. 293-96.
80. *Ibid.*, pp. 302-3.
81. Leon B. Poullada, "The Failure of American Diplomacy in Afghanistan", *World Affairs* (Washington), Vol. 145, No. 3, Winter 1982/83, p. 282.
82. Quoted in Bradsher, No. 4, p. 27.
83. Leon B. Poullada, "Afghanistan and the United States: The Crucial Years", *The Middle East Journal*, Vol. 35, (1981), p. 187.
84. Quoted in Gunther Nollau and Hans Jurgenwiche, *Russia's South Flank* (New York: Praeger, 1963), p. 136.
85. Fletcher, No. 8, p. 261.
86. United States, *American Foreign Policy: Current Documents* (Washington, D.C.: Government Printing Office, 1968), p. 608.
87. *Ibid.*, p. 609.
88. *Ibid.*
89. *Ibid.*
90. *Ibid.*
91. *Ibid.*, p. 610.
92. Newell, No. 68, p. 147.
93. Abdul Tawab Assifi, "The Russian Rope: Soviet Economic Motives and the Subversion of Afghanistan", *World Affairs* (Washington), Vol. 145, No. 3, Winter 1982/83, p. 255.
94. *Ibid.*, p. 256.

95. Alvin Z. Rubinstein, "The Last Years of Peaceful Co-existence: Soviet-Afghan Relations 1963-1978", *The Middle East Jonrnal*, Vol. 36, No. 2, Spring 1982, p, 170.

96. *New York Times*, 8 June, 1969.

97. Foreign Broadcasting Information Service (hereafter FBIS), FBIS/USSR, 21 March, 1972.

98. FBIS/USSR, 26 May, 1983.

99. *Kabul Times*, 31 July, 1973.

100. Ghaus, p. 159.

101. Bradsher, No. 4, p. 64.

102. *Kabul Times*, 6 June, 1974.

103. *Ibid*.

104. Ghaus, No. 6. p. 165.

105. A.G. Noorani, Soviet Ambitions in Soviet Asia", *International Security*, Vol. 11, Winter 1979-80, p. 41.

106. Ghaus, No. 6, p. 166.

107. *Kabul Times*, 9 June, 1974.

108. *Ibid*.

109. *Ibid*.

110. Abdul Tawab Assifi, "The Russian Rope: Soviet Economic Motive and the Subversion of Afghanistan", *World Affairs* (Washington, D.C.), No. 145, Winter 1983, p. 263.

111. *Ibid*.

112. Ghaus, No. 6, p. 168.

113. *Ibid*.

114. *Ibid*., p. 169.

115. *Foreign Broadcast Information Service (FBIS). USSR*, 10 December, 1975.

116. Ghaus, No. 6, p. 170.

117. FBIS/USSR, Part III, 17 December, 1975, pp. S. 1-3.

118. Louis Dupree, "Afghanistan 1977: Does Trade Plus Aid Guarantee Development?" *AUFSR*, Vol. 21, No. 3, August 1977, p. 3.

119. Ghaus, No. 6. p, 172.

120. *Ibid*., p. 173.

121. *Ibid.*

122. Alfred Monks, *The Soviet Intervention in Afghanistan* (Washington, D.C.: American Enterprise Institute, 1981), p. 14.

123. Ghaus, No. 6, p. 174.

124. Bradsher, p. 65.

125. *FBIS/Soviet Union*, South Asia, III, 13 April, 1977, p. J. 4.

126. *Ibid.*, p. 5.

127. Ghaus, No. 6, p. 177.

128. *FBIS/Soviet Union*, South Asia III, 13 April, 1977, p. J. 6.

129. Cited in Ghaus, No. 6, p. 179.

130. *Ibid.*

131. Thomas T. Hammond, *Red Flag Over Afghanistan* (Boulder: Westview Press, 1984),

132. Bradsher, pp. 65-66.

133. *FBIS/Soviet Union*, 18 April, 1977, pp. J. 1-3.

134. *Ibid.*, p. J. 4.

CHAPTER IV

AFGHAN-U.S. RELATIONS

Afghanistan's relations with United Stated are of recent origin. The formal diplomatic relations between Kabul and Washington were established in 1940s but efforts in this direction were initiated during King Amanullah's time. However it was during the middle of nineteenth century that some American missionaries made efforts to establish contracts with Afghanistan. The American Presbyterian missionaries made a pioneering attempt to establish direct contact with the Afghans.[1] They established a mission at Ludhiana, where several prominent Afghan refugees including the former Amir Zaman Shah and Shah Shuja were staying.[2] However, the American missionaries failed to establish contacts among "the exiled Afghan leaders or their retines."[3]

Until the advent of the regime of King Amanullah in 1919, there were virtually no direct or indirect contacts between Kabul and Washington. King Amanullah gave a new direction to Afghan foreign policy by seeking to establish friendly relations with Soviet Union, United Kingdom (UK) and Turkey. Amanullah sent his personal emissary to explore the possibilities of establishing friendly relations with the United States and other European countries,

In July 1921, an Afghan mission headed by Mohammed Wali Khan visited the United States.[4] On his arrival in New York on 11 July, 1921, Mohammed Wali Khan said that he had come to explore the possibilities of establishing friendly relations between Afghanistan and the United States.[5] Prior to his meeting with the then US Secretary of State, Charles E. Hughes, Wali Khan told the press on 17 July, 1921 that the establishment of relations between Afghanistan and the United States would provide ample opportunities for American businessmen to invest in Afghanistan.[6] However despite all such optimistic pronouncements Wali Khan was not sure about the success of his mission.[7] Leader of the Afghan mission met some officials of the State Department of the US before he could meet the Secretary of State. However, the *New York Times* commented that the welcome accorded to the Afghan Mission by the United States could not be interpreted as US recognition of King Amanullah's regime in Kabul.[8] The then US Secretary of State Charles E. Hughes, wrote to the US President on 18 July, 1921: "Apparently we have, hitherto, had no relations with Afghanistan directly as formerly our dealings with that country were through Great Britain. In 1919 Great Britain "recognized the independence of Afghanistan."[9] However, the UK did not like Afghan policy of foreign relations with other European powers. Hughes in his letter to the President conveyed the British feelings about Afghan Mission that "the British Government did not look with favour on its (Afghan Mission's) activities or its endeavours to conclude agreements with other Governments, as Afghanistan, though ostensibly independent, was still within the British 'sphere of political influence'."[10]

The US Secretary of State expressed the view that there was no way of having relations with Afghanistan "at that time unless they are had directly and there is nothing in the British position which precludes our reception of the (Afghan) Mission."[11] The US was aware of Afghanistan's Treaty of Friendship with Soviet Union, signed in September 1920, and ratified by Afghanistan in August 1921. The US Secretary of

State, Hughes, expressed the view that Afghanistan's relations with the Soviet Union did not prevent the United States to establish relations with Kabul. He wrote to President Hardinge that "the Soviet Government had dealings with other powers with which we are in relations and I do not believe that the Soviet Treaty with Afghanistan furnishes a reason for precluding ourselves from the opportunities which otherwise might be open in that country."[12] Thus the US Secretary of State advised the US President to receive the Afghan Mission and opined that he did not think "however, that pending further inquiries, it is necessary or advisable to go beyond their courteous reception."[13]

Consequently, the Afghan Mission was received by the Secretary of State on 20 July, 1921. Secretary Hughes in another letter to the President Hardinge on 21 July, 1921 informed the latter that the Afghan Mission was in the United States for the establishment of diplomatic relations."[14] There did not prevail or exist formal or informal diplomatic relations between Kabul and Washington. In view of the fact that the Great Britain had "relinquished her protectorate"[15] over Afghanistan, the United States could establish direct relations with Afghanistan. But the then US Secretary of State did not favour the establishment of direct diplomatic relations with Afghanistan. He advised the President that "nothing further should be said at this time and that the matter will be taken under careful consideration."[16]

The Afghan Mission met the US President Hardinge on 26 July, 1921. Mohammed Wali Khan, leader of the Afghan Mission, handed over a personal letter from the Afghan King, Amanullah, to President Hardinge. Amir Amanullah wrote: "As I used to have the sincere wish to establish permanent friendly relations between Afghanistan and the high Government of the United States, I expected that Your Excellency's high Government may be satisfied with the keeping of that friendly relations too."[17] President Hardinge in his reply to Amanullah's letter wrote:

> It is my wish that the relations between the United States and Afghanistan may always be of a friendly character, and I shall be happy to cooperate with Your Majesty to this end. I am constrained, however, to confirm to Your Majesty, what was stated orally to G. Mohammed Wali Khan, that with respect to the United States, the question of the creation of a Diplomatic Mission and of the appropriate action to that end by the Congress of the United States must be reserved for further consideration.[18]

In 1922, Cornelius Van H. Eugert, an American diplamat stationed in Persia, who paid an unofficial visit to King Amanullah's court and was accorded friendly welcome "as the first American official to visit Afghanistan, wrote a detailed report to State Department strongly recommending recognition of Afganistan. It was filed away and ignored."[18a]

It becomes clear from the above analysis that the United States had deferred the Afghan request of establishing diplomatic relations between Kabul and Washington. The fact that the US did not recognize Amanullah's regime in 1921 could not be interpreted as the negation of US interest in Afghanistan.

There occurred a spell of about four years when there was discernible effort on either side to resume negotiations on establishing diplomatic ties between the two countries. In October 1925, the Afghan Ambassador to France, Nadir Khan, contacted the US Ambassador in France, Merrick, in that connection. On 30 October, 1925, Nadir Khan wrote a letter to Merrick urging him to resume negotiations regarding the establishment of diplomatic relations between the two countries.[19] The Afghan Ambassador in his letter had also attached a draft proposal for a treaty to be concluded between the two countries which incorporated provision for Ambassador level relations and increased economic cooperation between the two countries.[20] Merrick forwarded Afghan Ambassador's letter along with the proposed draft treaty to the US State Department.[21] The US Secretary of State, Frank B. Kellogg informed Merrick to convey to the Afghan Ambassador the appreciation of US Government's appreciation of friendly sentiments towards the United States and also enclosed a draft reply purported to be sent to Afghan Ambassador.[22] The proposed note, a copy of which was handed over to Nadir Khan on 20 February, 1926 in Paris, conveyed the appreciation of US Government towards Afghanistan's friendly sentiments and assured that "careful consideration will be accorded to the draft treaty which you have presented".[23] In 1927 and 1928, the exchange of communications between Kabul and Washington used to be through either French Ambassador in Kabul or through their respective missions in Paris.

In the wake of the downfall of King Amanullah in April 1929, the process of negotiations between Afghanistan and the United States suffered a setback.[24] Nadir Shah who succeeded Amanullah as the new King of Afghanistan could remain in power from the end of 1929 to 1933. During this period the Government of Afghanistan did make certain efforts to establish diplomatic relations with the United States. In 1931, the Afghan Ambasador in London made attempts to contact the US Ambassador in London. Consequently, the US Ambassador in London informed the Department of State and requested for further instructions.[25] However there was no positive response by the State Department to Afghan proposal. The Secretary of State directed the US Ambassador in London that if Afghan Ambassador raised the question of recognition "you should state that you are not authorized to discuss the matter with him."[26]

The Department of State was informed in September 1931 by the US Ambassador in Italy, Kirk, that the Afghan Government believed that the United States might be inclined to establish official relations with Afghanistan.[27] The Afghan Ambassador in Rome had contacted Ambassador Kirk there and conveyed to the latter his government's desire to "establish relations with the United States Government and was prepared to negotiate a treaty".[28] The Afghan Ambassador had further informed that in case the US Government gave due weightage to the Afghan proposal, his government would undobtedly empower him to undertake preliminary negotiations in Rome.[29] Thus the Department of State was requested by the US Ambassador in Rome to issue instructions to the latter in this matter.[30]

The US Secretary of State in his reply to Ambassador Kirk wrote that the Afghan Ambassador could be informed that "no recent consideration has been given to by his Government to the question of the establishment of official relations with the Afghan Government and the present moment is not considered to be opportune to negotiate a treaty".[31] The US Department of State regarded the question of establishing official relations with Afghanistan at that time as premature "since the present regime in Afghanistan has not yet been recognized by this Government."[32]

Consequent upon the death of King Nadir Shah, in 1933, Zahir Shah took over as the new King of Afghanistan. The new King adopted measures to improve Afghanistan's relations with Japan, Italy, France and Czechoslovakia and also made efforts to procure economic assistance from these countries.[33] In July 1934, King Zahir Shah sent a letter to the US President through Afghan Ambassador in Paris expressing his desire to strengthen political and economic relations between Afghanistan and the United States.[34] The then US Acting Secretary of State, william Phillips, wrote to the US President Roosevelt that although the US had never entered into direct diplomatic relations with Afghanistan, President Hardinge in 1921 received an official mission from that country by which it was generally accepted that "recognition had been accorded to the regime of King Amanullah who was then in power".[35] However the US reluctance to establish diplomatic relations with Afghanistan was evident from his statement: "We have been naturally conservative on the subject of establishing relations with Afghanistan owing to the primitive conditions in that country, the lack of capability or other guarantees to the safety of foreigners and the absence of any important American interests."[36] However the Acting Secretary of State further wrote that he could see no reasons "why we should withhold recognition of Afghanistan."[37] President Roosevelt in his reply sent to King Zahir Shah wrote: "I cordially reciprocate the sentiments which you express in extending recognition to Your Majesty's Government, take this opportunity of assuring you of my hope that friendly relations will always exist between the United States and Afghanistan."[38] Thus it was for the first time that the United States accorded recognition to Afghanistan. A friendship treaty between Afghanistan and the United States was proposed by the former in October 1934.[39] The then US Secretary of State in his reply to US Ambassador in France, Straus, wrote that although the United States was not opposed to "concluding a treaty of friendship and commerce with the Government of Afghanistan, it considers that the purpose which the two Governments have in mind might be accomplished more expeditiously and satisfactorily by the conclusion of a less formal agreement."[40]

Subsequently a draft proposal envisaging proposed US amendments to the Afghan draft treaty was sent to Afghanistan. The proposed agreement consisting of seven articles envisaged political and economic relations between washington and Kabul.[41] The resultant impact of these negotiations was that on 26 March, 1936, the agreement was signed between Kabul and Washington at Paris.[42] Thus by March 1936, the United States had recognized the Afghan Government and both countries had signed a formal agreement. Accordingly on 4 May, 1936, Hornybrook, presented his credentials to the Afghan Government at Kabul as the first US Ambassador, in Afghanistan, with his headquarters at Tehran.[43]

The year 1937 marked the beginning of the economic cooperation between Kabul and Washington when Afghan Government granted its first concession to the American Inland Exploration Company a 75-year option on the exploration of the Ore resources available in Afghanistan. However, negotiations in this regard had started in October 1936 and on 20 November, 1936[44] an agreement was signed between the representatives of the Inland Exploration Company and the Afghan Foreign Minister, Faiz Mohammad Khan.[45] Under the terms of this agreement, the US Company acquired the rights of exploring oil in Afghanistan and the agreement proved very useful for the Company.[46] Reports indicate that German Foreign Office and Berlin-based Soviet Ambassador made frantic attempts for thwarting the conclusion of this agreement.[47] Realizing that their efforts in thwarting the conclusion of the said agreement could not succeed, the Soviets adopted other measures to exert pressure on Afghanistan. Consequently, Moscow laid clai n over Afghan territory along the Afghan-Soviet border, which was refused by the then Afghan Government.[48]

Such reports also emanated from Moscow. The acting US Ambassador in Moscow, in a letter to the Secretary of State, informed the latter that within a few days after the American Company had concluded oil exploration agreements with Iran and Afghanistan, the Afghan Ambassador in Moscow told the former that the Soviet officials were annoyed because of having not been consulted by Tehran and Kabul in connection with conclusion of such an important agreement.[49] The Soviet attitude might have been governed by the fact Moscow regarded Afghanistan under its sphere of influence and hence it disliked any third country to become its rival.[50]

At the same time, Moscow also did not allow transition facilities to Afghanistan. There also did not exist any treaty or agreement between Kabul and Moscow in this regard. The Afghan Ambassador in Moscow is on record of having said that it would have been better if the Americans avoided using Soviet rail transport for supplying their material to Afghanistan, otherwise Moscow could exert undue pressure on Afghanistan.[51] The Afghan Ambassador had further observed that Russia was not prepared to provide transition facilities through its territory because Moscow was trying to impose a trade agreement on Afghanistan which could have undermined Afghan interests.[52] The US Company was also accorded the right to explore the mineral deposits subject to further negotiations. The Inland Exploration Company on its part agreed to pay $ 3,30,000 in the first years of the concession and 20 percent of the concessions thereafter.[53] However within a year, the Inland Company surrendered its concessions pleading that the rich oil deposits of Afghanistan were virtually inaccessible and would require about $ 300 million to exploit them.[54] Even the global situation was not suitable for foreign investment in Afghanistan. By 1938, the possibilities of the outbreak of hostilities in Europe had become almost certain. The management of the Inland Company thought that in the even of war, oil fields in Afganistan could be vulnerable to Soviet attack and thus their investment would be wasted.

The Inland Company's decision served a blow to Afghan policy of seeking support, services and investments from distant countries which were, it was hoped, politically disinterested in Afghan affairs. In the wake of US disinterestedness in large scale and long-term investments, Afghanistan became determined to disallow concessions to the Soviets and British nationals and rather thought of relying on German, Italian, Japanese and Czech investment and technicians.[55]

Impact of Second World War

In the wake of the outbreak of Second World War, the Afghan economy was adversely affected because its exports of Karakul to the Western Europe had almost stopped. During 1940-41, out of 2 hundred thousand hide-skins, Afghanistan could export only 38,940 skins to Germany and Soviet Union.[56] At this crucial juncture, the United States came to Afghanistan's rescue to help it export its Karakul in American markets.

By January 1941, the US had not established any diplomatic mission in Kabul. Murray, the Chief of State Department's Near Eastern Affairs Section, had observed that as long as the US interests continued to be slight, there was no possibility of the United States establishing diplomatic mission in Kabul.[57] It was only in December, 1941 that the US initiated a move to establish a diplomatic mission and it was on 6 June,

1942 that the US diplomatic mission was inaugurated in Kabul.[58] While addressing the *Loya Jirgah* on 15 June, 1942, King Zahir Shah, welcomed the opening of US mission in Kabul and expressed the hope of better economic and political relations between Kabul and Washington.[59] On 25 July, 1942, Cornelius H. Van Engert presented his credentials as US Ambassador in Kabul to King Zahir Shah. Ambassador Engert and King Zahir Shah exchanged views on mutual cooperation and world peace.[60]

In August 1942, the Afghan Foreign Ministry urged the US Government to help it in exporting 900 bales of Karakul, 100 bales of Fur, 250 tonnes of Wool and 40 tonnes of Pistachiu, which were lying at the Karachi port to the American markets.[61] The Afghan Government also expressed hope of similar US cooperation in future. The US Ambassador in Kabul even suggested to station some US Air Force bombers in Kabul during the war period with a view to boost the morale of Afghan Government.[62] However, the US Government rejected this suggestion.[63]

The US State Department had come out in December 1942 with a proposal of constructing a motorable road passing through India, Afghanistan and the Soviet Union to reach China with a view to supply material to China through road transport.[64] Consequently a US official, Gordon Bowles, reached India to explore the possibility of such a plan.[65] Following the Soviet refusal to allow any American national on its territory even for survey purpose[66] and Afghan reluctance to do so,[67] the US had to abandon such a plan.

As is well-known, the Afghan Government had declared to pursue policy of strict neutrality during the Second World War. In this regard, King Zahir Shah had issued a *farman* on 17 August, 1940, proclaiming the continuance of the policy of neutrality.[68] During the war period, there had been no major breakthrough in political or economic relations between Afghanistan and the United States. In April 1944, John L.

Savage, a US engineer, visited Afghanistan to help the latter in devising its irrigation plans.[69] In the beginning of 1945, the US envoy in Kabul, presented a memorandum to the Afghan Government urging the latter to bring the production of opium in that country under strict control for exclusive use in medicine and other scientific purposes. The Afghan Government, while acceding to American request, declared that it was going to ban the production of opium from 21 March, 1945.[70]

Thus during the period of Second World War, the relations between Afghanistan and the United States had become friendly and formal. During this period, the US diplomatic mission was established in Kabul. Afghanistan while promoting its diplomatic and economic relations with the United States, pursued a policy of strict neutrality during this period.

US-Afghan Relations After the Second World War

During the immediate postwar years, the era of good feelings lingered and Afghan leaders realized that "the United States would be the ideal substitute for receding British power, since distant. America was no imperialist threat to Afghanistan".[71]

In May 1946, the Afghan premier, Shah Mahmud Khan, had given gestures of cementing bonds of relations between Kabul and Washington. He said that he was "convinced that America's championship of the small nations guarantees my country's security against aggression. America's attitude is our salvation."[72]

Even when the clouds of war had not completely faded in 1944, the US Ambassador in Kabul Cornelius Von H. Engert, had recommended to the State Department:

> With a view to further consolidate our gains. it is essential to continue our present policy during the war period and subsequent period of reconstruction. I am little worried about the fact that during the immediate period preceding

> the war, the requirements of Afghanistan may not get due priority to US foreign policy. Therefore, I request the Department of State, Washington and future policy makers to take into consideration the fact that Afghanistan, besides being an independent Muslim country, is also strategically important for the United States' policy in the Middle East.[73]

Immediately after the conclusion of the Second World War, the Afghan Government asked the United States to send American teachers and engineers. In 1946, an agreement was signed between the Afghan Government and the Morrison-Knudsen Company of the United States worth $ 17 million for repairing the dams and their reconstruction, and the construction of 350 miles long highway.[74] All these plans were to be implemented in the Helmand Valley region. The Helmand Valley Project was so far the most ambitious project undertaken by the Government of Afghanistan. It was the multipurpose water and land development scheme for which initial surveys had been done by the Japanese engineers in the 1930s.[75]

By the end of 1948, the Afghan Government after having launched ambitions developmental projects, fell short of foreign exchange and thus required foreign assistance. Consequently, it turned to the United States. Accordingly, in 1949, Abdul Majid Zabuli, the Afghan Minister of National Economy, and a financial genius visited Washington to negotiate loans for Afghan economic development plan. Zabuli asked for the loan worth $ 118 million.[76] The US Department of State instead of acceding to his request, rather made him shuttle to the US Export-Import Bank (Exim Bank) "which completely failed to understand the quality and integrity of his plan and offered instead to finance the ongoing work of the Morrison-Knudsen Company in the Helmand Valley",[77]

As compared to original Afghan request for $ 118 million, the Exim Bank sanctioned only a loan of $ 21 million.[78] Even this loan was also sanctioned because of the Morrison-Knudsen Company's political influence.[79] Zabuli insisted that such unbalanced development would be a mistake and that the long payback of a multipurpose reclamation project like the Helmand would cause serious problems for Afghanistan. So he recommended to his Government to decline the loan, "but his Afghan superiors overruled him because they wanted to establish close economic relations with the United States for political reasons".[80]

Zabuli had also requested the United States to provide American weapons so that Afghanistan could modernize its armed forces in the wake of possible Soviet anger. He said:

> . . . Properly armed, and convinced of US backing, Afghanistan could manage a delaying action in the passes of the Hindu-Kush which would be a contribution to the success of the armed forces of the West and might enable them to utilize bases which Pakistan and India might provide. . . When war came Afghanistan would, of course, be overrun and occupied. But the Russians would be unable to pacify the country. Afghans could and would pursue guerrilla tactics for a indefinite period.[81]

However, Zabuli's request for US arms assistance was rejected. Even the Afghan Government seemed to have not taken a serious view of Zabuli's requests and US offers and rejections. Kabul rather accepted the meagre loan offered by the United States. Even Afghan Prime Minister, Shah Mahmud had observed in a conversation with the US President, Truman: "The Afghan Government tends to think of the loan as of political as well as of economic importance, possibly increasingly so in the light of manifestations of Soviet interest and offers of assistance to Afghanistan."[82] Repeated requests for weapons were put off, even though in 1949 Afghan officials suggested that "unless US gave Afghanistan more assistance, Afghans might turn to USSR".[83]

Actually, Afghanistan had made requests for US arms assistance as far back as in 1944.[84] Since then the repeated Afghan requests for American arms had been ignored by the

United States. According to Leon B. Poullada: "Afghan overtures to America were met at first with bureaucratic and legalistic evasions and finally with a clear negative response. True, the Afghan approaches were often naive and awkward, but sophistication on the tortuous ways of American policy making could hardly be expected."[85] The US Embassy in Kabul recommended arms sales on 4 January, 1950 "to exclude Soviet influence, cement Afghan-American friendship, maintain internal security and promote settlement of differences with Pakistan."[86] However, in Washington the policy makers were underscoring the strategic significance of Afghanistan. As is revealed from an assessment made by the US National Security Council in early 1951:

> The Kremlin apparently does not consider Afghanistan's relatively meagre assets to be worthy of attention and probably believes that it can take Afghanistan easily whenever its broader objectives would be served. There is little doubt that Afghanistan could be conquered regardless of its will to resist. In the event of an invasion, it is possible that certain elements—particularly the Afghan (Pathan) tribesmen, would continue to resist.[87]

However, the then US Assistant Secretary of State, George McGhee, visited Kabul on 12 March, 1951 and discussed the Afghan defence requirements with Sardar Mohammad Daoud, then Minister of War. George McGhee suggested a formal request by diplomatic note with a detailed list of desired equipment attached and assured Daoud that it would receive "sympathetic consideration".[88] Poullada claims that Daoud understood it to mean that approval was assured.[89] The Afghan Government had never made a formal official request unless it was assured beforehand that it would be approved.

The Afghan Prime Minister, Shah Mahmud, during his visit to the United States in April 1951 took the matter with US President, Truman. However, even prior to the visit of Afghan premier, the US Department of State in a note to the President on 21 February, 1951 had observed: "Afghanistan continues tc maintain toward the USSR an attitude of cautious correctness combined with firm resistance to Soviet efforts at penetration... So far, Soviet pressure has not been severe not has the Soviet influence in Afghan territory contiguous to the Soviet Central Asian Republic (sic) been extensive".[90] The State Department further advised the US President that the Afghan requests for arms were being ignored rather than refused. President Truman was further advised to tell the Afghan Prime Minister of "the limitations of the ability of the US to furnish military assistance" to stress reliance on collective security within the United Nations, and to hold out hope for more financial and technical aid".[91] But the Afghan Government still insisted on procuring arms from the United States and by August, 1951, a formal request with arms list was presented to the United States. On 27 November, 1951, the US Government instructed its Ambassador in Kabul to tell the Afghan Government that "the arms requested will cost $ 25 million. They will have to be paid in cash. Transit through Pakistan will have to be arranged with no help from the United States. The sale will have to be made public, and it would help if the Pushtunistan claim is dropped."[92] It appeared that the US was ready to supply arms to Afghanistan on cash payment and simultaneously it expected Afghanistan to strike a deal on Pushtunistan, a step which no Afghan Government could ever undertake. Thus there was a clear indication that US was reluctant to supply arms to Afghanistan. At the same time, such a stipulated bargain was also not acceptable to Afghanistan. Shah Mahmud called it "a political refusal". And the issue was shelved for the time being by both sides.

With the onset of 1952, when the relations between Afghanistan and Pakistan over the issue of Pakhtoonistan had become tense the Kabul Government sought to good offices of the United States to help resolve the dispute. It is worth mentioning here that on 6 November, 1950, Washington had approached the Governments of Afghanistan and Pakistan with an expression of concern over the tension between the two and made an offer to act as an informal "go-between in seeking agreement by the two governments on the basis of following four points:

(i) To cease attacks upon each other by officials or through official channels and to use their best efforts to prevent such attacks in the press or from other non-official sources:

(ii) To use their influence to prevent incidents among the tribes which were likely to affect good relations between the two governments. The two governments would further agree that, if despite their efforts, incidents did occur, they would consult together through diplomatic channels and avoid public statements on such incidents;

(iii) To exchange ambassadors within two months;

(iv) To designate representatives to meet within three months for informal exploratory discussions of their differences without a previously agreed agenda or stated preconditions. The two governments would further agree that there should be no publicity concerning these discussions without prior agreement between them.[93]

On 25 January, 1952, Ali Mohammad Khan, the then Foreign Minister of Afghanistan told the American Ambassador in Kabul that Pakistan should be urged to "accept unequivocally" the US proposal of 6 November, 1950. To this, the US Ambassador told the Afghan Foreign Minister that Washington considered "the November 6 approach to be a dead issue, had no further proposal to make and feel that it was upto the two countries concerned to negotiate directly. . ."[94] This showed that even after two years of US offer, Afghanistan was still willing to utilize the good offices of Washington in improving its relations with Pakishtan but United States had by then become reluctant. Even in early July 1952, Abdul Hamid Aziz, First Under Secretary in Foreign Office in Kabul in his talks with the US Charge in Kabul expressed the hope that "US will not withdraw its interest in settling the differences between Pakistan and Afghanistan."[95]

During the last week of August 1952, a meeting between the Afghan Ambassador to India and First Secretary in the US Embassy in India took place in New Delhi. The Afghan Ambassador expressed his country's disappointment at the limited amount of US economic and technical assistance provided for Kabul and expressed the fear that "the progress already made in Afghanistan may be jdeoparized if additional assistance is not obtainable."[96] The Afghan Ambassador further added that the political and economic life in Afghanistan was threatened with being crushed between the "upper and nether mill stones" of Soviet and Pakistan pressures.

On 7 August, 1952, the Soviet Charge d'Affaires in Kabul, Shepedko, had delivered a stiff *aide memo're* to the Afghan Government, which *inter alia* noted that the Soviet Union would regard Afghan plan for oil drilling in northern part by a French firm under UN auspices "to be an unfriendly act and specific violation of the non-aggression treaty of 1931".[97] While referring to the Soviet *aide memoire* Afghan Ambassador Najibullah Khan told the US diplomat that his Government would by no means yield to such pressures in a matter involving Afghan sovereignty and internal affairs. However, he expressed the fear the Afghan rejection of Soviet representation would be followed by drastic economic sanctions in the curtailment or even "the termination of the current barter agreement between Afghanistan and the USSR, upon which the Afghanistan is dependent for the critically needed petrol supplies. . . the only practical alternative source of such supplies is from or through Pakistan."[98]

While reiterating his Government's willingness to resume negotiations with Pakistan, the Afghan Ambassador hoped that "the US may be willing to take initiative in bringing them about".[99] At that stage, Kabul wanted United States to play two-fold role—(a) to provide the initiative in having the negotiations resumed; and (b) to act as "observer" and to render friendly "advice" to either party when it appeared that either side was taking a wrong stand. In this regard, the US diplomat told the Afghan Ambassador that Washington had made a protracted but "unsuccessful" effort to assist in a solution between 6 November, 1950 and the latter part of 1951 and suggested the involvement of a third party which was most probably the United Kingdom.[100] To this Ambassador Najibullah Khan reiterated his conviction that only a great power such as the United States was competent to sponsor the negotiations and "Afghanistan hopes¦ that) the US will become permanently interested in the survival of South Asian countries against threatened communist domination."[101] He also pointed out Afghanistan's "present state of defencelessness" which could prompt Moscow to intervene militarily on or without a pretext at any time.

The above analysis makes it clear that Afghanistan was keen to further strengthen its relations with the United States. Imbued by this desire, Kabul wanted to utilize US good offices to ease Afghan-Pakistan tension and safeguard Afghan interests from any eventuality of Soviet attack or intervention into Afghanistan. However, Washington had categorically declined to mediate between Pakistan and Afghanistan and until August end 1952, it had been taking the growing Soviet influence in Afghanistan not very seriously. It was only during September, 1952 that Washington started taking serious notice of Soviet manoeuvres in Afghanistan. On 9 September, 1952, the US Charge d'Affaires in Kabul, Horner, in a despatch to the Department of State wrote: "Over past year Embassy (US) has reported evidences of increasing Soviet interest in Afghanistan. . . It may suffice to say that we have felt earlier estimates of relative Soviet non-interest in this country to be in need of radical revision."[102]

On 9 September, 1952, the then Afghan Foreign Minister, Ali Mohammad Khan, in a conversation with Philip Beck and Louis de Laive, two members of the United Nations (UN) technical assistance mission, confirmed that the Soviet Charge d'Affairs in Kabul, Shpedko, had delivered a stiff *aide memoire* to the Afghan Government on 7 August, 1925. During the first week of September the Soviet Foreign Minister Vishinsky had called the Afghan Ambassador in Moscow, Sultan Ahmad, and warned him orally "in a severe tongue lasting".[103] However, on 8 September, 1952, the Afghan Government in a written reply handed over to the Soviet Charge d'Affaires in Kabul asserted that the proposed oil exploration "was purely an internal matter"[104] of Afghanistan. The Afghan Foreign Minister regarded the Soviet *demarche* regarding oil as having broader implications.

The US Ambassador in Kabul further noted that any US advice to Kabul in that regard depended upon evaluation of overall Soviet intentions and he solicited the views of the Department of State on the matter.[105] In his view it was difficult to imagine that Soviet Union would take any overt steps against Afghanistan at that particular juncture. The Afghan Government seemed to be disturbed over the Soviet *demarche*. The First Under Secretary in Afghan Foreign Ministry, Abdul Hamid Khan Aziz, told the US Ambassador in Kabul on 9 September, 1952: "Afghanistan considered US her really true friend and counts on US (USA) to help Afghanistan take her place among free and democratic nations of the world."[106]

The US Secretary of State, Dean Acheson did not feel that the Soviet *demarche* was precursor of any immediate Soviet threat to Afghanistan.[107] He regarded the Soviet *demarche* as the first step in Soviet campaign to prevent the entry of Westerners in north of Hindu Kush "in line with long standing Soviet policy and an endeavour to prevent economic improvement amongst peoples who are potentially exploitable by the Soviets on ethnic grounds."[108]

In middle of September 1952, the Afghan Government announced its plan to construct modern roads in the north Afghanistan. The US Ambassador in Kabul recommended to the Department of State to provide $ 1 million worth of economic assistance to Afghanistan in this regard.[109] In its view, the granting of such assistance would:

(i) strengthen Afghan will to resist Soviet presence;

(ii) provide additional incentive towards development of north;

(iii) provide effective means for overall economic strengthening of Afghanistan;

(iv) reduce the possibility of the success of Soviet economic pressure on North Afghanistan;

(v) increase Afghan potentiality to combat subversion and subversive rebellion in north;

(vi) . . . . ;

(vii) 110

Strangely enough the US Department of State instead of considering seriously the recommendations of its Ambassador in Kabul, rather note that Afghanistan, aside from a desire for friendly advice from the United Kingdom and the US, "may well be capitalizing on *demarche* in attempt to achieve (i) increased economic assistance; (ii) military assistance; and (iii) US-UK pressure on Pakistan to negotiate Pushtunistan agreement with Afghanistan".[111] It further noted that the Soviet *demarche* when considered in historical perspective, did not pose any threat to Afghanistan. However, Ambassador Horner while expressing his doubts over the instructions of the Department of State asserted that "no account seems to have been taken of Afghan psychology or existence of important elements here willing to come to terms with the Soviets".[112] He further informed the State Department that the Afghan cabinet was coming around to view that "accommodation with Soviets must be sought at almost any cost".[113] Thus Ambassador recommended that "we should not promptly and positively and not wait until enemy (Soviet Union) is already within gates."[114]

The available evidence shows that Washington did not take Soviet *demarche* to Afghanistan seriously and only expressed its moral support in that regard. It also expressed its inability to provide increased economic assistance to Afghanistan.[115] Besides, in the wake of these developments, the US did not apprehend any danger of Afghanistan's falling "into Soviet camp".[116]

Despite the initial American silence over Soviet *demarche*, Afghanistan did not slacken in its efforts to keep Washington informed. On 24 October, 1952, Afghan Ambassador in Washington, Sardar Mohammad Naim in his meeting with the US Acting Secretary of State, Bruce, provided a background to Soviet *demarche*. Sardar Naim explained that Afghnistan's one of the outside needs was gasoline and in view of Pakistan's "economic blockade", it had only two sources opened to it. It could either explore for oil within its own boundary or it could look to the Soviet Union as a supplier.[117] After the Second World War, Kabul concluded a barter arrangement with the Soviet Union to procure petroleum products from that country for the northern area of Afghanistan. The resumption of oil exploration activities, which had begun shortly before the World War II but suspended when hostilities broke out, using French technicians under UN auspices, had provoked the Soviet *demarche.* Reiterating that he was not playing on the theme of Soviet menace, Sardar Naim said:

> The fact remains that the Soviet know that Afghanistan's sources of supplies from the south are 'blocked' and that it must rely upon the Soviets for essential items. This is the position that Afghanistan finds itself in today . . . his Government has instructed him to explain the position to the State Department and to ask for its 'opinion.'[118]

The US Acting Secretary of State while emphasising on the "wise and proper course" to follow, asked Sardar Naim as to what Soviets could do if Kabul went ahead with its programme of oil exploration despite Soviet *demarche.*[119] In this regard, Afghan Ambassador said that it was not a question of what the Soviets might or might not do under given circumstances, "but it is a question of what the Soviets know they can do since the Afghans are 'sealed off' in the south and must depend upon the Soviets for essential supplies."[120] The United States regarded the Afghan problem in the wake of Soviet *demarche* as being of political nature and "accordingly a solution would seem to lie in the improvement of relations between Pakistan and Afghanistan."[121]

During the last week of October 1952, a meeting of Afghan delegation led by Mohammad Kabir Ludin, Chairman of the Afghan Delegation to the UN General Assembly was held in New York with American delegation comprising US Secretary of State and other members. Sardar Mohammad Naim, Afghan Ambassador in USA also participated in the meeting. During the discussions held between the delegations of the two countries, the Soviet *demarche* to Afghanistan also figured in the talks.[122] Ludin while presenting Afghanistan's case, observed that the Soviet authorities, who were fully aware of Afghan predicament, might wish to exploit it realistically in a political sense. Thus there existed a "critical situation for Afghanistan, far-reaching in its influence for peace and security in that part of the world."[123] While referring to Afghanistan's reply to Soviet explanations with regard to *demarche*, Ludin said that his Government was "also conscious of the risks of such an answer to the Soviet Government."[124] After the leader of the Afghan delegation had concluded his statement, the US Secretary of State wanted to know precisely "what it was that we were being asked to express an opinion on."[125] With a view to further elaborate Afghan stand, both Sardar Naim and Ludin referred to the great assistance rendered by the Good Offices of the United States in connection with the Helmand River Problem with Iran in February 1948 and US "good offices" with regard to Pakhtoon issue in November 1950 and further added that "Afghanistan had stood ready to accept them but Pakistan had refused. They now hoped that the United States would be able to suggest means by which the Pashtoonistan issue could be solved."[126]

Angus Ward was designated as new US Ambassador to Afghanistan, on 27 June, 1952 and he assumed his new assignment in early November of the same year. On 8 November,

1952 he presented his credentials to the King of Afghanistan, Zahir Shah. The Afghan King expressed his admiration for US friendship and also expressed thanks for constructive American economic assistance.[127]

Since 1951, the United States had been involved in establishing a military alliance in the Middle East to strengthen its position. The news reports that Pakistan would join the proposed US defence alliance created worry and anexiety in Afghanistan. The proposed alliance was named as Middle East Defence Organization (MEDO). The Secretary of State informed the US Embassy in Afghanistan that the MEDO was conceived to be military planning organization only, not involving formal alliance or commitments. He further added that when the organization was established "perhaps it would invite other nations of general area for example, Afghanistan or Pakistan, if they are then interested."[128] However the Department of State wondered whether Afghanistan would join MEDO in view of its geographic proximity to the Soviet Union and Article 2 of the Afghan-Soviet treaty of June 1931.[129]

At this stage, US Ambassador in Kabul, Angus Ward suggested to the State Department that while reassessing US policy towards Afghanistan, "consideration must necessarily be given to the possible accession of Pakistan to MEDO and its resultant effects."[130] On 19 February, 1953, Sardar Naim, then Afghan Ambassador in Washington during his talks with the officials of State Department that Afghanistan was concerned about the prospects of the participation of Pakistan in any kind of a Middle East defence organization prior to the solution of Pushtoonistan issue.[131]

During the last week of June 1953, Afghan Ambassador to India, Najibullah Khan, had handed over a memorandum on the Pushtoonistan question to the US Department of State wherein Afghanistan expressed concern over the prospects of military aid and other assistance being given to Pakistan. The Memorandum further added:

> There is reason to believe that the apparent determination of the United States to shore up the economy of Pakistan, as well as the possibility of early solution of Pakistan's difficulties with India, have aroused fears among Afghan officials that these developments possibly leading to a more economically and politically stable Pakistan, may have a detrimental effect on Afghan plans to alienate the tribes from their connection with Karachi.[132]

The year 1953 marked a change of leadership in Afghanistan when on 6 September, 1953, Sardar Mohammad Daoud Khan took over as Prime Minister of Afghanistan. In the United States, John Foster Dulles had taken over as the Secretary of State. Dulles provided a new impetus to American cold war policies by establishing defence alliances with active US support and involving countries having geographic proximity to the Soviet Union and People's Republic of China. By 1953, Pakistan had started receiving massive economic and military aid from the United States which was bound to create an alarm for Afghanistan which had strained relations with Pakistan over the issue of Pushtunistan. However the United States still ignored the strategic significance of Afghanistan. It is evident from a secret study conducted in 1953 by Joint Chiefs of Staff which *inter alia* concluded:

> Afghanistan is of little or no strategic importance to the United States. Its geographic location coupled with the realization by Afghan leaders of Soviet capadilities, pressages Soviet control of the country whenever the situation so dictates. It would be desirable for Afghanistan to remain neutral because otherwise it might be overrun as an avenue to the Indian subcontigent. Such neutrality will remain a stronger possibility if there is no we.tern-sponsored opposition to communism in Afganistan, which opposition in itself might precipitate Soviet moves to take control of the couutry.[133]

Despite these developments, Afghanistan was still willing to utilize "good offices" of the United States with regard to improving relations with Pakistan. Such a stance was reiterated by Mohammad Hashim Maiwandwal, then Afghan Charge d'Affaires in Washington during his talks with the State Department officials. Maiwandwal expressed "the hope that the United States was still willing to use its informal good offices to improve relations between Pakistan and Afghanistan . . . the United States has always been interested in the improvement of Pakistan-Afghan relations . . . (and) this US interest is a continuing one and the US would be willing to use its informal good offices to help the two countries to improve their relations. . . ."[134]

In early October 1953, it was announced in Washington that US Vice-President Richard M. Nixon would embark upon a goodwill tour of Far East and South Asian countries including Afghanistan.[135] The State Department prepared a background note on Pushtunistan on 28 November, 1953 for Vice-President Nixon suggesting the line he should take on the Pushtunistan issue during his visit to Kabul.[136] In this regard, US Secretary of State, John Foster Dulles asked the US Embassy in Kabul to suggest Vice-President Nixon during the course of his proposed visit to Afghanistan that the United States considered most desirable course that bilateral negotiations between Pakistan and Afghanistan.[137] He further suggested: "If Afghans bring up old chestnut of looking to USSR, if US unwilling to support Afghanistan, Vice-President may wish to observe it difficult to believe that Afghanitan with its familiarity with USSR and its reputation as freedom loving nation, would commit political suicide over a dispute with a friendly Muslim neighbour."[138]

In the meanwhile, Sardar Mohammad Naim, Afghan Foreign Minister inquired on 3 December, 1953 from US Ambassador in Kabul about the validity of press reports that The United States and Pakistan were about to enter military pact. The Afghan Foreign Minister said that the US military assistance to Pakistan would undermine the Afghan interests on two counts: "(i) It would strengthen the neighbour which has not demonstrated desire for harmonious existence with Afghanistan; and (ii) It would prompt the USSR to take defensive measures at the expense of Afghanistan."

During the early part of second week of December 1953, the US Vice-President, Richard Nixon, paid a visit to Afghanistan in his our of northern-tier countries. Nixon's visit made excellent impression on Afghan officials and the Afghan people.[140] During the talks between the visiting US Vice-President and Afghan leaders, no direct mention was made about the quantum of aid to be given to Afghanistan, Exim Bank loan or alleged US-Pakistan military cooperation. The substantial points on which the two side held discussions were: Afghanistan's need for outside assistance for its economic, educational and social development and the Pushtunistan question. During his talks, Vice-president Nixon firmly reiterated US unwillingness to become involved in Pushtunistan dispute or to play the role of a mediator. He rather laid stress on the need for direct negotiations between Kabul and Pakistan.[141] Afghanistan was assured of continued US help for Helmand Valley Project but not assurance was given regarding the military assistance.[142]

On 5 January, 1954, the Afghan Ambassador in Washington, Mohammad Kabir Ludin, along with Mohammad Hashim Mainwandwal held a meeting with the US Secretary of State and other senior officials of the State Department [143] During this meeting, the Afghan Ambassador presented a note on behalf of Afghan Government which expressed Kabul's concern over US economic and arms assistance to Pakistan and its implications for Afghanistan. The note also reiterated Afghan hope for better ties with the United States.[144] During the talks, the Afghan Amassador said that his Government was prepared to cooperate with the United States, Pakistan and others to realize the defence of the region, "however, a prerequisite to such cooperation is a solution of the Pushtunistan issue with Pakistan."[145] Ambassador Ludin further added that if the issue of Pushtunistan remained unresolved, while Pakistan's economy, productivity and military strength increased, as a result of US aid, the increased imbalance of strength between Afghanistan and Pakistan "would be of serious concern to Afghanistan."[146]

While appreciating Afghan apprehensions, the US Secretary of State in his reply told Ambassador Ludin that a military aid programme for Pakistan would have the objective of increasing the defence capacity of that nation "and that it is not our desire to make one country strong at the peril of a neighbour . . . in any agreement with Pakistan adequate safeguards would be provided for against the aggressive use of its increased military strength."[147]

In early 1954, the military cooperation pacts were signed between Pakistan and Turkey and Pakistan and United States. The Mutual Defence Assistance Agreement was signed beween Pakistan and the United States of Karachi on 19 May, 1954.[148] In the wake of these developments, the belief was growing in the Afghan Governmental circles that "the US has turned its back to Afghanistan."[149] Thus US Ambassador in Afgganistan, Ward, expressed the view that the Soviet Union had been taking moves to strengthen its ties with Kabul through trade on terms very favourable to the Afghans and through credits for economic development accompanied by technical assistance.[150] He further asserted that should Soviet efforts be intensified and in the absence of any effective counter move by the United States, "We can expect the Soviets to establish effective control in the trans-Hindu Kush area of Afghanistan within the fore-seeable future."[151] Thus he emphasized that there should be an appraisal by the appropriate US military authorities of the importance of Afghanistan, both direct and indirect, for the United states. Ward recommended the supply of US military assistance to Afghanistan in the context of a regional arrangement—an association with Turkey or Pakistan or both in arrangements similar to those existing between Pakistan and Turkey.[152] He also suggested to the Department of State: "We should be forth right in making clear to Afghanistan that we can make no commitments beyond the language of the mutual defence assistance agreement. We cannot guarantee Afghanistan borders."[153]

He also cautioned not to overlook the fact that the Soviet Union might react to US move of providing arms assistance to Afghanistan and asserted that "this possiblity exists whether or not we extend military assistance to Afghanistan."[154]

The United States also seemed to be worried about the growing Soviet economic penetration into Afghanistan. A note prepared by the US Department of State in June 1954 entitled "United States and Soviet Interests in Afghanistan," noted that the dangers of the increased Soviet activity in Afghanistan included the military aspects of road and oil storage construction and the subversive activity by Soviet "technicians" who were of the same racial stock as the Afghans.[155] The note called for a review of US economic policy in Afghanistan to counter the mounting Soviet influence. It *inter alia* suggested the three following alternatives:

(i) keeping our presented policy without significant increases or decreases in our aid;

(ii) minimize our losses by gradually recuding our activity and our aid to a minimum consistent with achievement of bare economic results; and

(iii) countering the Soviet moves so as to preclude infiltration by Soviet technicians or mitigate their achievements.[156]

However with regard to the third alternative, the note envisaged that it might be expensive as it would probably be possible only upon US acceptance of likely Afghan requests for substantial additional US economic aid and US military aid on certain guarantees.[157]

The Afghan Ambassador in Washington met the US Assistant Secretary of State for Near Eastern, South Asian and African Affairs on 27 July, 1954 and expressed his Government's willingness to consider US military assistance on a bilateral basis without reference to a regional organization, with the avowed objective of bolstering its internal strength and of improving its capacity to resist aggression from whatever direction it should come.[158] Byroade while accepting that the Middle East being a vulnerable area was threatened by increasing Soviet interest, added that the conclusion of a US-Afghan military and programme might provide a very strong Soviet reaction thus undermining the interests of both the countries.[159] The Afghan Ambassador also met the US Secretary of State on 27 July, 1954 and told the latter that the United States had not yet taken any decision on Afghan request for American arms [160] The Secretary of State told the Afghan Ambassador that his country should proceed slowly in the matter "... (and) some of the more immediate imponderables in considering military aid for Afghanistan were the nature of the aid programme for the coming year, the character of our current commitments and future contingentis. . . .[161]

In October 1954, the National Intelligence Estimates Committee, an inter-departmental wing of the National Security Council (NSC) and Central Intelligence Agency (CIA) prepared a report entitled "Outlook for Afghanistan".[162] The report note that the growing Afghan reliance on Soviet Union for trade and loans with technical assistance made it highly vulnerable to Soviet pressures.[163] Afghanistan's participation in a Western-backed defence arrangement or its acceptance of substantial Western military aid was bound to evoke adverse Soviet reaction. It was further observed that the USSR could easily take over Afghanistan if it chose to do so, but openly aggressive action against Afghanistan would "almost certainly entail anti-Soviet reactions elsewhere, particularly in the Arab-Asian bloc which the USSR would wish to avoid".[164] However the report expressed the hope that the Afghan Government was likely to continue with its fundamental policy of attempting to play off the great powers to Afghanistan's advantage, meanwhile continuing its association with the Arab-Asian bloc in the United Nations.[165] However the report also noted the future policy which Afghanistan might pursue:

> Afghan leaders will attempt to obtain additional Western economic aid to counterbalance that received from the

> USSR and will probably display continuing interest in the idea of participating in Western-backed military aid programmes. However, it is unlikely that the Afghans would actually accept membership in a Western: backed area defence arrangement since they almost certainly realize that no foreseeable arrangement could furnish them sufficiently realistic protection against Soviet attack to compensate for the increased Soviet hostility towards them which would almost certainly ensue.[166]

In October 1954, the Afghan Foreign Minister, Sardar Mohammad Naim met the US Secretary of State, John Foster Dulles and pleaded for the supply of US arms to Afghanistan. However Dulles replied: "After careful consideration, extending military aid to Afghanistan would create problems not offset by the strength it would generate. Instead of asking for arms, Afghanistan should settle the Pushtunistan dispute with Pakistan."[167] Thus by the end of 1954, it had become evident that the United States was reluctant to provide arms assistance to Afghanistan. Leon B. Poullada has observed that "American failure between 1942 and 1954 to respond to the genuine economic and security needs of a friendly and pro-Western Afghan government, and to understand the political imperatives behind the Pushtunistan problem, set the stage for the stunning success of Soviet diplomacy."[168]

On 16 December, 1954, the US Acting Secretary of State emphatically said that the United States would not, for present, extend military aid to Afghanistan. However it could consider doing so upon "attainment of improved Afghan relations with Pakistan and Iran."[169]

This stance remained preeminent in US foreign policy towards Afghanistan in the years to come. On the one hand, Washington showed anxiety as well as concern over the growing Soviet influence in Kabul while on the other it rejected repeated Afghan requests for arms assistance and rather insisted on Afghan-Pakistan rapprochement on Pushtunistan. On 15

February, 1955, the US Secretary of State, Foster in a communication to US representative in the United Nations, Cabot Lodge, wrote that the US support to Kabul on the Pushtunistan issue, would mean to abet "the partition of another friendly country."[170] The US State Department believed that a closer cooperation between Afghanistan and Pakistan was the only sound basis for improving the situation in the region. The Secretary of State opined: ". . . the urgency of the problem requires that we consider providing assistance to cooperative economic projects which would draw the the two countries together, strengthen Afghanistan's ability to resist Soviet enticements and in this way bring Afghanistan closer to the West."[171]

The ambiguity in US foreign policy towards Afghanistan was noticeable during the beginning of 1955 especially when Secretary of State, Foster Dulles wrote: "While we do not wish at this time to incur the risk of a strong Soviet reaction in Afghanistan nor to back the Afghans against the Pakistanis. We are most interested in drawing Afghanistan closer to the free world. . . ."[172] He did not spell out as to "how" the US could do it. Washington likened its relations with Afghanistan with that of US-Pakistan relations. It always linked its relations with Kabul to that of Afghan-Pakistan relations. In view of the deteriorating Afghan-Pakistan relations during 1955, United States regarded cordial Afghan-Pak relations as a precondition for Afghan-US relations. Such a feeling was conveyed by Secretary of State Dulles to US Embassy in Kabul on 2 April, 1955 when he wrote: "It (US) is deeply concerned over recent manifestations of some deterioration of relations between these two countries. This trend is contrary to the best interest of both nations and of the whole free world."[173]

Pakistan during that period regarded Prime Minister of Afghanistan Sardar Mohammad Daoud as the main stumbling block in nrmalizing Pakistan-Afghan relations especially in view of Sardar Daoud's uncompromising position of the issue of Pakhtoonistan. Thus Pakistan was interested in the removal of Daoud Government and in this regard Pakistan's Ambassador to Kabul, A S.B. Shah met the US Ambassador in Kabul and sought the help of United States, UK and Turkey in persuading the King of Afghanistan to dismiss the Daoud Government.[174] In this regard the US Ambassador in Kabul, Ward, wrote to the US Department of State while endorsing A S.B. Shah's proposal that "the situation sufficiently serious warrant our direct action"[175] and sought instructions whether to approach the Afghan King individually or collectively. The State Department in its reply instructed the US Ambassador in Kabul to approach the Afghan King separately to "avoid dangers of adverse reactions to joint approach."[176] The US Ambassador, Ward, was also instructed to seek audience with the Afghan King and tell the latter that the United States sincerely desired continuation and strengthening of its ties of friendship and common purpose with Afghanistan. The telegram further envisaged that the US "has observed with greatest concern recent signs of deterioration in relations between Pakistan and Afghanistan both of which are subject to the threat of communist imperialism."[177] In the wake of these developments, US Secretary of State, Dulles, expressed the opinion that the ouster of present Royal family of Afghanistan "without alternative regime available to maintain and pursue reasonable policies in relations with Afghanistan's neighbours would probably result in reversion, period of uncertainty and chaos similar (to) those characterizing political interregnums of past."[178]

On 26 April, 1955, Ambassador Ward informed the US Department of State about his meeting with the Afghan King and the then Afghanistan's Acting Foreign Minister, Ali Mohammad. Ambassador Ward informed the State Department that the Afghanistan's King expressed the hope that Afghanistan would continue to enjoy "US interest, aid and favour."[179] While expressing Afghanistan's "every willingness" to re-establish normal relations"[180] with Pakistan, the Afghan King asserted that his government was eager to take any step toward restoration of normal relations provided it was not incompatible with Afghanistan's dignity.[181]

In the beginning of May 1955, the US Ambassador in Kabul informed the US State Department that he had been approached by the Afghan Government to inform both the US President and Secretary of State that Afghanistan wanted the US Government to mediate in the Pakhtoonistan dispute.[182] While commenting on Afghan request for US mediation, Ambassador Ward wrote that Afghanistan would probably attempt to use "mediation to inject US into Pushtunistan controversy."[183] He also cautioned that Afghanistan was seeking to place the burden for any further deterioration in Pakistan-Afghanistan relations on the United States and "US mediation would likely give Daud a new lease of life."[184] However Ambassador Ward seemed to be ambiguous in his approach on the issue of US mediation when he expressed his belief about actual US mediation "probably unwise" and at the same time opined that 'refusal to attempt mediation would undoubtedly have serious repurcussions on US-Afghanistan relations particularly if Daoud survives.'"[185]

In this regard, US Secretary of State, Dulles, in his telegram to US Embassy in Afghanistan on 5 May, 1955 endorsed the view of Ambassador Ward and wrote that United States should not attempt role of mediator in Afghan-Pakistan dispute.[186] At this stage, the US Ambassador in Pakistan informed the Department of State that the most useful contribution US could make at that juncture would be to assist in getting across ideas to the Afghan King and other appropriate members of the Royal family that Pakistan could be expected to become more reasonable and cooperative if Afghanistan had new Prime Minister.[187] It was clear indication that US should press on Afghan King to dismiss Daoud Government.

During the third week of June 1955, Sardar Mohammad Naim, brother of Afghan Premier, Daoud, and Deputy Prime Minister and Minister for Foreign Affairs of Afghanistan visited United States and held discussions with the US Secretary of State and other senior officials of the Department of State. The Afghan Ambassador in Washington, Mohammad Kabir Ludon was also present. During his discussion with the US officials, Sardar Naim expressed his keen desire to "understand the US Government's attitude towards Afghanistan."[188] He further added that until recently the US had maintained a natural position on the Pushtunistan issue "but that a few weeks ago, when Afghanistan asked the United States to mediate in current critical dispute with Pakistan. . . the United States considered the Pushtun question an internal Pakistani matter,"[189] which had come as a considerable shock to Afghanistan. He further declared that Afghanistan's long-range interests were entirely similar to those of the US and his country recognized that the greatest overall danger to Afghanistan emanated from the North.

While explaining Afghan stand on Pushtun issue and relations between Afghanistan and Pakistan, Sardar Naim said: "Afghanistan did not ask for one inch or territory from Pakistan and would be quite satisfied if the Pakistan Government would make it clear that at some future date, perhaps ten years off, the eight million Pushtuns in Pakistan would be given an opportunity to decide their own fate."[190] He further declared that if Pushtuns in Pakistan voted freely to adhere to Pakistan then his country would not raise the issue again.

The Memorandum of Conversation between the visiting Afghan Foreign Minister and US Secretary of State referred to the Afghan request for US military assistance and American refusal to comply with it and further noted that it "left the Afghans in a quandary as to the American Government's attitude towards them."[191]

Though the US Secretary of State appreciated Afghan stand and desire for friendly relations with the United States but there was no tangible outcome.

In view of estrangement of relations between Afghanistan and Pakistan and the economic blockade imposed by the latter on the former, an Afghan economic delegation had gone to Moscow in May 1955 to discuss a Soviet offer to provide transit facilities and other economic assistance to offset

Pakistani economic pressure. While reporting this development to the Department of State, the US Embassy in Kabul reported on 20 June, 1955 that Prime Minister Daoud was trying to counteract Pakistani economic pressure by seeking to substitute the Soviet Union as a trade route.[192] In the wake of this development, the US Ambassador in Kabul expressed his fear that Afghanistan might "make irretrievable commitments to the Soviets." Thus he recommended that Pakistan should lift the economic embargo on Afghanistan. In this regard, the State Department in its reply to the US Embassy in Kabul expressed its reluctance to urge Pakistan to make important concessions to reach agreement with Afghanistan because "it is US as well as Pak interests to see Daoud replaced."[193]

However, the US State Department, at the same time, seemed concerned about Afghanistan falling under Soviet control. It also expressed the speculation that either the Soviets would disappoint Afghans or the latrer might recoil from stringent Soviet terms. The US Embassy in Kabul was asked to keeps the developments under close watch andkeep it posted with new developments in that regard. It further added that when the real possibilityof Afghanistan sliding into the Soviet orbit would exist on account of necessity for relieving economic pressures applied by Pakistan, then the United States would consider urging Pakistan to make concessions to Afghanistan.[194]

The State Department was also curious to know about the likelihood of Daoud's downfall or weakening of Daoud's position or about King's determination to replace him.[195] The US Ambassador in Kabul informed the State Department on 27 June, 1955 that there were 50 per cent chances of Daoud's downfall if Pakistan continued its present policy.[196] On 7 July, 1955, the US Ambassador in Kabul informed the State Department about signing of a Afghan-Soviet transit agreement which in the event of a Pakistani blockade would permit nearly all Afghan goods to move through the Soviet Union. He further added that the agreement showed Afghan "willingness to accept closer economic ties with the Soviet Union as a solution the present impasse"[197] but expressed his inability to predict as to at what point those commitments would result irretrievable Afghanistan drift into Soviet orbit.

In this regard the US Secretary of State expressed the fear that deteriorating Afghan-Pak relations could create a situation which might endanger Afghan ability to resist Soviet penetration.[198] He further added that Afghanistan's inland position made it almost inevitable that it would turn orthward for aid if its access to south continued to be cut off and under such an eventuality "Pakistan would be in much worse situation than at present."[199] Thus the US Ambassador in Pakistan was instructed by the State Department to urge Pakistan to lift embargo on shipments needed for Morrison-Knudsen Coporation, an American Company operating in Afghanistan which "is one of chief influences which maintains Afghan connections with the West (and) its departure would create vacuum which Soviets would be anxious to fill."[200]

Following the reopening of consulates and trade agencies between Afghanistan and Pakistan during the second week of September 1955, the United States expressed hope of commencement of a new period of cordial relations between the two countries.[201]

On the other hand, United States took a serious view of growing Afghan-Soviet economic cooperation. The Soviet economic aid programme in Afghanistan during 1955 included the construction of a gasoline pipeline from a Soviet terminal into Afghanistan, construction of grain storage elevators paving of streets and a number of other projects—a most comprehensive Soviet programme of direct economic development aid in the free world and "Soviet penetration into Afghanistan."[202] Subsequently, the US National Security Council recommended that one of the most effective measures which Washington could adopt to counter Soviet penetration was to encourage the growth of closer economic and political relations between Afghanistan and Pakistan.

The recommendation provided for US technical and economic assistance to be give to Afghanistan for those project which would tend to strengthen Afghanistan ties with Pakistan. These cooperative projects, estimated to cost $ 10 million annually over a three-year period, included establishment of a free port and improvement of habour facilities in Karachi, furnishing additional equipment for Pakistan railways facilitate transit of Afghanistan goods, improvement of the road between the Pakistan border and Kabul, and development of an international curline, linking Kabul with Karachi and other cities in neighbouring countries.[203] The State Department hoped that initiation these projects would assist in forestalling Soviet efforts to extend its influence in the region.

On 15 October, 1955, the Afghan Foreign Minister, Sardar Naim had long discussions with US Ambassador in Kabul. Sardar Naim informed that the King of Afghanistan had sent a "special message" to President Eisenhower inviting latter's attention to deteriorating Pak-Afghan situation and calling for US intervention.[204] From his discussion, Ambassador Ward gathered that Sardar Naim's purpose was to assure that Washington had full understanding of Afghan views, "including the view that only hope for Afghan's future lies in US assistance in solving 'vital' Pushtunistan question."[205]

Ambassador Ward further informed the State Department that Sardar Naim eanted Afghanistan's association with the "free world," the form of which depended on US wishes. Ward further added: "He (Naim) said he does not ask for US arms, for role this country can play must be determined by higher "free world" policy. Then developmentof Afghanistan from economic security standpoint.."[206]

Sardar Naim in his talks with Ambassador Ward expressed surprise over the fact that Washington based its "judgements" on rumours. He also criticised the US policy of "non-interference in Pakistan-Afghan dispute. However he vigorously contended that United States was "the only agency which can secure solution to Pakistan-Afghan issue regarding Pushtunistan."[207] In his assessment, Ambassador Ward recommended to the State Department to assure Afghanistan about the continued US friendship and persuade the latter to seek direct negotiations with Pakistan.

Afghanistan Government's efforts to use the good offices of the United States to help restore normal relations between Afghanistan and Pakistan continued during the closing months of 1955 despite American reluctance. The Afgnan Ambassador in Washington, Mohammad Kabir Ludin, had been authorized by his Government to deliver "an oral message" to the US President who was then not keeping good health. Accordingly on 20 October, 1955, the Afghan Ambassador in Washington met the US Secretary of State and other officials of the State Department and handed over to them a letter of his own drafting based on Afghan King's "oral message" to be delivered to the US President which *inter alia* mentioned that Afghan-Pakistan relations had again become critical.[208] It further added that having in mind" the enormous prestige of the President and the confidence with which the United States is regarded by both government" the King of Afghanistan had wished to call this situation to the President's attention and to express the hope that the US would not withhold its efforts to bring about friend relations between the two countries.[209]

Consequently during the last week of October 1955, the US State Department circulated a draft reply to be sent to Afghan King to its Embassy in Kabul for comments.[210] The US Ambassador in Kabul in his telegram 431 of 1 November, 1955 to the State Department suggested several minor revisions in the Department's draft reply to the King including a cautionary note about "recent Soviet overtures."[211] On 2 November, 1955, the US Embassy in Kabul in its communication to the State Department with regard to latter's impending reply to be sent to the Afghan King suggested that it should include in the proposed reply that "the United States will give sympathetic consideration of granting of economic aid to Afghanistan if it curtail present pro-Soviet policies, and if Afghan differences with Pakistan can be adjusted."[212] It further added: "Role of Daoud should not be considered of primary importance. . . if United States pursues active policy of what is right for US and Afganistan, putting principles above personalities, Daoud will either have to cooperate with inevitable or fall."[213] At this juncture Ambassador Ward appeared to be bold enough to criticize the draft reply of the State Department being full of "reluctance and timidity" and asked the question as to what extent was United States interested in Afghanistan? It suggested two options. In the first option if the interest was only normal then "President's reply would preferably be simple acknowledgement of King's appeal and reiteration that Pakistan-Afghan affairs is none of our business."[214] In the second option, Ambassador Ward suggested: "It it is important for United States to keep Afghanistan outside the Soviet orbit, we must be prepared to pay price which involves not only economic assistance but also greater heed to local preoccupations such as Pushtuonistan as well as basic determinations as to this country's role in regional defence."[215] It was a bold and practicable suggestion which if implemented could have removed the ambiguity in US position and policy towards Afghanistan. While realizing the predicament of State Department in this regard, the US Ambassador in Kabul further added:

> Hard decisions regard US interest and paying price seem to be confronting us throughout Middle East these days and we realize difficulties which these choices confront us. However, need for such decisions regarding Afghanistan has been accentuated by increasing Soviet attention to this country, particularly following Iran's adherence to Baghdad Pact.[216]

Subsequently on 18 November, 1955 the US Ambassador in Kabul, Ward, delivered the letter of US President to Afghan King. On 19 November, 1955 Ambassador Ward informed the State Department that after receiving the reply from the US

President, the King of Afghanistan expressed his appreciation of "good intentions" expressed in the letter.[217] Anticipating the reaction of Afghan Government to the communication from American President, the State Department observed: "One of the most important considerations affecting the US as to the action which it might take following the King's reply is the evaluation of the chances that the Soviet Union would increase its influence in Afghanistan to the extent that it became dominant if the US did not intervene with the Pakistan Government in Afghanistan's behalf."[218] It further noted that such evaluation would be a continuing one affected by unfolding events such as the pending visit of Bulganin and Khrushchev, both Soviet leaders, to Afghanistan in December 1955.

It is worth mentioning here that CIA and State Department, especially CIA Director, Allen Dulles and, US Secretary of State, John Foster Dulles, generally dubbed Prime Minister Daoud as pro-Soviet. While speaking at the meeting of the National Security Meeting on 1 December, 1955, CIA Director, Allen Dulles said that the situation "in Afghanistan was reminiscent of that which had prevailed in Iran. . . there was a strong-minded Prime Minister who for the moment had been playing the Soviet game. The Afghan King seems either unable or unwilling to control Prime Minister Daoud. . ."[219] On an inquiry from the US President whether, what was going on in Afghanistan was the work of a single individual or of a "Junta", the CIA Director replied that it was the work of a single individual—Prime Minister Daoud. He regarded Pakistan as pro-West and "in the all-too familiar pattern, Afganistan was looking to the Soviet Union."[220] However Governor Stassen while taking an objective stock of the situation, suggested that the United States should try to mediate between Afganistan and Pakistan and also provide a little more economic assistance to Afghanistan.[221] Reacting to this suggestion, Secretary of State Dulles expressed doubt as to the wisdom of offering US's good offices to settle the dispute of Pushtunistan "on ground that the Afghan Government did not really appear to welcome our mediation."[222] On 12 December, 1955, the US President in his reply to Afghan King's letter of 22 November, 1956 expressed appreciation for Afghanistan's "warm feelings" and hoped for better relations between Pakistan and Afghanistan.[223] In this regard, the Soviet Department asked its embassies in Kabul and Karachi to take appropriate steps to keep entire President—King correspondence as confidential otherwise it "would seriously hamper if not make impossible efforts of United States to render effective assistance in Afghan-Pakistan dispute".[224]

On 14 December, 1955, US Ambassador in Kabul, Ward, handed over US President's letter addressed to Afghan King, to the Afghan Foreign Minister, Sardar Mohammad Naim. Later during the talks when Armin H. Meyer, a Counsellor in US Embassy in Kabul, said that an arms deal with Soviet bloc by Afghanistan during the visit of Soviet leaders visit to that country would be construed by whole world "as clear evidence that Afghanistan is becoming Soviet satellite",[225] Sardar Naim replied that arms were merely for self-defence and 'as for statellite status, Afghan leaders would never concur."[226]

The US Counsellor Meyer again asserted that it was not matter of what Afghan leaders had in mind but intentions of the Soviets. Egyes of the world will be on Bulganin-Khrushchev visit this week. If visit is highlighted by arms deal, as well as probable Soviet statements supporting Afghan claim regarding Pushtunistan, whole world will be led to believe that Soviets are "using Afghans" preparing another Korea in this country. He should know by this time that Soviet arms offer as well as any Soviet statements regarding Pushtunistan are not made because of Soviet love for Pushtuns or Afghans but are obviously designed to exacerbate Pakistan-Afghan troubles for ultimate benefit of Soviet imperialism."[227] The Counsellor further added that Afghanistan by insistence on "extremism" regarding Pushtunistan seemed to destroy Afghanistan itself and "facilitate Soviet expansion to this whole part of Asia".[228]

To this, the Afghan Foreign Minister, Sardar Naim remarked that "outside world, including Washington, would have no right to consider arms deal as anything but simple uncomplicated matter of Afghanistan's self-defence . . . with Pakistan having unsheated sword could any body dispute its (Afghan) right to use small knife?"[229]

Without conceding Afghan standpoint, the American Counsellor continued reiterating its own interpretation. Even Ambassador Ward in his comment observed the similar stance: "Naim's attitude reflects clearly that highest government decision has been made to enter arms deal with Soviet bloc, probably during Bulganin-Khrushchev visit".[230] He further added that the US President's letter to Afghan King was very timely: "It should have some effect, but even if it does no one including Afghans can ever say we did not try to save this country. . ."[231]

As mentioned in the preceding pages, the State Department, especially the Secretary of State Dulles had been obsessed with the downfall of Premier Daoud. In this regard it is worth mentioning here that Ambassador Ward played dubious role in the early months of 1955 by sending such assessments which influenced the State Department in adopting "hostile" attitude towards Prime Minister Daoud On 24 May, 1955, Ambassador Ward in a telegram to the State Department had outlined several alternatives for US policy *vis-a-vis* the Daoud Administration. In his opinion, Ambassador emphasized that "the entrenchment of Daoud in power would be inimical to US interests in the area since it would likely lead to closer ties between Afghanistan and the Soviet Union. . .Daoud was a poor investment for US support."[232] However on 14 December, 1955, Ambassador Ward seemed to have changed his mind about Daoud Administration when he wrote to the State Department that "Daoud has withstood all pressures brought to bear no him and emerged each time stronger than before. . . Daoud now has 'national backing from Loe Jergah. . ."[233]

With a plea to State Department to revise US policy towards the Daoud regime, Ambassador Ward durther wrote that unless the United States was willing to take allout measures against Daoud,". . .Embassy firmly believes that we must accept Daoud regime as a reality. . ."[234]

While expressing his views about the possibility of "get touch policy' by the United States along with Pakistan and United Kingdom (U.K.) against Daoud regime, Ambassador Ward said that such a course would not only be dangerous but most probably useless. "United States is prepared, it necessary to go all the way and write off Afghanistan should Daoud eounter such pressures by committing irrevocably to Soviets."[235]

Commenting on the presumption that faced with the solid US Pakistan British front followed by a threat of complete US withdrawal from Afghanistan, "Daoud might knuckle under, reject furlher Soviet overlares, adopt a reasonable posture on Afghanistan and compose differences with Pakistan."[236] Ambassador Ward said that given the nature of man (Daoud) and his past performances it was highly improbable. In this connection Ambassador Ward further added that the United States and its allies should not overrate leverage of the threat of withdrawal of US aid to Afgnanistan on three counts: In the first place the US aid which primarily cosisted of advisers had produced but little economic or political impact in Afghanistan. Secondly the US EXIM Bank loan to Afghanistan was viewed as "commercial banking deal" and Afghan Government was also disillusioned by US attitude on Helmand project. In the third place, in case of US withdrawal of aid, "Daoud would count on Soviets to replace US aid. Soviets thus far have shown every indication willingness to do so and Daoud's hope will undoubtedly be raised to higher pitch by Bulganin-Khrushchev visit".[237]

Ambassador Ward further noted that the possibility of deposing Daoud had "less chance of success now than six months ago". While counting on the advantages accruing to

United States in case Afghanistan was written off by the latter, Ambassador Ward observed that such a deventuality would:

(i) . . .spur a consolidation of anti-Daoud forces and smoke out leaders willing to really lead a movement to depose him;

(ii) strengthen US position with our declared allies, especially Pakistan;

(iii) serve as a stern warning to fence-sitters, would-be blackmailers and those countries who now apparently believe that best way to extract US largesse is to work both sides of street;

(iv) Soviet takeover in Afghanistan would probably shake India's neutralist tendencies to core and might induce Nehru to repulse Soviet overtures to India all of which undoubtedly be of great importance to US interests than Afghanistan;

(v) similar salutory effect might result in committed Muslim nations when they see one of their numbers swallowed up by Soviets;

(vi) US write off of Afghanistan would put all nations in area on notice that US cannot and will not go beyond certain point to help countries who are not willing to help themselves.[288]

While counting the disadvantages accruing to United States in case it wrote off Afghanistan and the latter was pushed into the Soviet orbit, Ambassador ward noted three eventualities:

(a) Be a severe blow to US prestige throughout free world;

(b) Probably result in Soviet outflanking northern tier security position by thrusting salient between Pakistan and Iran and bring Soviet influence to Pakistan's backdoor;

(c) Have serious repercussions in US political scene where loss of one more country to communists almost certain to raise controversial foreign policy issues in election year.[239]

After having enumerated all these probalities, Ambassador Ward warned that any US move to even throw "sunday punch" at Daoud would present United States "with a set of unpleasant alternatives".[240] Accordingly he recommended the need for bringing Afghanistan and Pakistan closer through negotiations to aviod any unpleasant alternative for the United States.

As described in the courth chapter, the Soviet leaders, Bulgain and Khrushchev concluded their five days visit to Afghanistan on 19 December, 1955. The Afghan Foreign Minister, Sardar Naim met the US Ambassador, Ward, in Kabul on 19 December, 1955 and apprised the latter about the contents of the letter sent by Afghan King in reply to the letter of US President, *inter alia*, mentioning that Afghanistan welcomed any effort by the United States would help in the settlement of dispute between Afghanistan and Pakistan.[241]

Ambassador Ward during his meeting with Afghan Foreign Minister, Sardar Naim on 19 December, 1955 reminded the latter of previous US warnings that wrong moves by Afghanistan during the visit of Soviet leaders would make US assistance to Afghanistan "difficult" and news of $ 100 million deal with the Soviets "would most certainly have adverse repurcussions. . :[242] Expressing suprise that the US Government should be concerned over Soviet-Afghan deal, the Afghan Foreign Minister reiterated that the said was "absolutely without any political conditions or implications.'[243] He further added that it was purely long term credit arrangement similar to US EXIM Bank loans and imposed no unreasonable terms. While protesting vigorously against mere thought that Afghanistan could ever be Soviet satellite, Sardar Naim said: "Whle world will be wrong in assuming Afghanistan is now on side of Soviets. . . Afghanistan's policy is clearly and firmly one of neutrality. . . At the same time unless United States stands by Afghanistan, there is little, if any, hope of preventing this country from being brought into Soviet sphere."[244] In an earnest plea,

Sardar Naim hoped that United States would continue its aid and particularly its efforts to facilitate Pakistan-Afghan rapprochement.

However Ambassador Ward in his comment wrote to the State Department: "One would think that Naim was deliberately prevaricating but like other top government officials he appeared to have naive conviction that Afghanistan was fully capable of completely controlling its destiny despite this huge long-term mortgage which Soviets have obtained."[245]

In the beginning of January 1956, an inter-departmental committee comprising CIA, State Department, Department of Defense etc. prepared a report under the caption National Intelligence Estimate on the situation in Afghanistan. The report noted that Afghanistan was currently drifting closer to the Soviet bloc which could threaten Afganistan's independence and its historic position as a buffer state.[246] In its assessment about Soviet game in Afghanistan, the report added: "However, the USSR is likely to be content for some to maintain close relations with and assist a 'benevolently' neutral Afghanistan rather than to accomplish a clear-cut takeover either by recognizable subversion or actual force."[247]

In its estimate, the United States had limited capabilities to induce Afghanistan to alter its policies. The US policy makers seemed to be skepticle about Afghan policy when their views as reflected in the report said: "Increased US aid might lend the Afghans to affirm their neutral benevolence toward the US as well as toward the USSR, but would probably also convince them that flirtation with the USSR was a good way to get US aid."[248] At the same time report also cautioned that a cut off of US aid or "other evidence of US unfriendliness" was likely to drive Afghanistan closer to the Soviet Bloc. It further observed that in case Western support of the "northern tier" concept was stepped up and particularly if the United States remained steadfast to the Baghdad Pact,[249] then the Soviet Union would attempt to counter these developments which might include increased efforts to ensure Afghanistan's orientation toward the Soviet Bloc.[250] With regard to establishment of American bases in Iran or Pakistan, the report worned that in such an eventuality Moscow would probably seek to gain control over Afghan foreign and military policy.

In view of the conclusion of $ 100 million loan agreement between Afghanistan and Soviet Union, there had been increased anxiety in Washington to know the implications of Soviet loan to Afghanistan. Consequently, the State Department in a telegram to the US Embassy in Kabul on 14 March, 1956 expressed its concern over "increasing indications USSR and Afghanistan intend to proceed rapidly towards implementation of $ 100 million loan agreement with possible result of Soviet domination in main sectors of Afghan economy. We are particularly anxious lest Soviets initiate projects in the southern part of the country which would provide opportunity for them (Soviets) to inject themselves in delicate situation arising out of bad State of Afghan-Pakistan relations."[251] In this regard the State Department suggested as one means of limiting extension of Soviet influence which might be initiation of economic development programme in Afghanistan which would effectively demonstrate continuing US interest in maintenance of Afghanistan's ties with the West.

The State Department asked the American Embassy in Kabul about the advisability of such programme. It was State Department's view that one of the main problems arising in consideration of such a programme was "our desire to prevent creation of impression that Afghanistan has only agreed to accept assistance from the Soviet Union in order to receive substantial aid from US."[252] The State Department further observed that while extending assistance to Afghanistan, the United States would have to take into account the impact of such a move on its relations with Pakistan: "It would be helpful if Afghans prior to any discussions with them of aid programme were to give some tangible evidence of their desire to continue cooperation with the free would."[253]

Before taking any decision regarding aid to Afghanistan, the State Department asked its Embassy in Kabul for comments on the following:

(i) Recent evidence if any of Afghan interest in US development assistance programme;

(ii) Desirability of initiating such programme in near future;

(iii) Composition of programme and assistance and method of approach to Afghan Government;

(iv) Probability of Afghanistan's willingness to proceed with projects requiring Afghan-Pakistan cooperative efforts.[254]

On 8 March, 1956, the communique issued by the Executive Council of the South-East Asia Treaty Organization (SEATO) stated:

> . . . the members of the Council severally declared that their governments recognized that the sovereignty of Pakistan extends upto the Durand Line, the international boundary between Pakistan and Afghanistan and it was consequently affirmed that the Treaty area referred to in Articles IV and VIII of the Treaty includes the area upto that line. . . .[255]

The United States had also endorsed the same stand. This was against the declared policy of Afghanistan which did not recognize the Durand Line as valid. It was inevitable for Afghanistan to protest against US move in recognizing the Durand Line. Accordingly on 2 April, 1956, the Afghan Ambassador in Washington, Mohammad Kabir Ludin, handed over a five-page note to the Department of State protesting against the reference to the Durand Line as the Pak-Afghan Boundary made in the SEATO's meeting at Karachi, as metioned above. The Government of Afghanistan had earlier on 20 March, 1956 handed over a protest note in this regard to the American Embassy in Kabul.

The Assistant Secretary of State for Near Eastern Affairs, George Allen told the Afghan Ambassador in Washington, Ludin, that the Durand Line question could have been avoided altogether by the SEATO Conference", however, the Bulganin statements supporting Pushtunistan which he supposed were not solicited by the Afghans had made it appear necessary for SEATO to 'set the record straight' so that there might be no misunderstanding."[256]

On 15 May, 1956, the US Department of State delivered an official reply to the Afghan protest note of 2 April, 1956. The US statement said:

> The Government of the United States has always regarded the Durand Line as the legal boundary between Afghanistan and Pakistan. . . by its participation in the SEATO Communique, the Government of the United States has reaffirmed its position with which the Government of Afghanistan is familiar.[257]

During the middle of May 1956, the US National Security Council held its 285th meeting in Washington which discussed the contemporary significant developments affecting the US security. While initiating discussion on Afghanistan, the then CIA Director, Allen Dulles said that the Soviets were making a major effort to extend their influence over Afghanistan. He further added: "Some $ 50 to $ 60 million of the $ 100 million loan recently made by the USSE to Afghanistan had already been allocated among thirteen different projects. . . truckloads of small arms were entering Afghanistan from the Soviet Union . . . as long as Afghanistan was cut off from the West by its feud with Pakistan, Afghanistan would turn more and more to the USSR. . . ."[258] Allen Dulles recommended strongly that the United States should try at least to maintain an air foothold in Afghanistan.

While participating in the discussions of the National Security Council, Governor Stassen laid emphasis on increased economic assistance to Afghanistan and "it was essential that a programme be worked out among Iran, Afghanistan and Pakistan if Afghanistan were to be saved from the USSR."[259] President Eisenhower observed: ". . . If there was one sentiment universally abroad in the world today, it was the sentiment nationalism. Accordingly the only course of action for the United States was to stress the significance of nationalism and to make clear to the Afghans that they will loose their national identity if they continue to go along with the plans of the Soviet Union."[260] He fur.her added "Nationalism and Moslem (Muslim) religion, were the only real influence in Afghanistan on which we could base our hopes. The United States could certainly not compete for Afghanistan with the Soviet Union in the economic sphere."[261]

On 6 August, 1956, the CIA Director, Allen Dulles, in a Memorandum to the Secretary of State expressed his concern over the increasing economic cooperation between Kabul and Moscow. He further opined that the "basic cause of closer Afghan-Soviet relations is Afghan Prime Minister Daoud's conviction that only from the USSR can he obtain the large-scale economic assistance required for the rapid modernization of his country and the political and military support to make his dream of Pushtunistan a reality.[262]

Afghanistan welcomed the Eisenhower Doctrine[263] and hoped for further strengthening of Afghan-US relations.[264] In this regard the State Department advised its Embassy in Kabul:

> . . . We fully understand the desire of Afghanistan to avoid actions which USSR could consider provocative. We are aware that outspoken endorsement by Afghan officials of doctrine and indication that the US was seeking to exclude USSR-Afghan relationship, might bring about Soviet presrures creating real hardships for Afghanistan. In circumstances it would appear wise for Afghanistan to avoid actions or statements *vis-a-vis* Soviets which might afford basis for Soviet retaliation, particularly since it

might be impracticable for the US to meet resultant Afghan requirements for security assurances and economic relief.[265]

On 1 March, 1957, Najib-Ullah presented his credentials as Afghan Ambassador to the US President. In his meeting with the officials of US Department of State, Ambassador Najibullah expressed the hope of continuing US economic assistance and cooperation.[266]

During the last week of March 1957, Richards, a State Department official, visited Afghanistan and met Afghan leaders. On the basis of his assessment, he sent a report to the State Department on 2 April, 1957 which *inter alia* mentioned "fixed determination of Afghan leaders to strive fiercely to maintain independence of country from any threat including international communism."[267] While referring to Afghan leaders being aware of Soviet manoeuvers in Afghanistan, the *Report* further added: "They probably desire to loose embrace of Russian bear but know that they must move slowly to avoid being crushed. They hope to develop relations with United States as form of insurance against USSR."[268] With regard to US policy towards Afghanistan, Richards suggested:

> I believe what we should strive for is really "neutral" Afghanistan on Swiss model. We should help the country to extract itself from Russian fold but at cautious pace to keep down likelihood of counter moves by the Soviets to tighten their hold. We need also to avoid arousing on part of Afghans expectations of support which in actual crisis it would not be practical for United States to extend. . .[269]

It is evident from the foreground analysis based on the recently published documents of the US Department of State that United States remained reluctant to accede to Afghan request for the supply of American arms. The US policy towards Afghanistan from early 1950s onwards was mainly determined by Pakistan factor. Pakistan had joined SEATO and CENTO. The differences between Pakistan and Afghanistan over the issue of Pushtunistan had been deteriorated and

Pakistan's preeminence in determining United States's policy towards Afghanistan had resulted in invoking lukewarm American response to Afghan request for US arms as well as US mediation in the Pushtunistan dispute between Pakistan and Afghanistan.

According to Leon B. Poullada, the American policy-makers dilemma to realize the potential of the Soviet diplomatic offensive in Afghanistan during 1950s was partly due to the inadequate operations of the American embassy in Kabul under the direction of Ambassador Angus Ward [270] It is worth mentioning here that Ward had been a hostage of the Chinese Communists when he was Consul-General in Mukden. Having passionate hatred towards Communism and "personal animus towards Daoud", Ward failed to correctly assess or report the extent of Soviet danger.[271]

Poullada's assessment is substantiated by the despatches he had been sending to the State Department in 1954-55, as analysed in the preceding pages. Though by the middle of 1956, Ward's doubts about Daoud's policies had been cleared to some extend and he tried to convince the State Department about Sardar Daoud's stability and inevitability in Afghan politics but it was too late to alter the "conditioned" thinking of American policy makers towards Afghanistan.

On the other hand the augmented US economic and arms assistance to Pakistan but rejection of Afghan request for the supply of arms by the United States had perturbed the policy makers in Kabul. Consequently in January 1955 Daoud approached Soviet Union regarding longstanding Soviet offers of military aid which Afghanistan had previously rejected.[272] However the visit of top Soviet leaders to Afghanistan in December 1955 which envisaged promise of augmented Soviet help for Afghanistan, perhaps prompted Washington to review its policy towards the region especially Afghanistan. The *New York Times* had opined that Moscow had challenged the US policy towards Afghanistan.[273] According to Zalmay Khalilzad, it was the combination of Daoud's premiership, the Afghan-Pakistan dispute, US assistance to Pakistan and Washington's reluctance to provide military assistance to Afghanistan that afforded Moscow a significant opportunity for greater influence in Afghanistan."[274] However, the present author is disinclined to agree with Khalilzad's assessment about Daoud's premiership. The question of Pushtunistan had been lingering on since the time of Amir, Amir Dost Mohammad and that legacy was inherited by Sardar Daoud who rather refused to compromise on it even at the American insistence.

The aftermath of these developments was the emegence of three schools of opinion in Washington regarding US policy towards Afghanistan. One school was of the view that the US should counter the Soviet influence in Afghanistan. The second school of thought favoured Afghanistan to be left to its own fate and in case it tilted towards Moscow, it would be a warning to other non-aligned countries.[275] The third school of opinion espoused for the continuance of incremental help to Afghanistan. Hamilton F. Armstrong, the editor of prestigious quarterly *Foreign Affairs* while supporting this view wrote in an article: "It would seem to indicate right position for us to take realistically and morally as well, but only in the conditions and up to the point."[276] He further expressed the view that the conditions were such that "the Afghans, who sinerely want to protect themselves from domination from any quarter, shall be intelligent and farsighted their steps to avoid dangers of crisis."[277] The author strongly pleaded for the supply of US arms to Afghanistan:

> . . .Afghans are tough and resilient lot and it is possible that even the subtle programme on which the Soviet Union seems to be embarked for disarming them economically and financially will fail. Nothing that we can do can guarantee that result. But we can encourage the Afghan leaders to feel that they are not alone, we can continue our aid in moderate amounts, giving them time to get their bearing; we can perhaps be of service to them politically, and we can warn against further steps which will end almost automatically

in delivering their country to foreign hands even if seeing that result as imminent they belatedly revolt against it.[278]

The augmentation of Soviet economic and military aid to Afghanistan had unnerved the US policy makers for a while. Recognizing this fact, the US Secretary of State, Dulles, said that the success of Soviet aid and resultant increase in its influence was discernible from the pace of developmental programme being carried out in Kabul.[279]

In view of the growing Soviet influence in Afghanistan, the failure of US policy to abate it had been subject to criticism at home. Lesley E. Crane, an American engineer, who had worked in Afghanistan, said in an interview with the *US News and World Report* that the United States had spent millions of dollors in Afghanistan without gaining any advantage.[280] There were some who favoured a positive attitude towards Afghanistan Adam C. Powell told the House of Representatives that by remaining neutral during the two world wars, Afghanistanh ad earned admiration of world community which was evident from the fact that Kabul's admission to the United Nations was done unopposed in 1946.[281] The official circles in Washington also acknowledged that Soviet package-aid deals had great impact on the developing countries of South Asia especially Afghanistan, but at the same time they expressed the view that Washington had not lost its interest in Afghanistan.[282]

The United States provided air-travel facilities to over 1000 Afghans for Haj pilgrimage in June 1956.[283] During this period Afghanistan was hit by food shortages and it urged the US to supply foodgrains to meet the shortage.[284] The International Cooperation Administration of the United States declared on 17 November, 1956 that Afghan Government had accepted the aid worth $ 100,000 for the reconstruction of a part or Habibia College and the *Department of State Bulletin* called it an expression of US friendship towards the people of Afghanistan.[285] William M. Routry, a senior official of the Department of State told the Committee on Foreign Relations that the US investments in Afghanistan in 1956 were to the tune of $ 15.6

million.[286] In 1957, the United States agreed to provide Afghanistan technical aid worth $3 million and 11.4 million for development purposes.[287] The International Cooperation Administration in cooperation with the Department of State prepared a report which analysed the impact of US assistance on Afghanistan. The report noted that the US aid provided instrumental in saving Afghanistan from being pushed into the Soviet camp.[288]

The pattern of Afghan-US trade had remained always uneven. In 1957, the Afghan US trade worth 994.66 million Afghanis. However during 1956-57, the Afghan imports from the United States accounted for only 3.4 per cent of former's total imports.[289] Afghan exports to that country during the same period accounted for 21.3 per cent.[290]

Afghanistan and Eisenhower Doctrine

The US President Dwight D. Eisenhower in a message to the US Congress on 5 January, 1957 said that the countries of the Middle East were facing the threat of communism. He further added that the United States in pursuance of its policy of global containment of communism, wanted to provide increased economic and military assistance to the countries of the Middle East with a view to stem the tide of Soviet communism. This message later came to be known as "Eisenhower Doctrine."[291] James P. Richards, a senior officer of the Department of State, visited Afghanistan in early 1957 as part of his tour to the Middle Eastern and South Asian countries, to explain the purpose of the Eisenhower Doctrine and its importance in safeguarding the independence of these countries.[292] Richards tried to convince the Afghan rulers the benefits of joining the US sponsored alliances under the Eisenhower Doctrine. However, Richard's mission was not in keeping with the wellknown Afghan policy of traditional neutrality. Afghan acceptance of the Eisenhower Doctrine meant renouncing its centuries old and timetested policy of neutrality which Kabul could not afford.

PRIME MINISTER DAOUD &s VISIT TO US

Sardar Mohammad Daoud, the Prime Minister of Afghanistan paid an official visit to the United States from 24 to 27 June, 1958. He was accompanied by Mohammad Hashim Khan Mainwandwal, Afghan Ambassador to the United States. A.R. Pazhwak, reasoned diplomat Permanent Representative of Afghanistan to the United Nations and others. On his arrival in Washington on 24 June, 1958, Sardar Daoud and other members of his entourage were given a warm welcome. While welcoming the Afghan Premier, the then US Vice-President Richard Nixon recalled his own visit to Afghanistan five years ago and said: ". . . We have been looking forward to the time when you would visit the United States in your official capacity as Prime Minister of your country."[293] The US Vice-President hoped that the talks between the Afghan and US leaders during the visit "will be mutually helpful in developing closer bonds of friendship which have been traditional between our two countries."[294]

The Afghan Prime Minister in his reply said that his visit to the United States reflected the common desire of the Governmenrs of Afghanistan and the United States "to strengthen and expand the close and cordial relations which have existed between our two countries since establishment."[295] He further added that the geographic distance between the two countries could not sere as a barrier in bringing them more closer Prime Minister Daoud categorically asserted: "The history of our relations from the beginning has been a history of goodwill, mutual confidence and respect for each other, economic and cultural cooperation and good understanding."[296] He also hoped that his visit to the United States would serve the purpose of continuation of close friendship between the two countries.

In his address to the American Senate on 25 June, 1958, Prime Minister Daoud expressed his sincere gratitude for the warm reception and cordial hospitality extended by the Government and the people of the United States. He further said that the message of friendship of the Afghan people to the people of tne United States "does not stem only from the good diplomatic relations existing between our two countries; it has a sounder source which is the conviction of our peoples in the principles which the Afghans and the Americans alike consider to be the basis of their existence with human dignity."[297] While commenting on the Afghan-US relations Sardar Daoud told the Senate:

> Our relations with the United States of America were established on the firm basis of true knowledge, on the part of Afghan people, of the principles which constitute the American way of life. Those relations have continued in ever-increasing measure, in a spirit of mutual respect, confidence and good understanding. The further strengthening and expansion of these relations is the sincere and living desire of the Afghan people.[298]

While detailing about his Government's determination to usher in alround progress of Afghan society, Sardar Daoud said:

> Our experiences in this connection have taught us not to forget our sufferings and not to trust any policy which might allow the dark days of the past to beset us again, but, rather to favour a policy through which we can look forward to an atmosphere of good understanding . . . I can say that the achievement of our national goal being dependent on international peace and security, our national and international aims are ultimately the same. . .[299]

While reiterating almost similar sentiments is his address to the US House Representatives, Sardar Mohammad Daoud said that the principles which were the true reflection of the spirit of the American people, as love of freedom and independence, was the most sacred tradition "by which our understanding of the American people is guided."[300] He further asserted that Afghan history was witness to the fact that the people of Afghanistan had tolerated many sufferings for the preservation of their independence and freedom. He further declared:

> At no time have we allowed any influence to damage our national prestige or hurt our national pride. We are determined to live this way, we cannot think of any materialistic factor that would persuade us to accept the slightest change in the course of our national determination for the preservation of our independence and of our freedom.[301]

Making a pointed reference to the Afghan-US relations, Prime Minister Daoud expressed the hope that friendly bonds between the two countries would further strengthen.

The discussions between the Afghan Prime Minister and the US leaders were marked by cordiality and genuine friendship, which characterized Afghan-US relations.[302] The US President explained the objectives of US policy in the field of international affairs and Prime Minister Daoud similarly described the attitude of his government in the field of international affairs including its traditional policy of neutrality and independence.[303] Afghanistan was assured of the continuing readiness of the United States to be of assistance to Afghanistan in its high objectives of developing the resources of the country for the welfare of the people. It was further agreed that cooperation which already existed in the development of Afghan civil aviation, the Helmand Valley, surface transportation projects and the Afghan educational system, would be continued with a view to making each of these projects as efficient and effective as circumstances would allow.[304] On 26 June, 19:8, a cultural agreement was signed between the two countries as a symbol of warm relations and as an indication of a desire of the two nations to base their relations on mutual understanding.[305] Both the sides expressed their desire to maintain and strengthen the cordial understanding between the two countries.[306] Thus the visit of Sardar Mohammad Daoud to the United States proved successful and a milestone in the Afghan-US relations.

PRESIDENT EISENHOWER'S VISIT TO AFGHANISTAN

In December 1959, US President, Eisenhower visited Afghanistan. The news of the visit of the US President was given the publicity in the Afghan media. *Anis* and *Islah* wrote that President Eisenhower was a great world statesman and President of a great nation who was due to visit Afghanistan.[307] *Anis* expressed the view that the proposed visit of President Eisenhower was significant on two counts. Firstly, because the countries of the region had differences on political and regional issues and secondly, the visit would help in ascertaining the US viewpoint on significant issues.[308] The paper further noted that the US President's visit to neutral Afghanistan was more significant because it was not a member of any US sponsored military alliance.[309]

The visit of President Eisenhower to Afghanistan was very short-just for five hours. President Eisenhower reached Kabul on 9 December, 1959. Welcoming the US President, the Afghan King Zahir Shah hoped that the vsit would help in strengthening the relations between the to countries.[310] President Eisenhower, while praising the valiant Afghans, hoped that his brief visit would help in understanding the great country of Afghanistan.[311] The United States provided financial and technical assistance to develop Kandhar International Airport as a major refueling point for flights across southern Asia. The United States provided $ 10 million in grants and $ 5 million in loans for Morrison and Knudsen to build the airport. Prior to the airport could be opened in December, 1962, modern jets had come into use and were speeding across the area without need to refuel.[312]

On 27 September, 1961, Mohammad Naim Khan, the Afghan Foreign Minister and brother of Prime Minister, Sardar Daoud during his meeting with American President, John F. Kennedy, sought American help in quickly developing an overland route through Iran so that Afghanistan could avoid complete logistical dependence upon Moscow. President

Kennedy instead of acceding to Afghan request rather added that the latter needed to make adjustments in its policy to resolve its problems with Pakistan, because no country could readily maintain its independence on one country like the Soviet Union.[312a]

AFGHAN KING ZAHIR SHAH'S VISIT US

The Afghan King, Zahir Shah paid an official visit to the United States from 4 to 16 September 1963. During the course of his visit, the Afghan King had an exchange of views with US President, John F. Kennedy, on matters of mutual interest to Afghanistan and the United States and the contemporary world situation.[313] The joint communique issued after Afghan King's visit to the US, noted that the US had followed with interests and sympathy the efforts being made by Afghanistan under the leadership of King Zahir Shah, to achieve economic development and social progress.[314] President Kennedy assured the visiting Afghan King of the "continuing desire of the US to cooperate with Afghanistan in economic and technical fields by so doing to contribute to the success of the efforts which Afghanistan is making to provide a better life for its people."[315] The joint communique further noted that in the sphere of international relations both the countries were dedicated to the furtherance of the cause of world peace and to bring about the elimination of reduction of tensions between nations. Both countries expressed their deep conviction of the indispensable role of the United Nations in advancing the cause of peace and of the necessity of suppprting is efforts directed to that end.[316] It also noted that "Afghanistan's traditional policy is the safeguarding of its national independence through non-aligment, friendship and cooperation with all countries. The US for its part places great importance on Afghanistan's continued independence and national integrity."[317] Both Washington and Kabul agreed that the visit of Afghan King had contributed to better understanding between the two countries.

PRIME MINISTER MANWADWAL'S VISIT TO THE US MARCH 1967

Mohammad Hashim Mainwadwal, the Prime Minister of Afghanistan, visited the US from 25 March to 9 April, 1967. He stayed in Washington from 28-30 March, 1967 and held talks with the US President Lyndon B. Johnson and other US officials. The US President in his welcome speech on 28 March, 1967 said: "... Afghanistan is far from us in miles and hours as we meet this morning. But for us it is no longer a distant, far off remote place."[318] The US President listed the following four commonalities between the two countries:

(i) your land, like ours has a strong tradition of freedom and independence;

(ii) your people, like ours cherish diversity, while they seek unity in mutual respect and justice;

(iii) you, like us, are experimental in the art of government and social reform;

(iv) and we share in common dedication to peace and to the idea of a world community based on freedom.[319]

President Johnson further added that the relations between Kabul and Washington had been close and cordial: "Today they are warmer than ever before. It is a very great honour and privilege to have you with us to discuss an even more productive future."[320]

The visiting Afghan Prime Minister in his reply thanked the US President for latter's "kind expressions of friendship toward Afghanistan."[322] The Afghan Prime Minister further said that despite the considerable geographic distance separating and us Afghanistan, "our common belief and devotion to liberty and respect for the inherent dignity of man has bridged this distance."[322] The Afghan Prime Minister expressed his confidence that this visit would serve to strengthen and promote the friendly and cultural relations which so happily had prevailed between Afghanistan and the US. He also appreciated the role of US assistance in the development of Afghan economy. The Afghan Prime Minister said: "Afghanistan follows a policy of active non-alignment and is determined to exercise the free judgement in international affairs. It endeavours wherever possible to serve the cause of international peace and the rights of nations and people in the firm belief that only in peace can the progress of all nations, including Afghanistan, be assured and that international understanding is the best way of insuring human prosperity throughout the world."[323]

The joint statement issued on 28 March, 1967, noted that the two leaders talked about current developments elsewhere in Asia, particularly the urgent need for peace and stability in South-East Asia.[324] they outlines their respective positions on the problems of Vietnam and agreed that a peaceful and just settlement is urgently needed.[325]

The United States and Afghanistan concluded an agreement on 18 July, 1967 for the sales of agricultural commodities under title of the Agricultural Trade Development and Assistance Act of 1954.[326] On 25 May, 1969, the US Secretary of State, William Rogers, had a brief stopover in Kabul, on his way to Paris to attend the Sixteenth Plenary Session on Vietnam. In his statement issued on 9 May, 1969 prior to his reaching Kabul, Secretary Rovers said: "I am also very pleased to be stopping in Kabul where I will be the first US Secretary of State ever to visit Afghanistan. The visit will give me an occasion to express our friendship for that country."[327]

Then followed the visit of the then US Vice President, Spiro Agnew to Afghanistan in early part of January 1970. On 6 January, 1970, Spiro Agnew reached Kabul. In reply to a toast at a reception given by Afghan Prime Minister, Nur Ahmed Etemadi, the US Vice-President said that many Americans having known Afghanistan had "made us eager to see this beautiful and spirited land and to meet, at first hand, its proud people with their strong tradition of freedom and jealously guarded independence".[328] Referring to the geographical distance between the two countries, the Vice-President further added: "We share a kindred spirit and many of the same aspirations. . . no vexing problems divide us nor diminish the respect we hold for each other nor lessen our ability to work together."[329] While making a reference to the striking similarities in the national character and outlook of the people between the two countries, Spiro Agnew said that both Washington and Kabul shared common aspirations of deep traditional devotion to freedom and national independence. While praising Afghanistan for having longer history of maintaining such traditions, he said:

> . . . We Americans are proud of our association with Afghanistan over the years in working toward a brighter fnture for Afghanistan we feel confident that Afghanistan will continue its drive to utilize its resources to build new and better institutions, to improve its agriculture, to broaden its industrial base and create more educational and employment opportunities for its people. As Afghans persevere in their efforts, we look forward to assisting in any way we can.[330]

It was evident that the US Vice President had assured the Government of Afghanistan of continued US assistance.

The concomitant development was the beginning of the period of detente between Washington and Moscow on the one hand and Sino-US rapprochement on the other. The resultant change in US policy towards South Asia as a whole was discernible in its decline in assistance to the region as a whole. While expressing interest in Afghanistan's independence and promoting better relations between Kabul, Tehran and Islamabad, Washington apparently went back to its pre-1955 analysis of relative insignificance of Afghanistan to its overall interests and power. According to a 1971 policy assessment by the US Mission in Afghanistan: "For the United States, Afghanistan has at present limited direct interest: it is not an important trade partner , , , it is not an access route for US trade with others, there are no treaty ties or defence commitments and Afghanistan does not provide us with significnnt defence, intelligence or scientific facilities."[331]

Between 1963, and 1973, the United States made no special effort to give strong visible support to the several Prime Ministers. During this period, Mainwadwal, Masa Shafiq and Noor Ahmed Etemadi served as Prime Ministers of Afghanistan. They had bitterly complained to Leon B. Poullada that "they had not been able to elicit encouragement or support from American officials during the period of democratic reform."[331a]

THE VISIT OF HENRY KISSINGFR

On 1 November, 1974, the then US Secretary of State Henry A. Kissinger, visited Afghanistan. During his visit, Kissinger had various of talks with Afghan Head of the State and Prime Minister, Sardar Mohammad Daoud and other Afghan officials. The joint communique issued after Kissinger's visit, the same day, at Kabul, noted that both the countries conducted frank discussions on a wide range of issues in the friendly atmosphere that "characterizes US-Afghan relations".[332] Both sides held that on the wide ranging issues which included bilateral relations, recent developments in the Near East and South Asian region, progress in international detente and mutual interests of both nations of securing a peaceful, stable and cooperative world.[333]

The Afghan officials apprised the visiting US Secretary of State about their Government's views on regional and global problems. Both countries agreed that "the way to find lasting, durable and peaceful solutions to existing problems and differences between states is through constructive and thorough discussions among all sides concerned".[334] While expressing his appreciation for that opportunity to visit Afghanistan, Henry Kissinger affirmed his admiration for progress being made by the Government and people of Afghanistan. Both Washington and Kabul laid stress on the importance of international cooperation in the field of economic and technical development and "its major role in strengthening international stability and peace".[335] Afghanistan expressed its "pleasure at the contribution towards this end being made by the United States in Afghanistan through bilateral economic, technical and educational cooperation".[336] The US Secretary of State, Henry Kissinger, expressed his government's continuing dssire to "cooperate with the Republic of Afghanistan in achiveing its economic development goals".[337] He further informed the Afghan Government that he would ask a senior official of the US Agency for International Development to visit Afghanistan in the near future to renew with the Afghan authorities joint programmes and progress in bringing projects to fruition.[338]

The US Secretary of State, Henry Kissinger again visited Afghanistan on 8 August, 1976 and held discussions with Sardar Mohammad Daoud, the then president of Afghanistan.[339] The talks were held in the warm and friendly atmosphere. There was friendly and fruitful exchange of views between the two sides on major international questions of mutual interest, especially the development of situation in South Asia and the Middle East. Both the leaders also exchanged views on Afghan-US bilateral relations and cooperation in different fields.[340] Both sides also reaffirmed the importance of the strengthening and expansion of friendship and cooperation between the two countries for preserving and consolidating the regional and world peace. The two sides noted the similarity of the "views and purposes of Aghan and American leaders and peoples regarding national independence and integrity".[341] The Government of Afghanistan pointed out that the traditional policy—based on positve neutrality, non-alignment and friendship and cooperation with all peace-loving countries was guarantor of Afghan independence. The US Secretary of State said that his government appreciated Afghanistan's position.[342]

In his discussion with other Afghan officials, Henry Kissinger, reaffirmed US interest in participating closely in Afghanistan's economic development and also noted with satisfaction the ongoing work in various spheres with American help.[343] The Afghan Government expressed its satisfaction at US contributions which had been and were being made through bilateral economic, technical and educational cooperation. Both sides expressed their desire to expand further existing cooperation, particularly in the technical and economic fields.[344] On this occasion, an agreement was signed between the two countris for the sale of edible oil to Afghanistan on concessional terms.[345]

The pattern of friendly relations between Afghanistan and the United States continued smoothly even after the advent of Carter administration in Washington. However in early 1977 the US mission in Kabul while retaining the old notions, added two additional reasons—the lack of interest on the part of the US private sector in investing in Afghanistan and a view of the country as "distant and primitive'.[346] While the Afghan Government wanted a "large and visible US presence to counter Soviet influence" the US Embassy saw the US role differently. It argued that there "can be no question of taking counterbalance literally. In terms of proximity, historical importance, trade relations, military supply and training, or economic assistance the balance overwhelmingly weigh on the Soviet side."[347]

During the summer of 1977, the efforts were made by both the countries to arrange a visit of Sardar Daoud to the United States. And finally the visit of Sardar Daoud to the US was tentatively planned for September 1978, a dream which never came true because of the Communist *coup* in April 1978 in Kabul. Washington had rather started making preparations for the forthcoming visit of Sardar Daoud. A senior State Department expert on Soviet Affairs, Adolph Dubs, who was then overseeing South Asian Affairs in the State Department, told a House of Representatives Subcommittee on 26 March, 1978, just six weeks before the *coup* in Kabul that "internally, the political situation is stable" in Afghanistan and "President Daoud remains very much in control and faces no significant opposition."[348]

The Communist's seizure of power in Kabul by staging a *coup* in April 1978 served a blow to the rapidly growing ties between Washington and Kabul. The *coup* had paved way for direct Soviet control of internal and external policies of Afghanistan. The United States had lost Afghanistan because of its own negligence and reluctance.

REFERENCES

1. Vartan Gregorian, *The Emergence of Modern Afghanistan* (California, 1969), p. 69.
2. For details see, Eugene Stock, *The History of the Church Missionary Society, Its Environment, Its Men and Its Work*, Vol. 4 (London, 1916). pp. 209-10.
3. Gregorian, No. 1, p. 69.
4. *New York Times*, 12 July, 1921.
5. *Ibid.*
6. *Ibid.*, 18 July, 1921.
7. *Ibid.*
8. *Ibid.*, 20 July, 1921.
9. United States, ''Secretary of State to President Hardinge'', 18 July, 1921, *Papers Relating to the Foreign Relations of the United States, 1921* (hereafter US Foreign Relations), Vol. 1 (Washington, 1930), p. 258.
10. *Ibid.*
11. *Ibid.*
12. *Ibid.*
13. *Ibid* , p. 259.
14. "Secretary of State to President Harding", 21 July, 1921, *ibid.*, pp. 259-60.
15. *Ibid.*
16. *Ibid.*
17. Amir Amanullah's letter to President Hardinge (no date), *ibid.*, p. 260.
18. President Hardinge to Amir Amanullah, 29 July, 1921, *ibid.* p. 261.

18A. Quoted in Leon B. Poullada, "The Road to Crisis 1919-1980—American Failures, Afghans Errors, and Soviet Successes" in Rosanne Klass (ed.), *The Great Game Revisited* (New York, 1988), p. 40.

19. Nadir Khan to Merrick, 30 October, 1925, pp. 557-58.

20. *Ibid.*

21. Merrick to Secretary of State, 4 Novemper, 1924, *ibid.*, 1926, Vol. I, p. 557.

22. Secretary of State to Merrick, 26 July, 1926, *ibid.*, p. 559.

23. Draft Note from Ambassador Merrick to the Afghan Ambassador in France (no date), *ibid.*, p. 560.

24. Gregorian, No. 1, p. 266.

25. Dawes to the Secretary of State, 15 April, 1931, No. 9 1931, Vol. I, p. 825.

26. Secretary of State to Dawes, 16 April, 1931, *ibid.*, p. 825.

27. Kirk to Secretary of State, 19 September, 1931, *ibid.*, pp. 825-26.

28. *Ibid.*

29. *Ibid.*

30. *Ibid.*, p. 826.

31. Secretary of State to Kirk, 24 September, 1931, *ibid.*, p. 826.

32. *Ibid.*

33. John C.L. Clare, "The West Eyes Afghanistan", *Asia* (London), Vol. 38, No. 1, p. 747.

34. Marriner to the Secretary of State, 30 June, 1934, No. 2, 1934, Vol. II, p. 747.

35. Acting Secretary of State to President, 21 August, 1934, *ibid.*, p. 749.

36. *Ibid.*

37. *Ibid.*

38. President Roosevelt to Zahir Shah, 21 August, 1934, *ibid.*, p. 750.

39. US Ambassador in France to Secretary of State, 13 October, 1934. *Ibid.*. 1935, Vol. I, p. 555.

40. Secretary of State to Ambassador Straus in France, 2 January, 1935, *ibid.*, p. 556.

41. For full text of the draft agreement, see *ibid.*, pp. 557-52.

42. Ambassador Strous to the Secretary of State, 26 March, 1936, *ibid.*, 1936, Vol. III, p. 7.
43. *New York Times*, 6 May, 1936.
44. US Ambassador in Germany's letter to the Secretary of State, 24 November, 1936, No. 9, 1937, Part II, pp. 597-98.
45. American Eeonomic Counsellor in Germany's letter to the Secretary of State, 30 November 1936, *ibid.*, pp. 598-99.
46. Memorandum by Raymond A. Hair of the Near-Eastern Affairs, 26 January, 1936, *ibid.*, pp. 599-601.
47. US Economic Vice-Counsellor in Karachi to Secretary of State, 13 March, 1937, *ibid.*, p. 602.
48. *Ibid.* p. 603
49. US Ambassador in Moscow to the Secretary of State, 3 December, 1937, *ibid.*, p. 756.
50. Head of the Near Eastern Division to US Ambassador in Tehran, 24 December, 1937. *ibid.*, p. 752.
51. *Ibid*, p. 757.
52. *Ibid.*
53. *Islah*, 3 May, 1937.
54. Gregorian, No. 1, p. 381.
55. Vasudeo B. Mehta, "Changing Afghanistan," *United Empire*, November 1939, p. 1109.
56. Government of Afghanistan, *The Five-Year Economic Development Plan of Afghanistan* (Kabul, 1956), p. 175.
57. Murray to US Ambassador in Tehran, 28 January, 1914, No. 9 Vol. III, pp. 255-58.
58. Thyes to the Secretary of State, 6 June. 1942, *ibid.*, 1942, Vol. IV, p. 50.
59. *Ibid.*, 17 June, 1942, p. 5.
60. Engert to Secretary of State, 25. July, 1942, *ibid.*, pp. 51-52.
61. Engert to the Secretary of State, 5 August, 1942, *ibid.*, pp. 53-54.
62. *Ibid.*, 7 August, 1942, p. 54.
63. Secretary of State to Enger. 29 October, 1942, *ibid*, pp. 57-58.
64. *Ibid.*, 9 December, 1942, (1943), Vol. I, p. 514.

65. Secretary of State to US Representative in India (Phillips), 28 January, 1943, *ibid.*, p. 618.

66. US Ambassador in Moscow to Secretary of State, 28 December, 1942, *ibid.*, p. 616.

67. Phillips to Secretary of State, 16 January, 1943, *ibid.*, p. 616.

68. Louis Dupree, *Afghanistan* (New Jersey, 1973), p. 480.

69. Engert to Secretary of State, 27 May, 1943, No. 64, pp. 54-63.

70. L.M. Goodrich and Mary J. Carole eds., *Documents on,* American Foreign Relations, *July 1944—June 1945* (Princeton, 1947), Vol. VII, pp. 695-99.

71. Leon B. Poullada, "Afghanistan and the United States: The Crucial Years", *Middle East Journal*, Vol. 35, Spring 1981, p. 181.

72. *Islah*, 9 May, 1946.

73. Engert to Secretary of State, 11 November, 1944. *Foreign Relations of the United States, Diplomatic Papers 1944* (Washington, 1965), Vol. V, p. 54.

74. Peter G. Franck, *Afghanistan Between East and West* (Washington, 1960), p. 36.

75. Richard S. Newell, *Politics of Afghanistan* (Ithaca, 1971), p. 120.

76. Franck, No. 74, p. 38.

77. Leon B. Poullada, "The Failure of American Diplomacy in Afghanistan", *World Affaris* (Washington), Vol. 145, No. 3, Winter 1982-83, p. 233.

78. Franck, No. 74, p. 39.

79. Poullada, No. 71, p. 182.

80. Poullada, No. 77, p. 233.

81. US, *Foreign Relations of the United States, 1948*, Vol. 5, Part I (Washington, 1975), pp. 491-93.

82. Cited in Poullada, No. 77, p. 233.

83. *The Economist* (London), 2 August, 1980, p. 4.

84. Poullada, No. 71, p. 186.

85. *Ibid.*

86. Airgram No. A-2, 4 January, 1950 from Embassy Kabul to Department of State, cited in *ibid.*

87. *Index of Declassified Documents* (Airlington, Virginia, 1978), No. 377A.

88. *Iibd.*

89. Poullada, No. 71, p. 186.

90. US, *Foreign Relations of the United States 1951*, Vol. VI, Part 2 (Washington, 1977), pp. 2005-10.

91. *Ibid* , p. 1995.

92. US, National Archives, File No. 890, 20/7-2048 as cited in Poullada, No. 71, pp. 186-87.

93. United States, *Foreign Relations of the United States, 1952-1954*, Vol. XI (Washington: Government Printing Office, 1983), p. 1366.

94. "Memorandum of Conversation, by the Charge in Afghanistan (Horner)", 2 January, 1952. *Ibid.*

95. "The Charge in Afghanistan (Horner) to the Department of State", 7 July, 1952. *Ibid.*, p. 1367.

96. "Memorandum of Conversation, by the First Secretary of the Embassy in India (Leach)", 31 August, 1952, *Ibid.*, p. 1370.

97. Cited in *Ibid.*, p. 1447.

98. *Ibid.*, p. 1371.

99. *Ibid.*

100. *Ibid.*, p. 1379.

101. *Ibid.*

102. "The Charge in Afghanistan (Horner) to the Department of State", 9 September, 1952, *Ibid.*, p. 1447.

103. *Ibid.*

104. *Ibid.*

105. *Ibid.*, p. 1448.

106. Horner to Department of State, 9 September, 1952, *ibid.*, p. 1450.

107. The Secretary of State to Embassy in Afghanistan, 12 September, 1952, *ibid.*, p. 1450.

108. *Ibid.*, pp. 1450-51.

109. Horner to the Department of State, 23 September, 1952, *ibid.* p. 1453.

110. *Ibid* , pp. 1453-54. The clauses vi and vii are deleted in the original.

111. Secretary of State to the Embassy in Afghanistan, 29 September, 1952, *Ibid.*, p. 1454.

112. Horner to the Department of State, 2 October, 1952, *Ibid.*, p. 1456.

113. *Ibid.*

114. *Ibid.*

115. The Secretary of State to the Embassy in Afghanistan, 11 October, 1952, *Ibid.*, p. 1462.

116. Memorandhm by the Assistant Secretary of State For Near Eastern, South Asia and Africa Affairs (Byroade) to the Under Secretary of State (Bruce, 10 October, 1952, *Ibid.*, p. 1460.

117. "Memorandum of Conversation, by the Acting Secretary of State", 24 October, 1952, *Ibid.*, p. 1376.

118. *Ibid.*, p. 1377.

119. *Ibid.*

120. *Ibid.*, p. 1378.

121. *Ibid.*

122. "Memorandum of Conversation, by William Witman of the United States Delegation at the United Nations", 29 October, 1952, *Ibid.*, p. 1378.

123. *Ibid.*, p. 1379.

124. *Ibid.*

125. *Ibid.*

126. *Ibid.*, p. 1380.

127. "The Ambassador in Afghanistan (Word) to the Department of State", 13 November, 1952. *Ibid.*, p. 1381.

128. Secretary of State to the Embassy in Afghanistan, 20 February, 1953, *Ibid.*, p. 1465.

129. *Ibid.*

130. "The Ambassador in Afghanistan (Ward) to the Department of State", 17 February, 1953, *Ibid.*, p. 1392.

131. "Memorandum of Conversation, by the Deputy Assistant Secretary of State for Near Eastern, South Asian ahd African Affairs (Ternegan)", 19 February, 1953, *Ibid.*, p. 1395.

132. Quoted in, "The Ambassador in Afghanistan (Ward) to the Department of State", 21 July, 1953. *Ibid.*, p. 1398.

133. *Index of Declassified Documents* (Airlington, Virginia, 1979), No. 33A.

134. "Memorandum of Conversation, by LeRoy F. Percival of the Office of South Asian Affairs", 20 September 1953. *Foreign Relations, 1952-54*, No. 93, pp. 1402-03.

135. *New York Times*, 8 October, 1953.

136. Memorandum by the Deputy Assistant Secretary of State for Near Eastern, South Asian and African Affairs (Ternegan) to the Acting Deputy Under Secretary of State (Murphy), 28 November, 195`. *Foreign Relations*, No. 93, pp. 1403-05.

137. "Secretary of State to the Embassy in Afghanistan", 3 December, 1953, *Ibid.*, p. 1406.

138. *Ibid.*

139. "The Ambassador in Afghanistan to the Department of State", 3 December, 1953, *Ibid.*, p. 1406.

140. "The Ambassador in Afghanistan (Ward) to the Department of State", 15 December, 1953, *Ibid.*, p. 1407.

141. *Ibid.*

142. Louis Dupree, "The Mountains go to Mohammad Zaheer", *American Universities Field Staff Reports (AUFSR)* (New York), Vol. 4, No. 6, June 1960, p. 3.

143. *New York Times*, 6 January, 1954.

144. For full text of the note see, *Foreign Relations, 1952-54*, No. 93. pp. 1409-11.

145. "Memorandum of Conversation, by the Acting Officer in Charge of Pakistan-Afghanistan Affairs (Metcalf)", 5 January, 1954, *Ibid.*, p. 1408.

146. *Ibid.*

147. *Ibid.*, pp. 1408-09.

148. For text of the Agreement, see US, *United States Treaties and Other International Agreements* (Washington, 1958), Vol. 5, p. 1954.

149. Memorandum to the Deputy Director, Office of South Asian Affairs (Smith) to Donald D. Kennedy of the Bureau of Near Eastern, South Asian and African Affairs, 23 June, 1954, p. 1474.

150. *Ibid.*

151. *Ibid.*, p. 1475.

152. *Ibid.*

153. *Ibid.*

154. *Ibid.*

155. Memorandum by the Officer in Charge of Economic Affairs, Office of South Asian Affairs (Flucker) to the Deputy Director of that Office, 25 June, 1954, *ibid.*, p. 1476.

156. *Ibid* , p. 1477.

157. *Ibid.*

158. Memorandum by the Assistant Secretary of State for Near Eastern, South Asian and African Affairs (Byroade) to the Secretary of State, 27 July, 1954, *ibid.*, p. 1479.

159. *Ibid.*

160. Memorandum of Conversation, by the Acting Officer in Charge of Pakistan-Afghanistan Affairs, 27 July, 1954, *idid*, p. 1480.

161. *Ibid.*

162. For details see, *ibid.*, pp. 1481-97.

163. *Ibid.*, p. 1482.

164. *Ibid.*, pp. 1482-83.

165. *Ibid.*, p. 1483.

166. *Ibid.*

167. Cited in Poullada, No. 77, p. 235.

168. *Ibid.*

169. The Acting Secretary of State to the Embassy in Afghanistan, 16 December, 1954, No. 92, p. 1497.

170. "Letter from the Secretary of State to the United States Representative at the United Nations", 15 February, 1955, *Foreign Relations of the United States, 1955-1957. Vol. VIII, South* Asia (Washington, D X.: Government Printing Office, 1987), p. 165.

171. *Ibid.*

172. *Ibid* , p. 166.

173. "Telegram from the Department of State to the Embassy in Afghanistan," *Ibid.*, p. 169.

174. *Ibid.*, p. 170.

175. *Ibid.*, p. 171.

176. "Telegram from the Department of State to the Embassy in Afghanistan", 12 April, 1955. *Ibid.*

177. *Ibid.*

178. "Telegram from the Department of State to the Embassy in Pakistan", 16 April, 1955. *Ibid.*, p. 174.
179. "Telegram from the Embassy in Afghanistan to the Department of State", 26 April, 1955, *Ibid.*, p. 176.
180. *Ibid.*
181. *Ibid.*
182. See UP Ambassador's telegram, No. 566 to US Department of State, *Ibid* , p. 179.
183. *Ibid.*
184. *Ibid.*
185. *Ibid.*
186. "Telegram from the Department of State to the Embassy of Afghanistan per cent, 5 May, 1955, *Ibid.*, p. 179.
187. "Telegram from the Embassy in Pakistan to the Department of State", 6 May, 1955, *Ibid.*, p. 183.
188. "Memorandum of a conversation, San Francisco", 24 June 1959. *Ibid.*, p. 185.
189. *Ibid.*
190. *Ibid.*
191. *Ibid.*, p. 186.
192. Cited in *Ibid* , p. 187.
193. "Telegram from the Department of State to the Embassy in Afghanistan", *Ibid.*, p. 187.
194. *Ibid.*
195. *Ibid.*, p. 188.
196. *Ibid.*
197. Cited in *Ibid.*, p 189.
198. "Telegram from the Department of State to the Embassy in Pakistan", 12 Juty, 1955, *Ibid.*, p. 188.
199. *Ibid.*, p. 189.
200. *Ibid.*
201. *Ibid.*, p. 191.

202. "Memorandum from the Director of the Office of South Asian Affairs (Jones) to Raymond Hare of the Bureau of Near Eastern South Asian and African Affairs", 6 October, 1955, *Ibid.*, p. 191.

203. *Ibid.*, p. 192.

204. "Telegram from the Embassy in Afghanistan to the Department of State", 15 October, 1955, *Ibid.*, p. 193.

205. *Ibid.*

206 *Ibid.*, p. 194.

207. *Ibid.*, p. 195.

208. "Memorandum of Conversation, Department of State, Washington, 20 October, 1955, *Ibid.*, p. 196.

209. *Ibid.*

210. This document is not printed in the present volume, *Ibid.*, p. 196.

211. See, *Ibid* , p. 197, note 2.

212. "Telegram from the Embassy in Afghanistan to the Department of State", 2 November, 1955, *Ibid.*, p. 1 8.

213. *Ibid.*

214. *Ibid.*

215. *Ibid.*

216. *Ibid.*

217. *Ibid.*

218. "Memorandum from the Director of the Office of South Asian Affairs (Jones) to the Assistant Secretary of State for Near Eastern, South Asian and African Affairs (Allen)", Washington, 23 November, 1955. *Ibid.*, p. 2 0.

219. *Ibid.*, p. 202.

220. *Ibid.* , p. 203.

221. *Ibid.*

222. *Ibid.*

223. "Telegram from Department of State to Embassy in Afghanistan", Washington, 12 December, 1950. *Ibid.*, p. 204.

224. *Ibid.*, p. 205.

225. "Telegram from the Embassy in Afghanistan to the Department of State", Kabul, 14 December, 1955. *Ibid.*, p. 206.

226. *Ibid.*

227. *Ibid.*, p. 207.

228. *Ibid.*

229. *Ibid.*

230. *Ibid.*

231. *Ibid.*

232. Telegram No. 635, 29 May, 1955 cited in *Ibid.*, p. 208.

233. Telegram from the Embassy in Afghanistan to the Department of State, Kabul, 14 Deeember, 1955. *Ibid.*

234. *Ibid.*, p. 209.

235. *Ibid.*

236. *Ibid.*, p. 210.

237. *Ibid.*

238. Summarized from *Ibid.*, pp. 210-11.

239. *Ibid.*, p. 211.

240. *Ibid.*

241. "Telegram from the Embassy in Afghanistan to the Department of State", Kabul, 19 December, 1955. *Ibid.*, p. 212.

242. *Ibid.*

243. *Ibid.*, p. 213.

244. *Ibid.*

245. *Ibid.*

246. "Probable Developments in Afghanistan's International Position", Washington, 10 January, 1956. *Ibid* , p. 217.

247. *Ibid.*, p. 218.

248. *Ibid.*, p. 219.

249. It later came to be known as Central Treaty Organization (CENTO), with Pakistan as one of its active members. The other members included Iran, Turkey, Iraq and USA.

250. *Foreign Relations 1955-1957*, No. 177, p. 219.

251. "Telegram from the Department of State to the Embassy in Afghanistan", *Ibid.*, p. 228.

252. *Ibid.*

253. *Ibid.*

254. *Ibid.*, p. 229.

255. For full text see, *Department of State Bulletin* (Washington), 19 March, 1956, pp. 447-49.

256. "Memorandum of a Conversation, Department of State", Washington, 2 April, 1956, No. 177, p. 230.

257. *Ibid.*, p. 232.

258. Memorandum of Discussion at the 285th Meeting of the National Security Council, Washington, 17 May, 1956, *Ibid.*, p. 233.

259. *Ibid.*, p. 236.

260. *Ibid.*

261. *Ibid.*

262. Memorandum from the Director of Central Intelligence (Dulles) to the Secretary of State, Washington, 6 August, 1956, *Ibid.*, pp. 241-48.

263. President Eisenhower in his Special Message to the US Congress on 5 January, 1957 declared more economic and military aid programme for the couutries of the Middle East. It came to be known as Eisenhower Doctrine, *Ibid.*, p. 247.

264. Telegram from the Department of State to Embassy in Pakistan, Washington, 9 March, 1957. *Ibid.*, p. 248.

265. Telegram from the Department of State to the Embassy in Afghanistan, Washington, 16 March 1957, *Ibid.*, p. 250.

266. "Memorandum of Conversation, Department of State", Washington, 19 March, 1957, *Ibid.*, p. 251.

267 Telegram from the Embassy in Afghanistan to the Department of State, Kabul, 2 April, 1957, *Ibid.*, p. 252.

268. *Ibid.*, p. 253.

269. *Ibid.*, p. 253.

270. Leon B. Poullada, "The Road to Crisis 1919-1980—American Failures, Afghan Errors and Soviet Successes", in Rosanne Klass (ed.), *Afghanistan: The Great Game Revisited* (New York: Freedom House, 1987), p. 47.

271. *Ibid.*

272. Poullada, p. 235.

273. *New York Times*, 22 December, 1955.

274. Zalmay Khalilzad, "The United States and War in Afghanistan", in Leo E. Rose and N.A. Hussain (eds.), *United States-Pakistan Forum: Relations with the Major Powers* (Lahore: Venguard, 1987).

275. "The Russian Moves in Afghanistan", *The Reporter* (New York), 5 April, 1956.

276. Hamilton F. Armstrong, "Noɹth of the Khyber", *Foreign Affairs* (New York), Vol. 34, No. 4, p. 619.

277. *Ibid.*

278. *Ibid.*, p. 618.

279. US, House, 84th Congress, Second Session, Subcommittee of the Committee on Appropriation, *Hearings on Mutual Security, Appropriation for 1957* (Washington, 1957), p. 35.

280. *US News and World Report* (Washington), 16 April, 1956.

281. *Congressional Record*, House 84th Congress, Second Session (Washington, 1956), Vol. 102, Part II, pp. 8976-77.

282. *Departmental of State Bulletin*, 28 May, 1956.

283. *Ibid.*, 2 July, 1956.

284. *New York Times*, 23 August, 1956.

285. *Department of State Bulletin*, 3 December, 1956.

286. US House, 85th Congress(First Session, Committee on Foreign Affairs. *Hearings on Mutual Security Act*), *1957* (Washington, 1957), Part I, p. 794.

287. *Ibid.* Also see *Department of State Bulletin*, 9 April, 1957.

288. *Ibid* , p. 615.

289. Government of Afghanistan, *Afghanistan: Survey of Progress 1960* (Kabul, 1960), p. 209.

290. *Ibid* , p. 205.

291. For details see, *Department of State Bulletin*, 21 January, 1957.

292. *The United States in World Affairs 1957* (New Yark. 1958), p. 181.

293. *Departm?nt of State Bulletin*, 21 July, 1958, p. 131.

294. *Ibid.*

295. *Ibid.*, p. 132.

296. *Ibid.*

297. *Ibid.*, p. 129.

298. *Ibid.*

299. *Ibid.*, p. 130.

300. *Ibid.*

301. *Ibid.*, p. 131.

302. *Department of State Bulletin.* 21 July, 1958.

303. *Ibid.*

304. *Ibid.*

305. *Ibid.*

306. *Ibid.*

307. Cited in Dupree, pp. 6-7.

308. *Ibid.*, p. 7.

309. *Ibid.*

310. *New York Times*, 10 December, 1959.

311. *Ibid.*

312. Henry S. Bradsher, *Afghanistan and the Soviet Union* (Durham, N.C.: Duke Press, 1983), p. 29.

312A. *Declassified Documents 1977*, No. 1108.

313. *Department of State Bulletin*, 7 October, 1963.

314. *Ibid.*

315. *Ibid.*

316. *Ibid.*

317. *Ibid.*

318. *Ibid* , 17 April, 1967, p. 627.

319. *Ibid.*

320. *Ibid.*

321. *Ibid.*

322. *Ibid.*, p. 628.

323. *Ibid.*

324. *Ibid.*, p. 632,

325. *Ibid.*

326. *Ibid.*, 28 August, 1967.

327. *Ibid.*

328. *Ibid.*, 23 February, 1970.

329. *Ibid.*

330. *Ibid.*

331. US Embassy in Kabul, "Policy Review: A U.S. Strategy for the 70s", Kabul A 71, 26 June, 1981, Confidential, declassified, 26 January, 1981, as cited in Khalilzad, No. 274, p. 177.

331A. Poullada, p. 53.

332. *Department of State Bulletin*, 25 November, 1974.

333. *Ibid.*

334. *Ibid.*

335. *Ibid.*

336. *Ibid.*

337. *Ibid.*

338. *Ibid*

339. *Ibid.* 6 September. 1975.

340. *Ibid.*

341. *Ibid*

342. *Ibid.*

343. *Ibid.*

344. *Ibid.*

345. *Ibid.*

346. US. Embassy in Kabul, "Assessment of US Msssion's 1977 Performance Regarding the Attainment of Its Goals and Objectives", Pt. (Secret), p 4, declassified, 26 January 1981, cited in Khalilzad, p. 177.

347. US Embassy in Kabul, "Annual Policy Assessment", 24 March, 1976 (Confidential), p. 2. declassified, as cited in *ibid.*

348. *Department of State Bulletin*, May 1978.

CHAPTER V

GLOBAL RESPONSE TO SOVIET INVASION OF AFGHANISTAN

The Soviet invasion of Afghanistan on 27 December, 1979 and the developments occurring in its aftermath wielded tremendously serious impact on the global as well as regional geopolitical developments. The Soviet invasion of Afghanistan was preceded by the seizure of power in Kabul by the Soviet-backed Communist Party, also called the People's Democratic Party of Afghanistan (PDPA) in April 1978 by staging a bloody *coup* which led to the overthrow of popular and nationalist government of President Mohammad Daoud.

The seizure of power by the Afghan communists with the over and covert backing of Moscow on 27 April, 1978 was in a way writing on the wall with regard to the ultimate designs of the Soviet Union to invade and occupy Afghanistan eventually which it did in December 1979. The legitimate government of President Daoud which had been in power since 17 July, 1973 was overthrown at the instance of Moscow and a pro-Soviet regime was installed in Kabul. With a view to have an indepth analysis of the Soviet role in the overthrow of Daoud regime, it deems appropriate to briefly analyse the foreign policy pursued by President Daoud and to identify the geopolitical developments occurring during the period which led Moscow to invate and occupy Afghanistan.

Sardar Mohammad Daoud founded the Republic in Afghanistan by overthrowing the monarchy in a peaceful transition of power on 17 July, 1973. On the occasion of the proclamation of the Republic, President Daoud in a broadcast from Kabul Radio said on 17 July, 1973: "Afghanistan's foreign policy will be based on neutrality, non-alignment in military blocs and free judgement of the people of Afghanistan themselves."[1] The Afghan President further added that the first pillar of the policy of Afghanistan "is a desire for peace and friendship with all the nations and people of the world."[2]

Sardar Mohammad Daoud after founding the Republic, had kept the office of the President and the Prime Minister unto himseif. We have seen in the third chapter that the pattern of Afghan-Soviet relations during the Daoud regime had remained almost that of a "cool off" stage because Daoud was steadfastly committed to the pursuit of independent, genuine and positive policy of non-alignment. With a view to pursue an independent and genuinely non-aligned foreign policy, Mohammad Daoud followed the policy of foriendship and cordiality with the neighbouring countries, Islamic and non-aligned countries. The objective of this policy was to reduce Afghanistan's dependence on Soviet Union and maintain a genuinely non-aligned and independend policy to safeguard the sovereignty, independence and territorial integrity of Afghanistan. And Mohammad Daoud succeeded in it to a large extent.

It has been suggested that Mohammad Daoud captured power in July 1973 with the help of the Soviet Union. However this analogy is misplaced. Given the patriotism and nationalistic commitments of President Daoud and the pattern of Soviet-Afghan relations between July 1973 and April 1978, it is wrong to surmise that President Daoud needed or had Soviet help in founding the Republic. This view is also shared by Abdul Samad Ghaus when he says: "I am, however, convinced, after years of association with Daoud and his colleagues, that the coup of 17 July, 1973, was definitely not a

Russian initiative. It was an Afghan venture in pursuit of purely Afghan aims."[3]

Relations with Turkey

Afghanistan under the dynamic presidentship of Mohammad Daoud pursued the policy of further strengthening the friendly relations with Islamic and non-aligned countries. In this regard, measures were taken to enhance the friendly and cordial relations with Turkey with which Afghanistan had centuries old traditional and cultural relations. On the occasion of the Fiftieth Anniversary of the founding of the Republic of Turkey, President Daoud in a congratulatory message to his Turkish counterpart said: "The ties of friendship and brotherhood, binding the peoples of Afghanistan and Turkey are unbreakable and deeply rooted in the history of our nations. We witness with pleasure that these ties in the course of past fifty years have expanded in various areas to the interest of our people."[4]

The relations between Afghanistan and Turkey registered further improvement when Afghanistan's Deputy Foreign Minister for Political Affairs, Waheed Abdullah paid an official visit to Turkey in early July 1974 to further promote the friendly ties between the two countries. While speaking at a reception in Ankara on 7 July, 1974, hosted by the Turkish Foreign Minister, Turen Gunis, the Afghan Deputy Foreign Minister said that the closely-knit ties, friendship, and cordiality between Turkey and Afghanistan "are neither new manifestations nor a requisite of the time."[5] While referring to the age-old ties between the two countries, Waheed Abdullah recalled that Afghanistan was the first country to accord recognition to the "new progressive regime of Ghazi Mustapha Kamal Attaturk in Turkey."[6] He further added that since then, "friendship and cordiality have been the major features of the ties between our countries. During these glorious years the heroic and freedom-loving people of Afghanistan and Turkey have bravely resisted foreign aggression and influence so that their epic struggles have consistently been a source of pride to their sons in the pages of history."[7]

The Deputy Foreign Minister of Afghanistan further added that fortunately the friendship and cordiality between the two countries had been coupled with "untrammelled and perpetual cooperation."[8]

The joint communique issued at the conclusion of Waheed Abdullah's visit to Turkey on 12 July, 1974 noted that the visit provided an opportunity for the leaders of both the countries to exchange views on the international situation and to study the questions concerning the two countries.[9] The communique further noted that the talks between the two leaders were held in an atmosphere of "sincere cordiality, reflecting the traditional friendship uniting the two countries, friendship which was based upon a strong foundation of a long-standing collaboration in the past and of the existence of very close historical and cultural ties".[10] Both countries examined the bilateral relations in all their respects and decided to speed up efforts with a view to further strengthening these relations, especially in the economic, commercial and cultural fields.[11]

Apart from these visits, the two countries also shared common views on major international issues. Turkey also used its good offices to facilitate a dialogue between Afghanistan and Pakistan to help resolve the issue of Pushtunistan during 1975.[12] However, Pakistan's intransigent attitude rendered the Turkish mediatory efforts futile. Thus during the Daoud regime, there was a marked improvement in Afghan-Turkish relations.

Relations with Iran

Afghanistan during its republican period made appreciable endeavours to expand and develop friendly and cordial relations with its immediate neighbour Iran. In July 1974, the Special Envoy of President Daoud, Mohammad Naim and the Deputy Minister of Foreign Affairs, Waheed Abdullah, visited Arab countries and Iran with a view to further consolidate the friendly relations between the two countries. During 1974, following the disappearance of a frontier demarcation pillar on the Iran-Afghan borfer, both countries decided to solve the problem through mutual consultation's. The progress in this regard was going on satisfactorily until the advent of communist *coup* in April 1978.

President Daoud paid an official visit to Iran from 26 to 30 April 1975. During his discussions with the then Shah of Iran, the possibility of a Kabul-Mashad railway to link Afghanistan with the Iranian State railway and through it to the West European network was also discussed.[13] This was Sardar Daoud's first state visit to Iran after he founded the Republic in Afghanistan. The other points discussed between the two leaders included the completion of $ 2 billion highway connecting Afghanistan with the Persian Gulf. Through this almost completed road, Afghanistan would have access to the Persian Gulf at the port of Bandar-Abbas where ample port facilities were available for Afghan use.

The joint communique issued after the conclusion of President Daod's visit to Iran, on 30 April, 1975, stated that the two Heads of State discussed regional and international issues as well as the promotion of bilateral trade and economic relations.[14] Both the sides declared their support for the UN Charter and reiterated that the establishment of a world order bound with peace and stability was not attainable but through pursuance of the principles of non-interference in the internal affairs of countries, respect for territorial integrity, non-resort to force in international relations and the elimination of differences.[15]

The Afghan President Sardar Daoud also expressed pleasure over the favourable development in relations between the two countries.

On 5 May, 1975, the Shah of Iran re-affirmed his country's support to Afghanistan.[16] On this occasion, the Shah of Iran also offered his good offices to mediate between Afghanistan and Pakistan to help resolve the issue of Pushtunistan. During his visit, the Afghan President, Mohammad Daoud, who prior to his Iranian visit, had visited Iraq in March 1975, also offered his good offices both to Iraq as well as Iran to help them resolve their dispute over the Shatt-al-Arab.[17] Thus President Daoud's visit to Iran had proved instrumental in comenting the bonds of friendship between the two countries.

This tradition of strengthening friendship between the Republic of Afghanistan and Iran during the presidentship of Mohammad Daoud got a further fillip when in 1977, both countries exchanged the instruments of ratification of the Hilmand Treaty which brought it legally into force and put an end to the dispute over the sharing of Hilmand waters. By the end of 1977, the Shah of Iran also accepted the invitation of Afghan Government to visit Afghanistan in July 1978[18] but the visit could not take place because of the advent of communist takeover in Kabul in April 1978. Had Daoud regime survived, the increasing cooperation between Iran and Afghanistan would have certainly strengthened the forces of peace and security in the region.

Relations with Pakistan

In pursuance of his policy of improving relations with neighbours, President Daouud also took initiatives to normalize relations with Pakistan. Though the couple of years succeeding the establishment of the Republic witnessed Pakistan's reluctance to take positive measures to improve relations with Afghanistan. As analysed in first chapter the only cause of friction between Afghanistan and Pakistan had been the issue of Pushtunistan. President Daoud in his broadcast to the nation through Radio Afghanistan on 17 July, 1973, the occation of founding the Republic, said: "Our relations with Pakistan. . . will be based on our permanent efforts to find a solution to the Pushtunistan problem."[19] There was no encouraging response from Pakistan which recognized the new republican regime of President Daoud on 22 July, 1973.

The improvement in Irano-Afghan relations also pave way for progress towards *entente cordiale* between Kabul and Islamabad because of the good offices of Shah of Iran. As stated earlier, Turkey had also been trying to bring Afghan-Pak rapprochement. The resultant outcome of Irano-Turkish efforts was that it was agreed that a meeting between the Deputy Foreign Minister of Afghanistan and Foreign Secretary of Pakistan would be held in Kabul in March 1975 The US Senator, Charles Percy also proved instrumental in arranging a meeting between Afghan Ambassador, Mohammad Naim and Pak Ambassador Aziz Ahmad, in Kathmandu in early 1975. The meeting between Naim and Aziz Ahmad was held in a cordial atmosphere Both sides agreed to tone down their hostile radio propaganda as a beginning to the betterment of their relations.

In the wake of disturbing development in the NWFP in February, the process of betterment received a jolt. However Iran and Turkey continued their conciliatory efforts to draw Afghanistan and Pakistan into a dialogue. However, there was no major breakthrough. In the wake of severe floods and earthquake in the northern Afghanistan, Pakistan offered aid in the form of foodgrains, clothes etc. which was accepted by Afghan Government. In May 1976, President Daoud sent an invitation to Pakistan Premier Z.A. Bhutto to visit Afghanistan which the latter accepted.

Consequently Premier Bhutto visited Afghanistan from 7 to to 10 June, 1976 and held discussions with President Daoud on bilateral relations. The statements issued by the two leaders on the eve of conclusion of Pakistani Prime Minister's visit, reflected the optimistic mood.[20] Both sides expressed their determination to pursue the dialogue until a satisfactory solution to the problem had been found. The subsequent period witnessed increasing economic interaction between the two countries. According to Ghaus, two important initial decisions by Pakistan, both procedural and substantive had "unlocked the door to the kinds of negotiations that Kabul had wanted."

These decisions were (i) the admission by Pakistan that a dispute existed between the two countries, and (ii) its recognition that Afghanistan had the right to be concerned about the fate of the Pushtuns living east and south of the Durand Line and, consequently, that it could discuss the fulfilment of their aspirations with the Government of Pakistan.

Further improvement in Afghan-Pakistan relations was registered in August, 1976 when President Daoud visited Pakistan from 20 to 24 August, 1976 and held discussions with Prime Minister Bhutto. While addressing a public meeting in Lahore, President Daoud said: "... The wish of the government of Afghanistan and my person is that our political differences be resolved, and our relations be brotherly and friendly and permanently based on good will. . ."[22]

During the discussions between the delegations of the two countries, Pakistani side pressed for a package deal which implied that it would release the political Pashtun and Balooch leaders who were under arrest and Afghanistan in return would recognize the Durand Line. However, the Afghan delegation declined to accept such a "deal". However, later on both sides agreed not to act in haste. The joint communique issued at the conclusion of Daoud's visit to Pakistan, reaffirmed their determination to continue their efforts to reach a final settlement. President Daoud's visit to Pakistan provided further impetus to the process of normalization of relations between the two countries. Transit trade was flowing smoothly. On 2 March, 1977 both countries agreed to restore their aid link,[23] which had been under suspension since early 1974.

On 9 June, 1977, Premier Bhutto on his way back from Tehran had a stop over at Kabul where he held talks with President Daoud. Premier Bhutto who was facing a political crisis in his own country on having been accused of heavy rigging in the March 1977 elections, told the Afghan President that the former would release the political leaders of the NWFP as soon as the confused situation returned to normalcy.[24] But this could not happen as Bhutto Government was overthrown by General Zia-ul-Haq on 5 July, 1977. The new government in Pakistan headed by General Zia reiterated its acceptance of the earlier two Afghan-Pak communiques of the predecessor regime.

In October 1977 General Zia visited Afghanistan and had exchange of views with Afghan President and other officials. This was an informal visit and nothing substantial result could be expected. However, it provided an opportunity for both sides to understand each other's views.[25] As a good will gesture, General Zia had released all the imprisoned Pashtun and Baluchi leaders. Thus, the first concrete step towards the normalization of relations between the two countries had been taken.

It was in the background of recently developed goodwill that President Daoud visited Pakistan during the first week of March 1978. During his talks with General Zia, President Daoud said that the establishment and preservation of cordial relations between Afghanistan and Pakistan was of primary significance.[26] He further added: "We are not here to ascribe blame to anybody for past mistakes, misrepresentations and suspiction. If we succeed in cementing our unity, the benefits deriving from it will make up handsomely for the years lost and the opportunities missed."[27] General Zia also expressed the similar sentiments and added that both countries had identical views regarding the necessity of cordial ties between the two Islamic neighbours. Both leaders laid emphasis on the need to take steps in the field of economic and cultural cooperation. While addressing a public meeting at Lahore, President Daoud declared:

> Your strength is our strength, your welfare is our welfare and your stability is our stability. . . . I pray that the day may come soon when brotherly ties already existing among us will transform themselves into a permanent. . . reality. I hope the friendship between Pakistan and Afghanistan will be permanent and everlasting.[28]

Such a spontaneous expression of warmth and solidarity with neighbouring Islamic countries by Daoud at that juncture, when viewed in retrospect, perhaps indicated the fear or a vision lurking in the mind of that extraordinary statesman about the coming events in which Soviet Union was to prop-up its stooges in Kabul and eventually invade and occupy Afghanistan.

Undoubtedly, Daoud's visit to Pakistan marked a watershed in the relations between the two countries. The overthrow of Daoud regime in April 1978 put an end to the newly attained *entente cordiale* between Afghanistan and Pakistan.

Relations with China

Afghanistan's relations with People's Republic of China also improved during the Daoud's presidency of the Republic. On 21 November, 1973, an agreement related to the construction of the hospital with the Chinese assistance was signed in Kabul.[29]

On 7 December, 1974, Mohammad Naim, the Special Envoy of President Daoud visited People's Republic of China. Naim met Chinese Foreign Minister, Chiao Kuan Hua and Vice-Premier Li Hsien-Nien and held talks on matters of interest to the two countries.[30] The Chinese Vice-Premier, Li Hsien-Nien hosted a dinner reception in honour of the Afghan Presidential Envoy in Beijing. While speaking on the occasion, Mohammad Naim expressed his pleasure for getting an opportunity for exchanging views on matters of interest especially "sincere and fruitful relations and cooperation between the two countries."[31] While spelling out the main features of the foreign policy pursued by the Republic of Afghanistan, Mohammad Naim added:

> The new order of Afghanistan in its foreign policy abides by the principles of peaceful coexistence and has unfailing belief in the policy of non-alignment to political and military groupings and free judgement on international

issues has always and everywhere supported right and justice and will do so.[32]

While referring to friendly and cordial relations between Afghanistan and China, the Special Envoy recalled the visit of Chinese Premier Chou Enlai to Afghanistan in January 1957 and the reciprocal visit by Afghan Prime Minister Mohammad Daoud in October 1957 to that country. Mohammad Naim also alluded to Sino-Afghan treaty of friendship and mutual non-aggression signed in 1960, border treaty of November 1963, and protocol on border demarcation of 1965, "which created formidable basis for friendship and good neighbourliness."[33]

The visiting Afghan Presidential Envoy expressed his pleasure on the expanding friendship and fruitful cooperation between the two countries. He also expressed Afghan gratitude "for the sincere and disinterested assistance"[34] rendered by China in the fields of aid industries, agriculture, and public health.

On 8 December, 1974, Mohammad Naim hosted a reception in honour of Chinese Vice-Premier, Li Hsien-Nien and Chinese Foreign Minister Chiao Kuan-Hua. The Afghan Ambassador to Peking, Chinese Ambassador to Kabul and other senior officials of the Chinese Foreign Office were also present on the occasion. The Afghan Presidential Envoy and the guests toasted to "further expansion of friendship between the peoples of Afghanistan and China."[35]

Mohammad Naim's visit to Beijing proved instrumental in further expanding the friendly relations between the two countries. Thus during the republican period, President Daoud took constructive and positive measures to expand and further develop Afghanistan's friendly relations with People's Republic of China.

Relations with Major Arab and Other Countries

In his policy of diversifying Afghanistan's relations with neighbouring Islamic and other non-aligned countries, President Daoud attached special significance to secure economic and political support in the Third World with a view to reduce Afghan dependence on Soviet Union and substitute it from other sources.

Most of the Arab countries had recognized the republican regime of President Mohammad Daoud within few weeks of its inception. Abdul Rahman Al-Aryani, the President of the Yemen Arab Republic in a telegram congratulated president Daoud and wished the Afghanistan people prosperity under the republican regime and for the friendly relations between our two countries more progress."[36] President Daoud in his reply to the President of Yemen Arab Republic wished the warming up of relations between the two countries.[37] Similar sentiments were expressed by the Chairman of the Revolutionary Council of Somalia, General Mohammad Sayed Dara[38] which were accordingly reciprocated by President Daoud.[39]

During the first quarter of 1978, President Daoud had an intense period of diplomatic activity. His goodwill and friendly visits to Libya, Kuwait, Saudi Arabia, Egypt and Yugoslavia bore fruitful results. Kuwait and Saudi Arabia committed financial assistance for Afghanist's Seven Year Development Plan. During his visit to Egypt, President Daoud held talks with President Anwar Sadat and expressed Afghanistan's solidarity with Egypt in its struggle against Israel and for the attainment of inalienable rights of the Palestinians. During his visit to Yugoslavia, President Daoud during his talks with President Tito had exchanged views on bilateral relations and ways of further strengthening the non-aligned movement.

It is evident from the foregoing that President Daoud strengthened Afghanistan's relations with the neighbouring, Arab and non-aligned countries. Even with Pakistan with which Afghanistan had strained relations over the issue of Pushtunistan, an *entente cordiale* had been envisaged during the republican regime.

COMMUNIST COUP OF APRIL 1978

The People's Democratic Party of Afghanistan (PDPA) seized power in Kabul on 27 April, 1978 by overthrowing the government headed by Sardar Mohammad Daud which had been saddled into power since 17 July, 1973. When Daoud had assumed power he had announced the replacement of monarchy by "a republican system, consistent with the true spirit of Islam."[40] Daoud, a seasoned statesman and a strategic thinker, pursued a "lukewarm" foreign policy in the initial years of his assumption of power. After securing his domestic position politically, he no more needed the "crutches" of the leftist groups of others. He openly declared that he was not adopting a leftist attitude or accepting the claims of any ideological faction. On 28 February, 1974 Sardar Daoud said: "We have no connection with any group, and linking us to any group or movement is a sin."[41]

On 27 April, 1978, a *coup* was staged by the PDPA and the same day Kabul Radio announced that "for the first time in the history of Afganistan an end has been put to the sultanate of the Mohammadzais (the Afghan Royal Family) and power has passed into the hands of the masses."[42] On 30 April, 1978, it was announced that power in Afghanistan was being exercised by a Revolutionary Council comprising military and civilians and headed by Noor Mohammad Taraki. On 1 May, 1978, the names of other ministers of the new government in Kabul with their portfolios were announced. Babrak Karmal was placed as number two and Hafizullah Amin as number three after Taraki.[43] On 9 May, 1978, President Taraki while announcing the foreign policy of the new Afghan Government, promised a foreign policy of non-alignment and good relations with all neighbours and also singled out such goals as "to further strengthen and consolidate friendly relations and all-round cooperation with the USSR."[44]

United States and New Regime in Kabul

There was no immediate official reaction by the United States to the Communist *coup* in Kabul. The US economic, cultural, educational and Peace Corps programme in Afghanistan continued. The United States rather faced with a policy dilemma as summed up by the then Assistant Secretary of State Harold Saunders, in a secret memo to Cyrus Vance, the Secretary of State, in the immediate aftermath of the Communist *coup* in Kabul:

> We need to take into account the mix of nationalism and communism in the new leadership and seek to avoid driving the regime into a closer embrace with the Soviet Union than it might wish On the other hand, anti-regime elements in Afghanistan will be watching us carefully to see if we acquiesce in or accept the communist takeover.[45]

He further noted that "Pakistan, Iran, Saudi Arabia and others of our friends in the area will see the situation clearly as a Soviet coup."[46] This dilemma was reflected in the US administration's two lines of thinking on the communist takeover in Kabul whether to react to it or to leave Afghanistan for the Soviets. Consequently a debate ensued within the Carter administration as to how washington should react to the situation in Kabul. This studied silence maintained by Washington showed that it was "unconcerned that another country apparently had joined the Soviet bloc."[47] While defending the US policy, Theodore Eliot wrote:

> The United States continued to keep an open mind towards assisting Afghanistan, maintained a dialogue in Kabul on possible new AID, Peace Corps or cultural programme and indicated a willingness to help to the extent proposals met out for legislative and developmental criteria. This policy made sense because cutting off these programmes unilaterally would duly reduce Afghan options and drive the Afghan Government deeper into the Soviet embrace.[48]

Moderate elements, led by Secretary of State, Cyrus Vance favoured self-restraint in Afghanistan so as to disallow the further increase in Soviet influence there. On other hand, the hard-liners led by the National Security Adviser, Zbigniew Brzezinski warned President Carter that to stand back from Afghanistan, especially in the wake of growing instability in Iran would "signal to the USA's allies in the region that it had been written off" as is essential to American interests."[49] The moderate view was expressed by the then US Secretary of State, Cyrus Vance, who wrote in his memoirs: "I concluded that our best chance to maintain a measure of influence in Kabul was to continue limited economic aid. To cut off all assistance or refute recognition would almost certainly weaken our position in Kabul."[50]

Though at the initial stage then National Security Adviser to the Carter Administration Brzezinski, had approved of the restrained response to the *coup* in Kabul, he said: "It was an internal *coup*, there was no evidence of Soviet involvement and hence there was no grounds of an American protest. The regime was undefined and not in consolidation, there was doubt as to whether it could hold power. As long as we could have some influence in Kabul, why cut off aid ? It was better to wait and see how things worked out."[51] Soon Brzezinski became a hard-liner. In the wake of faced by dilemma, President Carter compromised by permitting Brzezinski to seek an alternative regional strategy while the State Department was to establish "correct" relations with the new Afghan regime. Consequently Brzezinski, through the National Security Council, sought to establish a support network for the resistance in order to prevent any potential Soviet advance in Afghanistan in view of the growing instability there.[52]

However, the former US Ambassador to Kabul, Neumann told the US Department of State that he had known the new leaders of Afghanistan for years and they were definitely communists and would follow orders from Moscow hence the US should stop all aid to the new regime.[53] Cyrus Vance also later realized that the US reaction to the new regime was too mild. He wrote:

> In looking back I think we should have expressed our concern more sharply at the time of the April *coup* that brought Taraki to power. There were reasons why we did not protest more vigorously. Although there was little question that Taraki government would make itself responsive to Moscow, there was room for doubt about whether the Soviets had planned the *coup* or were involved in its execution. And there was reason to think the strong Afghan nationalism of Taraki, and even more of Hafizullah Amin, might keep Afghanistan from becoming a Soviet satellite. . . We concluded that our interests would best be served by letting Afghanistan continue to its traditional balancing act between East and West. The United States had few resources in the area and historically we had held the view that our vital intetests were not involved there. Moreover, our firiends in the region had adopted a wait and see attitude. There was no disposition on their part to add to the instability by supporting opponents of the Marxists in Kabul. Although we were contact from time to time about Coup plots, my advice was that we not get involved.[54]

Though there was some confusion in washington aboutthe political identity about the protagonists of the *coup* in Kabul, the US embassy also seemed uncertain. On 27 April, 1973, the US Embassy in Kabul in a cable, while expressing uncertainty about those involved in the overthrow of President Daoud advised the State Department "against any premature conclusion that the new leaders are communists".[55] In a message circulated by the State Department on 28 April, 1978 to various US Embassies, the State Department reflected its Kabul Embassy's doubts by arguing that "fragmentary evidence suggests that they (coup leaders) may be leftists and/or strongly Islamic nationalists".[56] According to Zalamay Khalilzad even when Washington was more certain about what had happened, "it did not regard the *coup* as having any important strategic or negative implications for US interests and power and its reaction was low-key."[57]

Though there was no official comment or reaction by Washington to the advent of communist *coup* in Kabul, the American press reacted very sharply to these developments. An editorial in the *New York Times* expressed concern that "a genuinely non-aligned country had fallen to an avowedly communist one that is likely to tilt towards Moscow."[58] The strategic analysts in the United States also quickly concluded that Afghanistan had been pushed into Soviet affairs opined: "The great game is over and the Russians have won it.'[59] Leon B. Poullada also regretted that no attempt was made by Washington to break relations with the communist usurpers nor to express official disapproval of such a shift in political power in a strategic country like Afghanistan.[60]

Brzezinski tried to expand US network in the region by involving the neighbouring countries of Afghanistan. In May 1978 he met the Chinese Premier Deng Xiaoping and reached an understanding on mutual security—an agreement which included Afghanistan in its provisions.[61] This discussion probably included Pakistan because by June 1978 "the first Afghan rebel camps were set up in Peshwar."[62]

However, this "token move" was not an effective measure either to deter the puppet communist regime in Kabul from pushing Afghanistan into the Soviet orbit or to checkmate growing Soviet political and military manoeuvres designed for virtual takeover of Afghanistan nineteen months later. Present writer's intimate knowledge about the Afghan resistance movement, the Afghans opposed to the communist regime in Kabul, had of their own established camps in Peshawar in June 1978 and not with US assistanc e.

Moscow and New Regime

Links of PDPA leaders, who assumed power after the *coup*, with Soviet Union were very clear. It is worth mentioning here that at the time of *coup*, there were about 350 Soviet military advisers in Afghanistan who played a significant role in the *coup*.[63] A broadcast from the Kabul Radio reported on 30 April, 1978 that one Puzanov of the Soviet Embassy in Kabul met Taraki and gave him a message of diplomatic recognition.[64] Moscow Radio finally reported on 3 May, 1978 about according Soviet recognition to Taraki Government but it cited Kabul Radio as the source.[65] On 3 May, 1978 Soviet leaders Brezhnev and Kosygin sent "hearty congratulations" to the Taraki Government and wished for its great success.[66] The advent of communist regime in Kabul had certainly raised high expectations for Kremlin. The Soviet daily *Pravda* while pronouncing the official Soviet attitude towards Kabul, wrote on 6 May, 1978: "The interests of social development demanded a fundamental break with obsolete social relations. . .complex task of forming the new power, the intrigues of internal and external reactionary forces and struggling for a better future for the Afghan people, lie ahead."[67] The reports appearing in the Soviet media by mid-May 1978 indicated that Moscow was happy with the regime.

Hafizulla Amin, the then Foreign Minister of Afghanistan, while on his way to attend the meeting of Foregin Ministers of the Non-aligned countries at Havana, stopped in Moscow on 18 May, 1978. He was greeted by the Soviet Foreign Minister Gromyko. The Soviet media, and the joint communique on their talks, identified the two men not only by their government position but also as members of the politburos, that controlled their respective parties, the Communist Party of Soviet Union (CPSU) and PDPA.[68]

During June-July 1978 Taraki managed to get rid of the leading Parchamites by appointing them as Afghan Ambassadors abroad. Nur Ahamad Nur was sent to the United States, Karmal to Czechslovakia, Anahita Ratebzad to Yugoslavia, A. Mahmud Barialay, Karmal's younger brother to Pakistan.[69]

During the initial months of 1978 Moscow tried to keep a low profile in Afghanistan. In July 1971, an agreement to provide $ 250 million worth of Soviet weapons to Afghan armed forces[70] was neither made public nor Soviet media made any reference to it.

Afghan-Soviet Treaty of Friendship and Cooperation

Despite its overt silence, Moscow was making every attempt to see that the PDPA remained in power and consequently Kabul in the Soviet orbit. A major milestone in this direction was laid during the first week of December 1978 when both countries signed a treaty of friendship and cooperation on 5 December, 1978 at Moscow.[71] The treaty was signed during Afghan President Noor Mohammad Taraki's visit to the Soviet Union from 4 to 7 December, 1978. This treaty was used as a pretext a year later by the Soviet Union to invade Afghanistan. Article IV of the said treaty, *interalia* said:

> The high contracting parties, acting in the spirit of the traditions of friendship and good neighbourness, as well as the United Nation's Charter, shall consult each other and take by agreement appropriate measures to ensure the security, independence and territorial integrity of the two countries In the interest of strengthening the defence capacity of the high contracting parties, they shall continue to develop cooperation in the military field on the basis of appropriate agreement concluded between them [72]

Under the treaty, though Moscow was not bound to prevent the downfall of the new communist regime in Afghanistan, it was already preparing the possibility of saving it from failure and keeping that country under Soviet influence even by force if needed. After the conclusion of the treaty, Soviet leader Brezhnev said that the relaticns between the two countries "have assumed a qualitatively new chapter permeated by a spirit of friendship and revolutionary solidarity."[73] The treaty came into effect with the exchange of instruments ratifications on 27 May, 1979.

The joint Communique issued after Taraki's visit observed that the contacts between the PDPA and the CPSU would be expanded.[74] Along with the friendship treaty, another agreement was also signed between Kabul and Moscow to establish a permanent inter-governmental commission on economic cooperation.[75] Thus Soviet Union had taken over the overall responsibility of Afghanistan's economic and military responsibilities even in December 1978.

Assassination of US Ambassador in Kabul

In the immediate aftermath of the *coup* in Kabul, there was no shift in Soviet policy towards the region. Washington rather discouraged both Iran and Pakistan, both neighbours of Afghanistan and allies of the United States, from following a hostile policy and from making "hasty moves" against Kabul's new rulers.[76] Khalilzad has maintained that Carter Administration was providing more aid to Afghanistan's communist government than to Pakistan.[77] The US Embassy in Kabul warned that the negative and "standaffish" attuitude carried with it the danger of making Kabul "totally dependent and aligned with the USSR."[78] However this phase of "engagement policy" ended following the assassination of US Ambassador in Kabul.

Adolph Dubs, the US Ambassador in Afghanistan was assassinated by four Afghans in Kabul on 14 February, 1979. He had presented his credentials on 17 June, 1978. Dubs's assassination cast a spell on the already deteriorating US-Afghan relations as there were supposed to be many unresolved questions about the role of Afghan Government in the affairs and its consequent uncooperative attitude.

The assassins of Dubs had held the US Ambassador as hostage in Kabul hotel and demanded from the Afghan Government the release of the arrested some leftist members in exchange for Dubs.[79] The US Embassy in Kabul advised the Afghan Government to prolong the negotistions while applying rescue operations. But the Afghan forces along with Soviet advisers stormed the hotel room which resulted in the death of

Dubs and the kidnapped.[80] According to Richard P. Cronin: "Soviet security advisers appeared to be directing the operation and the Afghan government disregarded US suggestion that an attempt to rescue Dubs by force be delayed."[81] The Afghan Government tried to underplay the incident by blaming some groups. As Beverley Male has also opined: "The choice of groups as the culprit appears a convenient ploy to divert attention from the real beneficiaries of the kidnapping and murder of the US Ambassador,"[82] However, the official organ, *Kabul Times*, in a defensive editorial wrote:

> The terrorists and the enemies of the people of DRA (Democratic Republic of Afghnistan) by committing such an inhuman and cruel act may think they would disturb or damage the ties between the two friendly countries . . . The people and the government of the DRA and the USA are fully aware of the acts of their enemies. They know that such provocative acts will not undermine the friendly relations between the two nations.[83]

Such a defence in an official daily was nothing but a move by the communist regime in Kabul to absolve itself from the responsibility of being involved in Dubs' murder and thus shift the blame to others. The outraged Carter Administration accused Moscow of involvement in the bungling that caused Dubs' death but Kremlin denied it. The US economic aid to Afghanistan was slashed.[84] On 23 July, 1979 Washington announced the withdrawal of most of its diplomatic personnel from Afghanistan because of "security reasons."[85] Although the Carter Administration had announced a drastic curtailment of US economic aid to Afghanistan but it was not totally stopped until in August 1979, when President Carter signed PL 96-53, the International Development Cooperation Act of 1979, into law.[86] Section 505 of the said Act prohibited any further assistance to Afghanistan unless the President certified to the Congress that the Afghan Government had officiary apologized and assumed responsibility for Ambassador Dubs and agreed to provide suitable protection for all US personnel in

Afghanistan.[87] Thus, in the aftermath of Dubs' assassination, the US relations with Afghanistan had reached the lowest ebb. The mild US response to Dubs episode helped crystalise the view that US policy was not working and thus it had "quietly acquiesced in the establishment of an avowedly communist government in Afghanistan."[88]

On 15 September, 1979, the Afghan Revolutionary Council announced that Taraki had asked to be relieved from party and state posts on health grounds,[89] and Hafizullah Amin became the new President of Afghanistan.

Soviet Union and Amin Regime

Amin had developed a distrust towards Moscow especially after what happened on 14 September, 1979 when an attempt on his life was made in the presence of Russian Ambassador. On 17 September, 1979, Soviet leaders, Brezhnev and Kosygin, while sending congratulation to Amin expressed the confidence that "fraternal relations between the Soviet Union and revolutionary Afghanistan will be further developed successfully on the basis of the treaty of friendship." The Moscow's message lacked the usual Soviet warmth. Another fact indicating Soviet disenchantment with Amin was that Soviet Prime Minister Kosygin after visiting in early 1979 on his way back to Moscow did neither stop over Kabul nor send usual message of greetings.[91]

Shah Wali, Foreign Minister in Amin's Cabinet accusedt he Soviet Ambassador in Kabul, Puzanov not only of harbouring four former ministers[92] but also of being involved in a conspiracy to assassinate Aimn and asked Moscow to recall the Soviet ambassador which was done in November 1979.[93] The new Soviet Ambassador in Kabul was Fikriat Akhmetdzhanovich Taibeev who assumed charge on 28 November, 1979.[94]

Prior to his assumption of power Amin, as a Foreign Minister and later on as a Prime Minister under Taraki, had seldom shown his disenchantment for Moscow in his public pronouncements. He said on 22 July, 1979: "Any person and any element who harms the friendship between Afghanistan and Soviet Union will be considered the enemy of the country, enemy of our people and enemy of our revolution. We will not allow anybody in Afghanistan, to act against the friendship of Afghanistan and the Soviet Union."[95] However, at the same time he also seemed worried about the increasing Soviet presence in Afghanistan. On 17 July, 1979 he said: "Those who boast of friendship with us, they can really be our friend when they respect our independence, our soil and our prideful traditions."[96] Male opines that Amin was too much of a realist to imagine that the PDPA could survive without Soviet assistance and in any case too good a socialist to wish to see relations with the Soviet Union deteriorate further.[97]

According to Western political analysts, Moscow was anxious to draft Karmal as Taraki' successor and it could be done only after eliminating Amin. And such planning was done in mid August 1979.[98] Taraki's visit to Moscow on 9 September 1979 had been utilized by the Soviet leadership to implement it. Amin never made public his distrust or disenchantment with Moscow but he seemed to be equally concerned with increasing Soviet influence in Afghanistan. In early October 1979, Amin, while acknowledging the Soviet military aid, said: "Soviet Union is providing whatever we can use . . . (to defend Afghanistan) . . . but we will defend our country. . . (and will never give this trouble to our international brothers to fight for us."[99] Thus, it can be srumised that Amin was interested in maintaining good relations with Moscow but at the same time was not opposed to increasing Soviet influence in Afghanistan.

United States and Amin Regime

After Adolph Dubs death, Washington had almost become lukewarm towards the communist regime in Kabul. Though the former national security adviser during the Carter Administration, recalled that the Special Coordination Committee

(SCC) of the National Security Council, on 9 April, 1979, in opposition to the State Department, decided that Washington should "be more sympathetic to those Afghans who were determined to preserve their country's independence."[100] But no details are available as to what concrete forms were adopted in this regard. According to Zalmay Khalilzad: "Publicly, the US government maintained that it did not support the insurgents in their efforts to overthrow the Kabul regime, privately it saw advantages in an overthrow of the Khalqis."[101] In August 1979, the US Embassy in Kabul in an assessment observed: "On balance, however, our larger interests, especially given the Afghanistan's close ties to Moscow, this regime's open hostility to the US, and the atmosphere of fear it has created throughout the country would probably be served by the demise of the Taraki-Amin Regime."[102]

On 11 September, 1979, Amin had told the American Charge d'Affaires, J. Bruce Amstutz, that he wanted to have "friendly relations" with the United States.[103] However, Amstutz did not take it seriously.

Following the assumption of power by Amin, on 15 September, 1979 the US State Department became more interested in the question of Amin's attitude toward the United States. Amstutz called on Amin on 27 September and found that the latter was "all charm and friendliness" and once more spoke in favour of better relations with the United States.[104] Shah Wali, Foreign Minister in Amin's Government, met the senior officials of US State Department in New York on 27 September, 1979. In early October 1979, Archer Blood, a US diplomat went to Kabul and met Amin. The former told that Amin "wanted American and without offering anything in return."[105]

The Carter Administration made the issue of "violation of Human Rights" in Afghanistan as a starting point with Amin.[106] The violation of human rights took place when Amin was in power. The report prepared by the State Department devoted six pages to violation of human rights in Afghanistan. The report contained sweeping generalizations without providing evidence of specific instances of atrocities which could be documents or checked.

Archer Blood in his assessment to the US Department of State reported that Amin was "content for the time being with a polite but limited relationship, which both countries would refrain from exacerbating by word or action."[107] Even the US Secretary of State, Cyrus Vance summed up: "At maximum we regard our current dialogue with the A fghans as a means of exploring the possibilities for a less contentious telationship and we are not overtly sanguine that even this limited objective can be sustained."[108] According to documents reproduced in the *Documents of the Den of Espionage* by the end of October 1979, the US Embassy in Kabul concluded: "We have been receiving clear signals that the DRA seeks better relations with the US."[109] Though the United States had started a dialogue with Amin as a means of exploring the possibilities for a less contentious relationship but without any tangible outcome.

The above analysis reveals that the US missed a golden opportunity by not making the strategic advantages of the situation. As Poullada has aptly absérved: "American weakness and complacence over development in Afghanistan convinced the Soviets that America had abandoned the field to them there, and that they could safely move into the vacuum with tacit American consent."[110]

SOVIET INVASION OF AFGHANISTAN

The world was taken by surprise by the events of 27-28 December, 1979 when sizeable number of Soviet troops equipped with sophisticated weapons invaded Afghanistan in which Hafizullah Amin was killed and Babrak Karmal was installed as a new ruler of Afghanistan. The foundations of Soviet invasion of Afghanistan had been laid much earlier and the December end 1979 episode was the final act.

According to Thomas T. Hammond, the information for preliminary planning by Moscow would have been collected when General A. Epishev, the head of the Main Political Administration of the Soviet armed forces, made an inspection tour of Afghanistan in April 1979.[111] This was followed by the visit to Afghanistan by General Ivan G. Pavloski, Deputy Minister of Defence from August 1979 to October 1979.[112] Pavloski had earlier undertaken a similar mission in Czechoslovakia in 1968 prior to the Soviet invasion of that country and he led the Soviet troops into Czechoslovakia. Thus he was a logical choice to make the assessment for launching Soviet invasion of Afghanistan.

Along with preparation of such strategic planning, there was also augmentation in the presence of Soviet military and civilian advisers in Afghanistan during October-November 1979. The Afghans had almost lost control of the essential levers of power to 1,500 or more Soviet officials in the civilian ministries and between 3,500 and 4,000 Soviet officials and technicians in the Afghan armed forces.[113] An estimated half of the 8,000 officers and non-commissioned officers of the Afghan army had been purged in October 1979.[114]

In late November 1979, Moscow put its troops in a stage of alert and reservists were called up to fill up understrength combat divisions in the central Asian military district. Bridging equipment was moved to the Afghan border.[115] The Warsaw Pact countries had also placed their troops on an advanced stage of readiness. By mid-December Moscow had airlifted about two battalions of troops with heavy weapons into Bagram Air Base, whose management had already fallen into the Russian hands.[116]

While making strategic and military preparations to invade Afghanistan, Moscow also continued efforts to make Amin agree to invite Soviet troops into Afghanistan. On 28 November, 1979, a Soviet deputy minister of internal affairs, Lt. General V.S. Paputin arrived in Kabul to discuss "mutual cooperation and other issues"[117] with the Government of Afghanistan.

According to Thomas T. Hammond, Paputin's real mission was to help prepare Kabul for the invasion by getting control of the Afghan police, to pressurize Amin to step aside in favour of Karmal, persuading Amin to invite the Soviet Union to send large numbers of Soviet troops into Afghanistan, if all those failed, assassinating Amin.[118]

On 17 December, 1979 there occurred a shooting incident at the official residence of Amin in which his nephew, Asadullah Amin was injured and then flew to Moscow for treatment.[119] Asadullah was the head of Afghan intelligence service and Amin's top security aide was thus removed. The airlifting of Soviet troops to Kabul had started by 23 December, 1979 and by 27 December, 1979, their strength was sizeable enough to take control of Afghanistan. Thus by the evening of 27 December, 1979, the Soviet forces had launched the invasion and asserted its control over Kabul and other strategic places in Afghanistan. A late evening broadcast, on 27 December, 1979 by Babrak Karmal as reported by Soviet news agency *Tass*, said:

> . . . who upto the present have been subjected to intolerable violence and torture by the bloody apparatus of Hafizullah Amin and his minions, those agents of American imperialism. . . . The day of freedom and rebirth. . . has arrived. . . . The central Committee of the united Peoples Democratic Party and the revolutionary council party of the Democratic Republic of Afghanistan proclaim true peoples power . . . we have once again raised the banner of national *Jihad*. . . a just war of the Afghan people for true democratic justice, for respect for the holy Islamic religion. . . for implementation of the aims of the glorious April revolution.[120]

In another broadcast on 27 December, 1979 the Kabul Radio announced the request of Afghan Government for Soviet armed assistance:

> Because of the continuation and expansion of aggression, intervention and provocation by the foreign enemies of Afghanistan, and for the purpose of defending the gains of *saur* revolution, territorial integration, national independence and preservation of peace and security, and on the basis of the treaty of friendship, good neighbourliness and cooperation dated 5 December, 1978 the Democratic Republic of Afghanistan earnestly demands that the USSR render urgently the political moral and economic assistance including military aid to Afghanistan. The Government of USSR has accepted the proposal of Afghan side.[121]

This statement was the justification for Soviet invasion of Afghanistan implying that Afghanistan requested Moscow to send their armed forces and the latter complied accordingly. The above sequence of events reveals that the Soviet Union occupied Afghanistan with the help of its armed forces and installed Babrak Karmal as a puppet in Kabul whose strings were in the hands of Kremlin. A statemnt published in *Pravda* on 31 December, 1979 stated that the Soiet Union had decided to grant Afghanistan:

> Insistent request. . . (for) immediate aid and support in the struggle against external aggression. . . and to send to Afghanistan a limited Soviet military contingent that will be used exclusively for aisistance in preventing the armed interference from the outside. The Soviet contingent will be completely pulled out of Afghanistan when the reason that necessitated such an action exists no longer.[122]

By 1 January, 1980, fifty thousand Soviet troops were in Afghanistan and more were on the way. Thus by January end 1980, the number of Soviet armed forces in Afghanistan was estimated between 80,000 to 1,00,000.[123]

The emergence of Karmal regime backed by Soviet troops pushed Afghanistan into Soviet orbit and its non-aligned status was completely undermined. Engineering of the April 1978 *coup* and signing of the Afghan Soviet friendship treaty in December 1978 were steps towards the final takeover of Afghanistan by Moscow in December 1979.

International Response

It is one of Newton's law that every action evokes reaction. Similar anology is applicable in international relations. The Soviet invasion of Afghanistan took the world by surprise and it severely condemned and criticized. The United Nations General Assembly and Security Council have passed resolutions condemning the "aggression" in Afghanistan and called for the withdrawal of "all foreign troops from Afghanistan." Besides, the European Economic Community (EEC), Organisation of Islamic Countries, Seventh and Eighth Non-aligned summits, and other countries have severely criticized the Soviet invasion of Afghanistan while calling for the unconditional withdrawal of Soviet troops from Afghanistan. However, the United States has played a leading role in this regard by not only condemning the Soviet invasion of Afghanistan but has taken certain steps since 1980 to help resolve the tangle. The succeeding pages present an indepth analysis of the international response evoked by Soviet Union by invading Afghanistan.

(A) The US Response

The Soviet invasion of Afghanistan was not only alarming but challenging as well for the United States. The US President Jimmy Carter, was surprised and his reaction was severe and spontaneous. He said that "we are the other Super Power on earth and it became my responsibility. . . to take action that would prevent the Soviets from (accomplishing) this invasion with impunity."[124] A day after the Soviet invasion, President Carter informed the leaders of France, United Kingdom (UK), West Germany, Italy and Pakistan about what had happened in Afghanistan and all leaders agreed that "the Soviet action is a grave threat to peace."[125] Sensing the magnitude of Soviet threat, President Carter, during the first week of January 1980, said that the Soviet act in Afghanistan posed a grave threat to peace because of the threat of further Soviet expansion in to neighbour countries in South West Asia and also because such an aggressive military policy is unsettling to other peoples throughout the world.[126] While refuting Soviet claim that they had not invaded Afghanistan but were "invited" President Carter said: ". . . The Soviet claims, falsely that they were invited in to Afghanistan to help protect that country from some unnamed outside threat."[127] President Carter did not confine US concern over developments in Afghanistan to make public pronouncements but also took up the issue with Soviet leaders. On 28 December, 1979, President Carter in a message sent to Soviet leader Brezhnev called for the withdrawal of Soviet troops and warned that if Afghanistan action was not corrected it "could have very serious consequences to United States—Soviet relations."[128] Finding that Brezhnev did not give a satisfactory answer, President Carter said on 31 December, 1979:

> He (Brezhnev) claimed that he had been invited by the Afghan government to come in and protect Afghanistan from some outside third-nation threat. This was obviously false because the person that he claimed invited him in, President Amin, was murdered or assassinated after the Soviet pulled their *coup*. He also claimed that they would remove their forces from Afghanistan as soon as the situation should be stabilized and the outside threat to Afghanistan was eliminated. So that was the tone of his message to me, which as I say, was completely inadequate and completely misleading.[129]

The Soviet invasion of Afghanistan also proved instrumental in changing US perceptions about Moscow. As President Carter said that "the Soviets have seriously misjudged our own nation's strength and resolve and our unity and determination and the condemnation that has accrued to them by the world community"[130] . . . . They undersetimated the courage and the tenacity of freedom in that country (Afghanistan), and they did not anticipate the world's quick and forceful response to their aggression."[131] The US reaction to these developments irked Moscow and the Soviet media especially *Pravda* accused the United States of "anti-Soviet hysteria reminiscent of the lamentable cold war times."[132] To this, President Carter added: "We do not want to return to the cold war, we do not want to have a confrontation with the Soviet Union. . . . The Soviets have tried to mislead the world, they have failed."[133] However, the Soviet media continued its criticism of Washington while concealing the real facts.

The above analysis reveals that the Carter Administration's reaction to the Soviet invasion was very sharp though belated. But now the question arises whether United States had prior information of what was going to happen in Afghanistan and if so why it failed to preempt the Soviet move. An answer to this question lies in the analysis of US policy prior to the invasion. As we have seen in the preceding pages, the US had reacted mildly to the advent of communist *coup* in April 1978 and until the assassination of Ambassador Dubs, the United States' flow of economic assistance to Kabul continued and it was drastically curtailed only after February 1979.

Between April 1978 and the Soviet invasion of Afghanistan in December end 1979, the US policy towards Afghanistan under Carter administration was mainly determined by Cyrus Vance, Secretary of State, Zbigniew Brzezinski, the National Security Adviser and other top officials of the State Department, particularly Christopher and Marshall Shulman, besides Carter himself.[134] The main difference of opinion towards Saviet Union existed between Vance and Brzezinski. Cyrus Vance and his chief Soviet expert Marshall Shulman were in favour of soft-pedalling towards Soviet Union to preserve the spirit of *detente* while Brzezinski who also favoured *det.nte* was, however, less optimistic of any outcome. Vance was perhaps convinced that the US should continue appeasing Moscow to get agreements like Strategic Arms Limitation

Treaty II (SALT II) approved by it. Thus he said in April 1978: "The Soviets may find it difficult to understand some of the things we do. They do not like many of the things we stand for. The future is going to depend a lot on whether or not we can begin to make progress on areas of central importance. At the heart of this lies SALT. If we can eventually reach a SALT agreement, which I believe we can, this will begin to change the whole character of the relationship, put it on the right track again."[135] Vance was honest enough to admit that he and Brzezinski had conflicting attitudes toward the USSR: "We have differences of view from time to time. . . . A different perspective with respect to the Soviet Union is the biggest set of differences. I believe it is essential we try to find common ground (with the Soviets). . . we should not be fearful of everything they do and automatically accept the thesis of the worst case motivations."[136]

On the other hand, Brzezinski was of the opinion that the relationship between Washington and Moscow was inherently competitive and even conclusion of any number of agreements including the SALT would not be able to alter Soviet determination to undermine the United States and make itself the dominant power on the globe.[137] In his opinion Moscow did not want true "peaceful coexistence" with the West and could not be trusted. He also regarded Vance and Shulman as accomodationists" who were willing to go much too far in "accomodating American Policies to please Moscow, in the vain hope that this would buy peace[138]

This difference in opinions among the advisers of Carter administration toward Soviet Union also determined their policy perspectives on Afghanistan after Communist *coup* of April 1978. Despite the increasing Soviet military activities during 1979, there were no public statements by the US State Department either to forewarn the US administration or to the world about impending Soviet invasion of Afghanistan. It was not until 21 December, 1979, that the US State Department finally revealed that the Soviets had assembled more than

30,000 soliders on the Afghan border and had flown three battalions of troops to an air base near Kabul.[139] Though one State Department official told the *New York Times* that the "Soviet preparation on the Afghan border show all the marks of a major military intervention"[140] but Cyrus Vance, on being asked whether Soviets were going to invade Afghanistan, replied, "That would be only speculation on my part."[141]

Lee Hamilton, Chairman of the House Sub-committee on Europe and the Middle East, in a letter to Marshal Shulman, on 18 March, 1980 asked that when the US Government knew in October 1979 about a high-level Soviet military visit to Afghanistan, "then why does our government wait until December (1979) to make any official presentation or protest to the Soviet government?"[142] Shulman replied that the actual Soviet movement of troops and equipment towards Afghanistan was observed only in late November 1979 "prompting us to make December approaches to the Soviets. . . . We acted as promptly and as forcefully as the evidence warranted."[143]

A detailed analysis of the divergent views among the policy makers of the Carter Administration towards Afghanistan prior to Soviet invasion, is beyond the scope of present study. It suffices to say that the lack of decisive action by the Carter administration "may have been due in part to the tradition of US government, whether Democratic or Republican of looking upon Afghanistan as an insignificant country."[144]

By January 1980, the Carter administration had realized that the Soviet invasion and subsequent occupation of Afghanistan posed a challenge to US strategic interests in the Gulf region and South West Asia and a direct threat to its security. As President Carter said on 14 January, 1980:

> Our own nation's security was directly threatened. There is no doubt that the Soviets move into Afghanistan if done without adverse consequences, would have resulted in the temptation to move again until they reached warm water port or until they acquired control over a major portion of

> the world's oil supplies. . . .[145] The Soviet Union has altered the strategic situation in that part of the world in a very omnious fashion. . . .[146] It places the Soviets within aircraft striking range of the vital oil resources of the Presian Gulf; it threatens a strategically located country Pakistan; (and) it poses the prospect of increased Soviet pressure on Iran and on other nations of the Middle East.[147]

Again on 23 January, President Carter in State in the Union address to the Congress, which was labelled as "Carter Doctrine", said: "Let our position be absolutely clear: An attempt to any outside force to gain control of the Persian Gulf region will be regarded as an assault on the vital interests of the United States, and such an assault will be repelled by any means necessary, including military force."[148]

The post-Dube assassination and pre-invasion period had witnessed the mounting Soviet influence in Afghanistan which gradually led to the decline in Afghan-US relations. Jack C. Nikolas, Deputy Assistant Secretary for Near Eastern and South Asian Affairs, in a statement before the Sub-Committee on Asian and Pacific Affairs of the House of Representatives, said on 15 May, 1979 that US relations with Afghanistan had regrettably deteriorated significantly.[149] He further added that as the Soviet Union had become more directly involved in Afghanistan, "we have detected a corresponding decline in interest in US programmes and in sensitively to our concerns. . . ."[150] Washington had made efforts to make clear to the Communist regime in Kabul that good relations were a two-way street which required concrete steps from both sides to demonstrate their interest in cooperation: "This distresses us that this is not the case in US-Afghan relations, particularly, because we know that there is still a great reservoir of good will among the Afghan people for the US and the Americans, as there is for Afghanistan in our country. . . ."[151] Niklos further opined that the existing state of affairs was not the US creation:

It is the inescapable result when one party to a relationship shows no interest in giving life and substance to these ties. . . . Because of the lack of interest we have reduced our economic assistance programme, terminated our military training programme and for the time being withdrawn our Peace Corps volunteers and staff.[152]

The increasing Soviet influence after the April 1978 *coup* in Kabul was detrimental to the United States' strategic interests in the region. Such an indication was given by Harold H. Saunders, Assistant Secretary for Near Eastern and South Asian Affairs in a statement before the Sub-Committee on Asian and Pacific Affairs of the House of Representatives on 26 September, 1979 when he said, "Our effort to encourage peace and stability in that troubled region is clearly made more difficult by Afghanistan's internal unrest and the exodus of refugees from Afghanistan. . . ."[153] The United States regretted the "reorientation in Afghan foreign policy. . . away from its traditional genuine non-alignment. . . ."[154] Washington also realized that direct interference in Afghanistan by any country including the Soviet Union, would threaten the integrity of that country as well as the peace in the region and it was a "matter of concern to the United States. . . ."[155] Saunders to the Sub-Committee that the US had no special interest in Afghanistan and at the same time "we have repeatedly impressed on the Soviet Government the dangers of more direct involvement in the fighting in Afghanistan."[156]

As has been described in the preceding pages, when Soviet Union invaded Afghanistan, the United States not only condemned the Soviet aggression but also took some measures to persuade Moscow to vacate the aggression in Afghanistan.

The specific US measures against the Soviet action in Afghanistan were envisaged in the announcement made by Ptesident Carter in his message to the nation on 4 January, 1980 suggesting US measures in this regard:

(i) Blocking grain sales to the Soviet Union beyond the 8 million metric tons already contracted. This means withholding an additional 17 million metric tons which the Soviets have already ordered;

(ii) Stopping the sale of high technology and strategic items to the Soviet Union, including computers and oil drilling equipment;

(iii) Curbing Soviet fishing privileges in US water. The catch allowed to Soviet fishing fleets in 1980 would be reduced from 3,50,000 tons to 75,000 tons, resulting in an estimated Soviet economic loss of $ 55 million to $ 60 million;

(iv) Delaying the opening of a new Soviet consulate in New York and an American consulate in Kiev;

(v) Postponing new cultural and economic exchanges between the two countries, now under consideration;

(vi) Boycotting the 1980 summer Olympics in Moscow. . .[157]

The United States imposed these sanctions while its allies and other friendly countries did not follow the suit. A study undertaken by the Congress Research Service (CRS) to assess the impact of sanctions imposed by the Carter administration against Soviet Union, concluded that Carter's sanctions might have had political benefits but:

> the economic punishment to the USSR was quite limited. . . while many nations supported the Olympic boycott, no other nations followed fully the US embargo and restrictive actions. This illustrates the difference between the United States and the other Western allies, which generally supported the political aspects of the sanctions while not supporting the principle of economic punishment adopted by the Carter administration.[158]

The United States did boycott the Moscow Olympic games and it claimed to have "helped to persuade 50 other countries to take similar action. . . ."[159] However, despite the US boycott, about 50 countries participated in the Moscow Olympic games and the Carter administration "could only be dissatisfied at the level of support for the boycott on the part of its traditional allies in Western Europe. . ."[160]

In the wake of sanctions declared by the Carter administration, the Soviet media launched a virulent propaganda against the United States. A statement issued on 6 January, 1980 by Soviet news agency *Tass* declared that, "if the White House decided to influence in some way the Soviet Union and its foreign policy, this is a hopeless undertaking. Such attempts flopped in the past and they will flop now. . . ."[161] The Soviet leader, Brezhnev in a statement published in *Pravda* dated 13 January, 1980 said that Carter's steps "show that Washington again, like decades ago, is trying to speak to us in the language of the cold war."[162] The statement further contended that:

> the arrogation by Washington as some sort of a "right to reward" or punish" independent sovereign states raised a question of a principled character. In effect, by such actions the US government deals a blow at the orderly international law system of relations among states. . . the world is increasingly forming the impression of the United States as an absolutely unreliable partner in interstate ties. . . These actions of the US administration will not inflict on us the damage obviously hoped for by their initiators. . . they will hit back at their initiators if not today then tomorrow.[163]

It had become evident that Moscow did not care for the United States' move of imposing sanctions against it or the criticism of the Soviet action in Afghanistan.

On 29 December, 1980, marking the occasion of the first anniversary of the Soviet invasion of Afghanistan, President Carter in a statement observed that the Soviet invasion of Afghanistan and attempted forceful occupation "of that fiercely independent non-aligned Moslem nation has had propoundly negative impact on the international community."[164] President

Carter further urged Moscow to respond to those countries which were urging withdrawal of Soviet military forces and inviting Soviet cooperation in thes earch of a political solution to the Afghanistan crisis: For our part, we have offered to join in the effort to find a political solution involving a Soviet withdrawal, and we repeat that offer to-day. . ."[165]

The Soviet invasion of Afghanistan had accelerated the process of reinforcements of some form of qualified globalism for the US policy. "The invasion appeared to challenge the United States to create a policy based on a new national consensus, one that required the necessary military power to support whatever role it determined to play."[166]

In 1981, when Ronald Reagan assumed the Presidency of the United States, the US policy toward Soviet Union on the issue of Afghanistan became more clear and practical. The main elements of President Reagan's policy towards Afghan crisis included humanitarian assistance to the Afghan refugees seeking shelter in Pakistan, diplomatic support for a political settlement along the lines of the United Nations Resolution, the resolutions passed by the Islamic Conference and Non-aligned Summit Conference.

The US Secretary of State, Alexander Haig said on 22 May, 1981 that the United States was in favour of convening an international conference to focus the world attention on Afghan crisis and take measures to defuse it.[167] While cautioning Moscow that it could not dominate the world by invading Afghanistan, Haig further added: "The people of Afghanistan overwhelmingly oppose the Soviet occupation and the Babrak Karmal regime. The vast majority of the world's nations are challenging the Soviets to come to the negotiating table, to agree to a political solution to withraw their forces and to restore Afghanistan a non-aligned status. . .[168] While urging the Soviet Union not to underestimate the potential Afghanistan resistance and international pressure he said: "By supporting initiative such as that of European community we offer the Soviet Union the alternative of an honourable solution. . ."[169]

The US Ambassador to the United Nations, J. Kirckpatrick, while addressing the UN General Assembly on 16 Novmber, 1981 on resolution on Afghanistan, called for:

(i) Immediate withdrawal of all foreign forces;

(ii) Restoration of the sovereignty, territorial integrity and non-alignment of Afghanistan;

(iii) Restoration of the right of the Afghan people to choose their own form of government and economic and social system, free from outside intervention, coercion or restrained; and

(iv) Return of the refugees to their homeland. . .[170]

She further added that Washington was firmly committed to the above mentioned terms: "The struggle of the Afghan nation for survival was consistent with the basic and most cherished purposes of the UN. . ."[171]

President Reagan also showed his grave concern over the developments in Afghanistan and the continued presence of Soviet troops on Afghan soil. While lauding the courage of Afghan people, President Reagan said that despite the presence of over 90,000 Soviet combat troops, "the courageous people of Afghanistan effectively deny Soviet forces control of most of Afghanistan. . ."[172] He further urged Moscow sincerely implement the proposals set forth by the UN General Assembly for the withdrawal of Soviet troops from Afghanistan "so that an independent and non-aligned nation can be re-established."[173]

President Reagan issued a proclamation on 10 March, 1982 designating 21 March as "Afghan Day" in the United States, to commemorate the valour of the Afghan people and to condemn the continuing Soviet invasion of Afghanistan. The proclamation said: "The International community, with the United States joining governments around the world, has condemned the invasion of Afghanistan as a violation of every standard of decency and international law and has called for a withdrawal of the Soviet troops from Afghanistan. . ."[174] The message further added that "Afghanistan Day" would serve to recall not only these events, but also the principles involved "when a people struggles for freedom to determine its own future, the right to be free from foreign interference and the right to practice religion according to the dictates of conscience. . ."[175]

Keeping in view the continued Soviet occupation of Afghanistan, the question has been raised as to what can the United States do to prevent more such Communist takeovers in the Third World countries. In this regard Thomas T. Hammond has suggested that "the US must be prepared to intervene diplomatically, economically and, if necessary, militarily. . ."[176]

The public opinion in the United States has strongly favoured the full US support to the Afghan freedom fighters. The National Association of pro-American, in its resolution on "support for Afghan Freedom Fighters," passed on 21 April, 1983, resolved that "President Reagan and the Congress should authorise support necessary to restore Afghanistan' independence and freedom. . ."[177] It also called for diplomatic and economic pressure to be brought against the Soviet Union to "immediately withdraw their forces from Afghanistan. . ."[178] Both the Houses of the US Congress—Senate and the House of Representatives, have also expressed their solidarity and support for the Afghan Mujahideen. On 6 October, 1983, the House of Representatives in a resolution passed unanimously observed that the Soviet invasion of Afghanistan was the first Soviet seizure of an independent territory since the 1940's and represented "a dangerous development in Soviet foreign policy. . ."[179] It further noted that the struggle for liberation in Afghanistan could succeed "if those of us believed in freedom could render support. . ."[180] The resolution envisaged that the policy of the US should be:

(i) To encourage and support the people of Afghanistan in their struggle to be free from foreign domination;

(ii) To provide ine people of Afghanistan if they so request with material assistance as the US considers appropriate to help them fight effectively for their freedom;

(iii) To pursue a negotiated settlement of the war in Afghanistan based on the total withdrawal of Soviet troops and the recognition of the inalienable right of the Afghan people to choose their own destiny free from outside interference or coercion so that the four millions of Afghan refugees return to their country in safety and in honour. . .[181]

The US Under Secretary of State, Lawrence Eagleburger, while addressing a forum on Afghanistan, sponsored by the US State Department and the Centre for Afghanistan Studies of the University of Nebraska, said that the Reagan Administration recognized that the invasion of and continued occupation of Afghanistan by Moscow was destroying the infrastructure of this poor country: "It has taken the lives of thousands of civilians while creating the world's largest refugee community—nearly three million Afghans now living in exile. . ."[182] While summing up the US policy, Eagleburger said:

> Our strategic interests as well as our humanitarian instincts make it absolutely essential that the Soviet aggression be checked. We continue to look for signs that the Soviet Union is willing to work seriously for a negotiated settlement that would return Afghanistan to its people. Until then, we will continue to support and be inspired by the spirit of the Afghan Mujahideen in their fight for freedom. . .[183]

The US support for Afghanistan, in the wake of Soviet occupation has been vigorous, constant and encouraging. It has increased with passage of time. While addressing the UN General Assembly on 15 November, 1984, the US Ambassador to the UN, J. Kirakpatrick, envisaged the American viewpoint:

> The elements comprising the honourable solution of Afghanistan. . .immediate withdrawal of foreign troops, the

preservation of the sovereignty, territorial integrity, political independence, non-aligned character of Afghanistan, the right of the Afghan people to determine their own form of government and to choose their enconomic, political and social system free from outside intervention, subversion, coercion or constraint, and the creation of the necessary conditions which would enable the Afghan refugees to return voluntary to their homes. . .[184]

Even President Reagan on 27 December, 1984, in a message marking the fifth anniversary of the Soviet invasion of Afghanistan, said that the United States had told the Soviet leaders "that their occupation forces in Afghanistan constituted a serious impending to improving US-Soviet relations. . ."[185] Recalling the five years of Soviet armed occupation of Afghanistan, the US President said that the Soviet Army had waged war in the proud and deeply religious people of Afghanistan and there was no end in sight as yet. "This fifth anniversary of Afghan defiance stands in stark contrast. . .yet there is a message of inspiration in the cauvel tale being written. . ."[186] While referring to the repeated condemnation of the Soviet occupation of Afghanistan by the United Nations, President Reagan said: "For our part, the US has made clear . . .(that) we cannot and will not remain silent on Afghanistan. We join our voice with other members of the world community in calling for a prompt, negotiated end to this brutal conflict . . .[187] He recalled that the history of independent Afghanistan went back more than 2,000 years and was far more being finished: "My deepest hope is to speak of freedom restored to Afghanistan by December 1985."[188] While expressing the hope that the valiant struggle being waged by the people of Afghanistan would bear the fruits success, the US President said: "we will not forget the people of Afghanistan who are struggling to live once again among the free nations of the world. These brave people will continue to have the support of all Americans in their noble struggle."[189]

The present day Afghanistan is reeling under terror. The US Congressmen and media have denounced the blatant violation of human rights by the Russians in Afghanistan. Mark D. Siljander, member of the House of Representatives, said on 18 September, 1985 that the "creeping cowardice syndrome" being played by the Russians in Afghanistan has gripped the US foreign policy since Vietnam."[190]

The Congressman Jim Courter has strongly pleaded for supply of US arms and ammunition for the Afghan Mujahideen. He acknowledged the courage of Afghan freedom fighters when he said on 26 September, 1985: "The Afghans have never before falt the crush of Red Army occupation. For 6 years now, they have resisted fiercely. Their pride and their religion are two firm guarantees that they wish to continue to do so."[191] On 8 October, 1985, Senator Gordon Humphrey, moved a resolution (S. Res. 237) in the US Senate which while condemning the Russian violation of human rights in Afghanistan, *inter alia* envisaged:

1. Strongly supports President Reagan's intent to discuss directly with the Soviet leaders American concerns with the Soviet presence in Afghanistan; and

2. Calls upon the President to reiterate the desire of the United States to achieve a negotiated political settlement agreeable to all interested parties in Afghanistan, which settlement should include—

   (a) the complete withdrawal of all foreign troops;

   (b) the restoration of the independent and non-aligned status of Afghanistan;

   (c) self-determination for the Afghan people;

   (d) the return of Afghan refugees with safety and honour.[192]

This resolution was passed by the US Senate unanimously on 25 October, 1985.

While drawing the attention of the follow Congressmen to the forthcoming Reagan-Gorbachev Summit meeting held in November 1985, Congressman, Norman D. Shunway told the House on 23 October, 1985: "... As we look forward the November summit meeting between President Reagan and Soviet General Secretary Gorbachev, I believe that the plight of Afghanistan should not be pushed to the back of our minds. . ."[193]

On 31 October, 1985, Congressman, Kemp, while introducing an identical resolution, as introduced earlier in the Senate (S. Res. 237) in the House of the Representatives, urged the fellow Congressmen:

> . . .Join us in this resolution to honour the great struggle of the Afghan people and proclaim their right to democracy and self-determination. And let us pray that someday the forces of tyranny will finally be lifted from the earth and all nations under God will respect the sacred and inalienable rights of mankind.[194]

The US President, Ronald Reagan, in his message on Afghan Day on 21 March, 1986, while reiterating his country's support for the Afghan Mujahideen said: "For the heroic Afghan people, it marks the beginning of yet another year in their struggle for national liberation against the ruthless Soviet military force that seeks to conquer them."[195] While paying his tributes to the Afghan freedom fighters, the US President further added that the sacrifices made by them could never be forgotton.[196] The US President also raised the issue during his summit meeting with Soviet leader Gorbachev at Rykvyk and urged the Soviet Union to resolve the Afghan crisis as soon as possible.[197]

On 17 September, 1986, Helmut Sonnenfeldt, a US representative to the Conference on US-Soviet relations at Riga,

Latvia, said that the United States had no special interest in Afganistan except to see it non-aligned and at peace with itself and with its surrounding neighbours.[198] On 8 October, 1986, the US Defence Secretary Weinberger in an interview on ABC Television in Beijing said that the Soviet offer of withdrawal of some of its troops from Afghanistan was only "a deceptive ploy". He further added that the Soviets had sometime ago inserted more troops into Afghanistan so that they could withdraw those same troops and leave their net strength the same.[199]

The Soviet proposal of withdrawing some of its troops from Afghanistan was only a "gimmick" because no exact information was made available about the *modus operandi*. The Western and other journalists, who were invited to cover the Soviet withdrawal of six regiments from Afghanistan, were kept under tight security and followed a closely monitored schedule.[200] On 30 October, 1986, the Director of the US Defence Intelligence Agency while addressing a press conference at the Pentagon said that the United States had clear and convincing evidence that Soviet claims of having withdrawn six regiments were a "sham and deception."[201] According to US Defence sources, the Soviet troops strength had only been reduced by 2,000 and not the 8,000 as claimed by Moscow.[202] On 31 October, 1986, the US President, Reagan, while commenting on the Soviet troop withdrawal accused Moscow of bad faith in its conduct in Afghanistan and added that "phony book-keeping would not end the war."[203]

The US Ambassador to the United Nations, Herbert Okum, in his address to the General Assembly on 6 November, 1986 regretted that despite the repeated calls given by the UN General Assembly for the withdrawal of Soviet troops from Afghanistan, the Soviet Union had not bothered to comply with these resolutions.[204] While denouncing the Soviet military adventures in Afghanistan, the US Ambassador said that the Afghan Mujahideen were giving stiff resistance to Soviet forces. He further added:

The Afghan people will never surrender. The magnitude of the Soviet threat—not only militarily, but for traditional Afghan religious and cultural values—has forged a unity of purpose among resistance fighters unparalleled in Afghanistan's history. Today, the resistance is cooperating more closely together than ever before joining forces, coordinating attacks, and sharing intelligence and battle techniques.[205]

He further said that if Moscow wanted to demonstrate its interest in a political settlement in Afghanistan, what it needed was to only respond to seven General Assembly resolutions which called for the immediate withdrawal of all foreign forces. While reiterating the US support for the efforts made by the UN Secretary General and his personal representative in conducting negotiations aimed at achieving a political settlement, the US Ambassador said: "... the United States firmly supports this process. We have made known our willingness, in writing, to play an appropriate guarantor's role with respect to a comprehensive and balanced settlement that protects the legitimate security interests of all concerned."[206]

The *New York Times* in an editorial has questioned the legitimacy of the Soviet backed communist regime in Kabul to speak for the whole of Afghanistan in the UN General Assembly.[207] The editorial further added that there was powerful case in logic, justice and precedent for seating the Afghan resistance because it spoke for more people and controlled more Afghan territory than the Kabul regime. On 28 November, 1986, Samuel Wise, the Deputy Head of the US delegation to the Conference on Security and Cooperation in Europe (CECE) in Vienna said that the Soviet conduct in Afghanistan called into question its commitments to every one of the solemn pledges it made in signing the Helsinki Final Act (1975).[208] The US delegated called upon the Soviet Union to stop genocide in Afghanistan and pave way for the political settlement of Afghan problem.

The US President Ronald Reagan in a statement on 27 December, 1986 marking the seventh anniversary of the Soviet invasion of Afghanistan, called upon the Soviet Union to accept the necessity for a political solution and self-determination for the Afghan people.[209] He further said: "If the Soviets truly want peace, let them present at Geneva realistic timetable for the withdrawal of their troops from Afghanistan."[210] While reiterating US support for a negotiated political solution to the Afghan tangle, the US President said that the United States "will place no barriers in the Soviet's way should they decide to negotiate seriously an end to their occupation of Afghanistan."[211]

After the Reykjavik summit meeting between the Soviet leader Gorbachev and US President Ronald Reagan, some hopes were generated about finding a permanent solution to Afghanistan question. However the US President was sceptical about the Soviet designs. He expressed his doubts while addressing the Los Angeles World Affairs Council in California on 10 April, 1987: "Not have the Soviets abandoned their strategy of trying to use these negotiations to divide our allies and friends in Europe and Asia from the United States."[212] Making a pointed reference to the military conflicts in the region of the developing world "where the facts of Soviet action are brutal, a danger to peace and our future relations", President Reagan while alluding to Afghan situation said: "Despite a claimed desire for peaceful settlement . . . and talk of national reconciliation, Soviet troops continue to wage a terrible war against the people of Afghanistan . . ."[213]

President Reagan claimed that the United States had elaborated a new policy of helping democratic insurgents in their battle to bring self-determination and human rights to their own countries. On 26 August, 1987 President Reagan said in California: "This doctrine was first spelled out in our decision to assist the people of Afghanistan in their fight against Soviet invasion and occupation."[214]

The joint statement issued after the visit of Soviet leader Gorbachev to the United States from 7 to 10 December, 1987 during which both leaders concluded Intermediate Nuclear Force (INF) treaty, did not contain direct reference to the Afghan question. It merely mentioned: "The General Secretary and the President engaged in a wide-ranging frank and business-like discussion of regional questions, including Afghanistan. . ."[215]

In the background of the conclusion of the INF treaty between United States and the Soviet Union, the steps for concluding an agreement between the two super powers over Afghanistan Question also got a fillip. By the beginning of April 1988, the indications in this regard had come visible. The talks at Geneva on Afghan question between Afghanistan and Pakistan under the aegis of the UN had made steady progress by that time.

As the Afghan question formed one of the key issues of negotiations between the two super powers and in view of the proposed Reagan-Gorbachev summit to be held in Moscow in June 1988, the official circles in Washington had started striking optimistic notes about the successful conclusion of Afghanistan negotiations in Geneva. On 8 April, 1988, a senior official of the US Department of State, while addressing a press conference at Santa Barbara, California, expressed the hope that a successful conclusion of the Afghanistan negotiations would be "a major achievement that will improve the general atmosphere" of the Moscow Summit.[216] The US official was of the opinion that the success in Geneva negotiations on Afghanistan might also increase the chances for progress in settling other regional conflicts including the Middle East.

Howard Baker, President Reagan's Chief of Staff of who also addressed the same Press conference, however, expressed cautious optimism about the withdrawal of some 115,000 Soviet troops from Afghanistan. He further added that President Reagan had made it known that the United States' assistance to the Mujahideen would continue as far as Moscow sends military supplies to the Kabul Government."[217]

At this stage it could be discerned from the statement of officials of the Reagan administration that they were more preoccupied with the successful outcome of the ensuing Reagan Gorbachev Summit to be held in Moscow in the first week of June 1988 rather than their ingenuity about the solution of Afghan question. In this regard Howard Baker's statement needs special mention, when he said that the conclusion of an accord on Afghanistan would mean an item less on the agenda of regional matters which President Regan and Soviet leader Gorbachev would discuss and it would have a salutary effect on the tone of the summit but, "I do not think it is likely to have a major impact on such other matters on the summit agenda as nuclear arms control, human rights and bilateral relations."[218]

Though ostensibly the officials of the US State Department in their statements frequently claimed that the Afghanistan question was an obstacle in the improvement of US-Soviet relations, but when it came to reality, they played it cool. When a press reporter asked to comment on a suggestion by the Soviet General Secretary Gorbachev that the Afghan accords could help resolve other regional conflicts around the world, the Deputy spokesman of the US State Department, Phyllis Oakley said in Washington on 8 April, 1988: "We have always said that Afghanistan was an obstacle in the improvement of US-Soviet relations. I think that this will remove a heavy burden from that relationship.''[219]

By the close of second week of April 1988, the draft aggreements on Afghanistan question had been ready. In one of the four agreements, United States and Soviet Union, were to be the guarantors of Geneva accord on Afghanistan. On 11 April, 1988 President Reagan announced that the United States had accepted the Afghan accord and he was sending the US Secretary of State, George Shultz, to Geneva to sign those accords on behalf of the United States.[220] While briefing the newsmen at White House on 11 April 1988, George Shultz said that the US policy, since the Soviet invasion of Afghanistan, had sought prompt and complete withdrawal of all Soviet troops, restoration of Afghanistan to independence and non-aligned status, self-determination for Afghans and return of refugees in safety and honour. He further maintained: "Those have been our objectives and those objectives have been registered year after year in overwhelming votes of the General Assembly of the United Nations."[221]

The Geneva accorded on Afghanistan were signed on 14 April, 1988 at Geneva. United States and Soviet Union also signed the accord as guarantors. The US Secretary of State, George Shultz, while commenting on the accords said that the Soviet Union was committed to firm dates to withdraw its forces from Afghanistan.[222] He further added that the stage had been set for the Afghan people to determine their own future, free of Soviet forces and for the return of Afghan refugees to their homes. The US Secretary of State further said: "The United States has associated itself with this settlement because we believe it will open the way for the restoration of Afghan control over Afghanistan."[223]

A statement issued by the United States with regard to the Geneva accords on Afghanistan, envisaged the US declaration that it agreed to act as a guarantor as long as the obligation undertaken by the guarantors were symmetrical. The statement further noted: "In this regard, the United States has advised the Soviet Union that the US retains the right, consistent with its obligations and guarantor, to provide military assistance to parties in Afghanistan . . . showed the Soviet Union exercise restraint in providing military assistance to parties in Afghanistan, the US will similarly exercise restraint."[224]

While commenting on the Soviet commitment to withdraw its troops from Afghan soil and its impact on US-Soviet relations, the US Secretary of State, George Shultz said:

> The presence of Soviet forces in Afghanistan has been an affront to the world community and a major burden to Soviet-American relations . . . The faithful withdrawal

> commitments embodied in the accords signed today will do much to improve the atmosphere for our bilateral relations and for the resolution of other regional conflicts.[225]

In terms of the Geneva accord on Afghanistan which came into force on 15 May, 1988, the Soviet Union announced the phased withdrawal of its troops from the Afghan soil. Moscow had fixed the initial target of withdrawing 30,000 of its troops stationed in Afghanistan by 29 May, 1988. In this regard the US Deputy Assistant Secretary of State, Robert A. Peck, while testifying before the House Subcommittee on Asian and Pacific Affairs on 19 May, 1988, said that history was being made as Soviet troops started pulling out of Afghanistan and "we can also take satisfaction from this achievement."[226] However, he suggested that much work was still needed to be done.

In the wake of coming into effect of the Geneva accords on Afghanistan and the phased withdrawal of Russian troops from Afghan soil, the United States declared that it wanted the Afghan people to determine their own political course. The US Under Secretary of State, Michael R. Armacost, while appearing before the Senate Foreign Relations Committee on 23 June, 1988 said: "The United States does support the efforts of U.N. Under Secretary General, Diego Cordovez to bring about a dialogue among the various factions in the country. Further, the United States expects to do its part in helping Afghanistan recover from the devastation of war."[227] Expressing the view that it was difficult to know what kind of government the Afghans would chosse, Armacost said that he was confident that "a free Afghan government will eventually emerge with which the United States will enjoy the friendly relations which characterized US-Afghan ties before the communist coup of 1978 and the Soviet occupation which followed."[228]

However in October 1988 the Soviet Union suspended the withdrawal of its troops from Afghanistan and instead inducted fresh reinformations and sophisticated arms and ammunition into Afghanistan. In this regard, Michael Armacost, US Under-Secretary of State for Political Affairs in a meeting with Soviet Ambassador in the United States on 31 October, 1988 expressed US's "grave concern about these recent Soviet actions in Afghanistan, including the deployment and use of newer and more sophisticated aircraft."[229] On 1 November, 1988, a statement issued by the US State Department contained American warning for Moscow about the growing concentration of Soviet military fire-power in southern Afghanistan. Charles Redman, a spokesman of the State Department said on 1 November, 1988 that what Afghanistan needed was the political settlement: "The tragic situation in Afghanistan calls for a political settlement that is acceptable to the Afghan people and reflects the realities on the ground. It cannot be resolved through indiscriminate bombing and more violence against the Afghan people."[230]

The unabated Soviet bombing inside Afghanistan was also criticized by United States US Ambassador to the United Nations, Vernon Walkers at the outset of his meeting with representatives of the alliance of Afghan resistance leaders in New York on 2 November, 1988 criticised the Soviet Union for escalating air attacks inside Afghanistan and called on Moscow to discuss plans for a broad-based government in Kabul with representatives of the Afghan Mujahideen.[231]

The announcement by the Soviet Deputy Foreign Minister, Alexander Bessmartnikh that the Soviet withdrawal of troops from Afghanistan was being suspended "in the wake of continuing attacks by Mujahideen forces", was criticised by the United States. Charles Redman, spokesman for the US State Department while briefing the newsmen on 4 November, 1988 in Washington said: "Of cource, suspension is disturbing, particularly if it indicates that the Soviets intend to continue the escalated level of violence. . . this kind of violence does nothing to contribute to a political settlement, which the Soviets themselves say is desirable."[232] The spokesman further asserted that the suspension of withdrawal underscrored Soviet commitment for living upto the Afghan Accords. He further maintained that the US still hoped that Moscow would honour its commitment of completing the withdrawal by 15 February, 1989.[233]

After the withdrawal of Soviet troops from Afghanistan on 15 February, 1989, the United States declared that there was no change in its policy towad Afghanistan and it would continue to support the Afghan Mujahideen. While elaborating US policy in this regard, Robert Flakes, the Director for Afghanistan, Pakistan and Bangladesh in the State Department's Bureau for Near Eastern and South Asian Affairs said that out of four objectives of US policy toward Afghanistan—(i) the withdrawal of Soviet troops; (ii) the return of the refugees in safety and honour; (iii) self-determination for the Afghan people; and (iv) the return of Afghanistan to its rightful place in the community of nations, only number one had been satisfied and that "the ability of the Afghans to exercise their right of self-determination had not yet been fully satisfied. Thus at the time this book is being published, there has bee no change in US policy towards Afghanistan question.

The United Nations Response

The issue of Soviet invasion of Afghanistan has been engaging the attention of the United Nations General Assembly and Security Council since January 1980.

In the early days of January 1980, a Six-Power draft resolution was introduced in the Security Council.[234] The draft resolution was mildly worded and it avoided "condemnation." It merely "deplored the recent armed intervention in Afghanistan" which it described as inconsistent with the fundamental principles of the UN Charter and it called "for the withdrawal of foreign troops from Afghanistan."[235] The Soviet Union was not referred to by name in the entire text of the draft resolution. When the Six-Power draft resolution was put to vote it failed to secure adoption because of the negative vote cast by Soviet Union. The voting pattern was 13 in favour and two against.[236] Consequently another draft resolution sponsored by 24 countries was introduced in General Assembly on 10 January, 1980 which was adopted by an overwhelming majority on 14 January, 1980. The voting was 104 in favour to 18 against[237] with 18 abstentions. The resolution strongly deplored "recent armed intervention into Afghanistan as inconsistent with a fundamental principle of the Charter" and called for an "immediate, unconditional and total withdrawal of foreign troops from Afghanistan in order to enable its people to determine their form of government and choose their economic, political and social system free from outside intervention, subversion, coercion or constraint of any kind whatsoever.''[238] The resolution also called for providing aid to the Afghan refugees through the UN High Commissioner for Refugees and also urged the Security Council to consider ways and means to assist in the implementation of the resolution.

On 20 November, 1980, the General Assembly again passed resolution against the Soviet invasion of Afghanistan.[239] But the second resolution was weak as compared to the first one. It used the phrase "grave concern" instead of "strongly deplores" withdrawal of foreign troops. On 11 February, 1981, the then Secretary General of the UN, Kurt Waldheim, appointed Javier Perez de Cuellar, who is the current UN Secretary General, as his special representative to seek negotiations over political settlement of Afghan issue in the context of the previous resolution passed by the General Assembly.

On 6 November, 1981, the Secretary General submitted his report on Afghanistan situation[240] which stated that the special representative of the Secretary General had thrice travelled to Afghanistan and Pakistan on 12-16 April, 1981 and 4-9 August, 1981 to hold discussions with the senior officials of Afghanistan and Pakistan. The report added that an understanding had been reached in August 1981 on the substantive issues to be negotiat-but on their format.[241] The report finally concluded that the approach adopted could facilitate the search for a fair political solution which would ensure that no Afghan people would be able to determine their own destiny, free from foreign intervention and interference.[242]

On 18 November, 1981, the General Assembly adopted a resolution 36/34 on Afghanistan situation by a recorded vote of 116 to 23 with 12 abstentions.[243] The countries which voted against the resolution were mainly the Soviet Union, its allies and client states. The resolution called for the immediate withdrawal of foreign troops from Afghanistan and reiterated that preservation of that country's sovereignty and territorial integrity was essential for a peaceful solution of Afghan tangle.[244]

The General Assembly has been continuously seized of the problem of Afghanistan. On 29 November, 1982, the General Assembly again adopted a resolution on Afghanistan, which *inter alia* said:

(i) Reiterates that the preservation of the sovereignty, territorial integrity, political independence and non-aligned character of Afghanistan is essential for a peaceful solution of the problem;

(ii) Reaffirms the right of Afghan people to determine their own form of government and to choose their economic, political and social system free from outside intervention, subversion, coercion or constraint or any kind whatsoever;

(iii) Calls for the immediate withdrawal of foreign troops from Afghanistan. . . .[245]

Abdul Rahman Pazhwak, a former Afghan diplomat and permanent Afghan representative to the United Nations, in an interview with the Voice of America (VOA), which was later published in a Pushtu language paper, urged for more amendments in the UN resolution of 29 November, 1982. Referring to "immediate withdrawal of foreign troops from Afghanistan", as envisaged in the UN resolution, Pazhwak said that instead the resolution should have included, "immediate, total and unconditional withdrawal of foreign troops."[246] He made various suggestions the incorporation of which could help the speedy solution of the Afghan problem. He laid emphasis on the fact that any solution to Afghan problem could be had only by involving the Afghan Mujahideen.[247] He further emphasized that any solution of Afghan problem without the participation of Afghan Mujahideen would be unacceptable to the people of Afghanistan.

The General Assembly in its resolution of 15 Novembe, 1984 called for the immediate withdrawal of the foreign troops from Afghanistan and reiterated that "the preservation of the sovereignty, territorial integrity, political independence and non-aligned character of Afghanistan was essential for a peaceful solution."[248] It also reaffirmed the right of the Afghan people to determine their own form of government and to choose their economic, political and social system free from outside intervention, subversion, coercion or constraint.[249] This resolution was adopted by a record vote of 119 in favour to 20 against with abstentions. The resolution also recognized the significance of the initiatives of the Organization of Islamic Conference and the efforts of the movement of non-aligned countries for a political solution. It also called upon all parties concerned to work for the creation of the necessary conditions which would enable the Afghan refugees to return voluntarily to their homes in safety with honour. It also renewed its appeal to all countries and national and international organizations to continue to extend humanitarian relief assistanee to Afghan refugees in co-ordination with the UN High Commissioner for Refugees.[250]

The General Assembly again passed a resolution in November 1985 with 122 votes in favour and 19 against with 12 abstentions.[251] The similar pattern was repeated in November 1986[252] and in 1987 as well. The following table reveals the voting pattern:

The below table reveals that when the issue of Soviet intervention in Afghanistan came up before the General Assembly in January 1980 it was supported by 104 countries and the number increased with the passage of time reaching upto 124 in November 1987. The number of countries voting against the resolution fluctuated between 18 to 23 and the majority of these countries belonged to Soviet bloc.

UN General Assembly Voting Patterns

Dates	*Votes for*	*Votes against*	*Abstentions*
January 1980	104	18	18
November 1980	111	22	12
November 1981	116	23	12
November 1982	114	21	13
November 1983	116	20	13
November 1984	119	20	14
November 1985	122	19	12
November 1986	122	19	11
November 1987	124	15	10

Source: UN Monthly Chronicle 1980-1987

However, the number of abstentions decreased gradually. In January 1980, there were 18 abstentions which declined to 10 in 1987. This shows that majority of the world community was opposed to the Soviet intervention in Afghanistan.

Following the summit meeting between US President Ronald Reagan and General Secretary of the CPSU, Mikhail Gorbachev in early December 1987 which resulted in growing detente between the two super powers, the ongoing process of negotiations at Geneva on the question of Afghanistan, as analysed in suceeding pages, between Pakistan and Kabul regime received a boost. The resultant out come was the signing of Geneva accords on Afghanistan on 14 April, 1981 which came into effect from 15 May, 1988. In this way, the annual ritual of adopting resolution on the situation in Afghanistan by the UN General Assembly had become a secondary objective as major emphasis had been shifted towards Geneva accords.

Geneva Talks on Afghanistan

The "Geneva talks" has been a part of the UN initiative to solve the Afghan tangle.

The Geneva talks to find a political solution to the Afghan question started in June 1982 in pursuance of the resolutions passed by the General Assembly. In the wake of ,Pakistan's refusal to recognize the Karmal Government in Kabul, the UN Secretary General and his personal representative, Diego Cordovez, made hectic efforts during 1981-82 to help hold "proximity talks" between Pakistan, Afghanistan and Iran. Diego Cordovez held indirect talks with the representatives of Pakistan and Iran which led to the first round of talks in Geneva in June 1982. Iran refused to take part in the negotations. There was no outcome of the talks which led to its postponement. However, it was agreed that the "proximity talks" veered round four main points: (i) withdrawal of foreign troops from Afghanistan; (ii) non-interference in the internal affairs of states; (iii) international guarantees of non-interference; and (iv) voluntary return of the refugees to their homes.[253]

Soviet Union was a silent observer while Iran preferred to be simply "kept informed". Until the middle of 1983, both Islamabad and Kabul had not relented. The proximity talks held in June 1983 resulted in the preparation of 23-page draft agreement for the consideration of "concerned parties."[254] The UN Special Representative Diego Cordovez claimed that 95 per cent of the agreement was in hand.[255] But there was no satisfactory outcome because of the differing opinions among the concerned parties. The fourth round of Geneva talks held in June 1985 also proved a failure.[256] However the eighth round of talks held in Geneva in the beginning of August 1986 was adjorned on 8 August, 1986[257] in view of the reported Soviet proposal to "withdraw some troops."

The Soviet leader Gorbachev in a major foreign policy statement made at the end of July 1986, announced that six regiments or about 8,000 Soviet troops would be withdrawn at the end of October 1986. The US supply of Shinger missiles to Afghan freedom fighters in late 1986 had turned the tide in favour or Mujahideen causing severe strategic and military blows to Soviet army in Afghanistan.[258] In the wake of these developments, Moscow seemed to have been convinced that a military triumph over the national Afghan freedom fighters was almost an uphill task which could not be established during the past seven years, hence political and diplomatic channels could be more effective means to solve the Afghan tangle. Accordingly, the Kabul regime was encouraged by Moscow to seek a political compromise with the Afghan Mujahideen. Suddenly on 1 January 1987, the Najib Government called for "national reconciliation" and announced a country-wide six-months ceasefire effectivefrom 15 January, 1987.[259] The Afghan freedom fighters rejected such offers and mere "ploys" to divert the public attention from the main issue.

In the meanwhile, Diego Cordovez, the Personal Representative of the UN Secretary General, continued shutting between Islamabad, Kabul, Washinton and Moscow to facilitate a negotiated settlement of Afghan crisis. He claimed to have achieved a breakthrough on major issues. However disagreement prevailed over the time-framework for Soviet pull-out. On 8 February, 1988, coinciding with a fresh round of Geneva talks, Soviet leader Mikhail Gorbachev announced that Moscow was prepared to begin the withdrawal of its troops beginning from 15 May, 1988 and to complete their withdrawal within 10 months if a final settlement could be hammered out at Geneva.[260] During the succeeding two months, ehtee ensued hectic activities which finally culminated in the signing of four series of accords between Pakistan and Kabul regime and it came to be known as Geneva accords.

Under the bilateral agreement between Pakistan and Kabul regime both sides agreed "to respect the sovereignty, political independence, territorial integrity, national unity, security and non-alignment of the other High Contracting Party, as well as the national identity and cultural heritage of its people."[261]

Both the United States and the Soviet Union signed the Geneva accords as co-guarantors. The accords were to be effective from 15 May, 1988 and the Soviet Union was to begin the withdrawal of its troops from that day from Afghanistan and the last Soviet soldier would leave Afghanistan by 15 February, 1989.

However, the Geneva accords on Afghanistan have been rejected as illegal, unjustified and unacceptable by the Afghan freedom fighters. A.R. Pazhwak, the seasoned Afghan diplomat and statesman who represented Afghanistan in the United Nations for obout two decades and now residing in the United States, had criticised the very mechanism of Geneva talks as devised by the UN Secretary General. He condemned the holding of Geneva talks as being "illogical, unjust and unacceptable."[262] He further argued that the parties represented in the socalled "Geneva talks" were not the real parties to the conflict. Under the norms and principles of international law and the provisions of the UN Charter, the negotiations for settling the dispute should be held between the two belligerent groups. In case of Afghanistan, the two belligerents were—Russia as an invader and national freedom fighters as defenders.[263]

A.R. Pazhwak and the Afghan Mujahideen have remained committed to their clear-cut stand on Geneva talks despite the fact that the Soviet troops have withdrawn from Afghan soil. In their view, the Geneva accord having been forced on the people of Afghanistan has done more harm than remedying the issue. It has helped the Soviets to withdraw their soldiers from Afghan soil thus as a face saving device to show the world that they are no more involved in Afghan crisis and secondly, Moscow's grip over Kabul remains steadfast in wake of the continued arms supplies by Soviet Union to its puppet regime in Kabul.

The Response of Organization of Islamic Conference

Ever since the Soviet invasion of Afghanistan, the Organization of Islamic Conference (OIC) has been seized of the Afghan problem and the OIC has played a prominent role by mobilizing the international public opinion against Soviet occupation of Afghanistan. It was but natural for the International Islamic Community to express its solidarity with the people of Afghanistan who had been subject to Soviet armed aggression.

The first extraordinary session of the Islamic Conference of Foreign Ministers which met in Islamabad, Pakistan, from 27-29 January 1980 unanimously adopted a resolution 1/EOS which *inter alia* noted that "the Soviet occupation of Afghanistan constitutes a violation of its independence, and aggression against the liberty of its people and a flagrant violation of all international covenants and norms, as well as a serious threat to peace and security in the region and throughout the world."[263]

While condemning the Soviet military aggression against the people of Afghanistan, the resolution denounced and deplored it as a flagrant violation of international laws, norms of the Charter of the UN and the Charter of the Organization of the Islamic Conference.[265] It called upon all peoples and Governments throughout the world to "persist in condemning this aggression and denounced it as an aggression against Human Rights and a violation of the freedom of people, which cannot be ignored."[266] Apart from demanding the "immediate and unconditional" withdrawal of all Soviets stationed in Afghan territories, the Conference reiterated that the Soviet troops should refrain from acts of oppression and tyranny against the people of Afghanistan.[267]

The Conference took the bold decision of suspending the membership of Afghanistan in the Organization of the Islamic Conference and urged the member countries to withhold the recognition to the "illegal regime" in Afghanistan and "sever diplomatic relations with that country until the complete withdrawal of Soviet troops from Afganistan."[268] It also called upon member countries to envisage through appropriate bodies not to participate "in Olympic Games being held in Moscow in July 1980 unless the Soviet Union in compliance with the call of the UN General Assembly and Islamic Conference, withdraws its troops forthwith from Afghanistan."[269]

The eleventh conference of Foreign Ministers of Islamic countries held in Islamabad in May 1980 adopted a resolution 19/11 SC on Afganistan which represented a substantial softening of the January 1980's emergency conference's strong condemnation of the Soviet invasion of Afghanistan. The resolution established a ministerial committee comprising Tunisia, Iran and Pakistan empowering them to open negotiations with all parties involved in Afghanistan, including Soviet Union, to solve the Afghan problem.[270] It also called for:" (i) the immediate withdrawal of Soviet troops; (ii) recognition of the Afghan people's rights to choose their own form of government and socio-economic-political system; (iii) respect for the independence, territorial integrity and non-aligned status of Afghanistan; and (iv) creation of conditions within that.''[271]

The OIC has continuously taken up substantial decisions on Afghanistan in its periodic sessions. The Third Summit Conference of the OIC held at Mecca, Saudi Arabia, from 25-28 January, 1981 also adopted a resolution 3/3-0 (IS) on the situation in Afghanistan.[272] The Conference viewed with "grave concern" the continued Soviet military occupation of the Islamic Republic of Afghanistan and the consequent impediments "which stand in the way of the Muslim people of Afghanistan to exercise their right to determine their political future according to their will.''[273] It strongly urged for the creation of appropriate conditions to enable the Afghan refugees to return to their homeland in safety and honour.[274] The resolution called for increasing all efforts to ensure that "Afghanistan remains an independent and non-aligned state and to enable its people to exercise in all freedom their right to express their will as regards the system of their own choosing.''[275]

The coordinating meeting of the Ministers for Foreign Affairs of the Organization of the Islamic Conference held at New York on 10 October, 1983 while expressing its serious concern over the deplorable situation in Afghanistan resulting from the fact of the continuing foreign presence in that country, evinced its interest in the "efforts exerted by the Special Envoy of the Secretary General of the United Nations and by the Islamic Republic of Pakistan, with a view to finding a solution for the problem which this strife tcrn Muslim country (Afghanistan) is experiencing."[276] It further demanded the cessation of the armed intervention by "foreign forces in the internal affairs of their brotherly country, and the retreat of these forces from Afghan territory; and reaffirms right of the Afghan people to adopt a system of government of their choice."[277]

The fourteenth Islamic Conference of Foreign Ministers was held at Dhaka, Bangladesh, from 6 to 10 December, 1983 and unanimously adopted a resolution 13/14-P.[278] The resolution expressed serious concern over the continued Soviet military intervention in Afghanistan and the consequent impediment thereof.

The Islamic Conference in its meeting held at Morocco in early February 1986 again called upon the Soviet Union to vacate its aggression in Afghanistan and also reaffirm the right of the Afghan people to adopt a government of their own choice.[279] When the Afghan freedom fighters formed the "interim government" in February 1989, the Islamic Conference during its session held at Taif, invited the representative of the interim government.[280] Many a Islamic countries have accorded recognition to it.

Response by the European Economic Community

The European Economic Committee (EEC) comprising 10 member countries of Western Europe have also taken a serious note of Soviet intervention in Afghanistan. During its annual meeting the EEC has frequently expressed concern over the continued Soviet occupation of Afghanistan and calling for the withdrawal of Scviet troops.

The Heads of State and Government and the Ministers of Foreign Affairs of the ten members of the EEC, met at Maastricht, the Netherlands, in March 1981. The resolution on Afghanistan passed by this meeting of the EEC noted with grave concern the military operations by Soviet troops against the Afghan people, "who are resisting this external interference."[281] The resolution further envisaged EEC's call "for the withdrawal of foreign troops from Afghanistan to exercise freely their right to self-determination and for Afghanistan thus to return to its traditional status as an independent state, neutral and non-aligned."[282] Similar stance was reiterated by the EEC in 1982[283] and 1933.[284] It called for the withdrawal of Soviet troops from Afghanistan and restoration of its non-aligned and independent status.

On 14 May, 1984, the meeting of the Ministers of Foreign Affairs of the member countries of the EEC was held in Paris. The meeting adopted a resoluiion on Afghanistan which reiterated the attachment of the EEC countries to the principles set forth in the resolutions adopted by the UN General Assembly calling for the withdrawal of foreign troops, self-determination of the Afghan people, voluntary return of the Afghan refugees and non-alignment being the conditions for an honourable, just and lasting settlement for all the parties involved.[285] The EEC also reviewed its appeal to Moscow to embark on that course and to contribute to the efforts undertaken to that end by the Secretary-General of the United Nations.[286]

While speaking on behalf of the EEC, as well as Spain and Portugal, the representative of Luxembourgh told the General Assembly on 12 November, 1985 that the large scale Soviet military intervention in Afghanistan in 1979 was a shock to the international community and "it remains one of the most serious violations of the Charter of the United Nations."[287] While expressing concern over the plight of Afghan refugees the Luxembourg's representative further added that "in order that a satisfactory solution to this serious humanitarian problem may be found, it is necessary that the refugees be enabled to return to their native land in dignity and safety."[288] In his opinion such an eventuality could be facilitated if the independent and non-aligned status of Afghanistan could be restored and the Afghans were allowed to exercise their right to self-determination.

While alluding to the efforts made by the UN Secretary General and his personal representative with regard to a negotiated settlement of Afghanistan, the representative further observed: "We note with interest the report that they have submitted to the Assembly, which shows that technical progress has been achieved in developing several international instruments. We shall continue support those mediation efforts and we anticipate that rapid, genuine progress may be achieved, especially towards an agreed timetable for the withdrawal of Soviet troops."[289]

Response of the Non-aligned Movement

The non-aligned countries were also alarmed over the Soviet intervention in Afghanistan. This alarm was manifested in February 1981 when the conference of Foreign Ministers of non-aligned countries was held in New Delhi. The final communique issued after the conference called for a political settlement on the basis of withdrawal of foreign troops and full respect for the independence, sovereignty, territorial integrity and non-aligned status of Afghanistan.[290] The communique also referred to the right of Afghan refugees to return to their homes in safety and honour. The conference urged all concerned to work towards such a settlement which would ensure that the Afghan people would determine their own destiny free from outside interference and which would enable the Afghan refugees to return to their homes.[291]

The Ministerial Meeting of the Coordinating Bureau of the Non-aligned countries which met at Havana from 31 May to 5 June, 1982 reiterated the urgent call made at the New Delhi Ministerial Conference held in February 1981, for a political settlement of Afghan problem on the basis of withdrawal of foreign troops and full respect for the independence, sovereignty; territorial integrity and non-aligned status of Afghanistan.[292] The other part of the resolution was similar in words and content as of February 1981.

The final declaration adopted by the Seventh Conference of Heads of State or Government of Non-aligned Countries held in New Delhi from 7 to 12 March 1983, viewed the situation in Afghanistan with grave concern. It reiterated the earlier calls given by the NAM Conferences for the withdrawal of foreign troops from Afghanistan.[293] The Heads of State or Government of the non-aligned countries expressed their appreciation for the sincere efforts made in the search of a political solution in Afghanistan and extended their support to the constructive steps taken in this regard by the UN Secretary General.[294] They regarded the discussions through the intermediary of the UN Secretary General as a step in the right direction and urged their continuation with a view to promoting an early political settlement of the problem in conformity with the ideals and principles of the non-aligned movement.[295]

The similar stance was reiterated in the final communique issued after the meeting of Ministers and Heads of Delegation of the non-aligned countries held at New York from 1 to 5 October, 1984.[296] The meeting of the Foreign Ministers of the non-aligned countries which was held at Luanda from 4 to 7 September, 1985 had also reiterated the old stand on Afghanistan.[297]

The final communique issued by the meeting of the Ministers and Heads of Delegation of the non-aligned countries held at New York on 1 October, 1985 while reiterating the earlier stand of the NAM hoped for an early solution of the Afghan tangle.[298]

The Ministerial meeting of the coordinating Bureau of the non-aligned countries which met at New Delhi in April 1986, while reiterating the NAM stand on Afghanistan expressed appreciation for the sincere efforts made in the search for a political settlement of the situation in Afghanistan and extended its full support to the constructive steps taken by the UN Secretary General.[299] It also called on all states to exercise restraint to avoid further endangering the peace and security of the region and to take such steps as would lead to the creation of conditions conducive to stable and harmonious relations among the countries of the region.

The Non-aligned Summit held in Harare, the capital of Zimbabwe in September 1986, reiterated its earlier stand on Afghan issue and called for the earlier solution of the Afghan problem. It also appreciated the efforts of the UN Secretary General in this regard and expressed the hope that the solution to Afghan problem would soon be achieved.[300]

The foregoing analysis reveals that the Soviet intervention in Afghanistan in December 1979 and the continued presence of Soviet troops in Afghanistan had been widely condemned by the United States, another Super Power, United Nations, Islamic Community, European Economic Community and the Non-aligned Movement (NAM). Though after the signing of Geneva accords which came into effect from 15 May, 1988, the Soviet troops have been withdrawn from Afghan soil, but the situation has not improved but deteriorated further. The continued supply of Soviet weapons to the Kabul regime has been instrumental in prolonging the struggle between Najibullah forces and Afghan freedom fighters. Thus the basic objective, as envisaged in the various resolutions of the UN—the establishment of a non-aligned, independent, sovereign Afghanistan to be free to choose its own form of social, economic and political system without any outside interference, has not been fulfilled.

REFERENCES

1. Government of Afghanistan, *The Afghanistan Republic Annual 1974* (Kabul : Government Printing Press, 1974), p. 3.
2. *Ibid.*
3. Abdul Samad Ghaus, *The Fall of Afghanistan* (Washington : Pergamon-Brassey, 1988), p. 107.
4. "President Daoud Congratulates Turks on Their National Day", *Afghanistan Republic Annual 1974* (Kabul, 1974), p. 109.
5. *The Afghanistan Repubic Annual 1975* (Kabul, 1975), p. 176.
6. *Ibid.*
7. *Ibid.*, p. 177.
8. *Ibid.*
9. *Ibid.*, p. 179.
10. *Ibid.*
11. *Ibid.*
12. Ghaus, No. 3, p. 124.
13. *Kabul Times*, 1 May, 1975.
14. *Ibid.*
15. *Ibid.* Also see *Kayhan International* (Tehran), 1 May, 1975.
16. *Kayhan International*, 4 May, 1975.
17. *Asian Recorder* (New Delhi), Vol. XXI, No. 31, 30 July—5 August, 1975, p. 12714.
18. Ghaus, No. 3, p. 149.
19. *Republic of Afghanistan Annual 1974* (Kabul, 1974), p. 4.
20. *Kabul Times*, 12 June, 1976.
21. Ghaus, No. 3, p. 134.
22. *Kabul Times*, 23 August, 1976.
23. *Ibid.*, 3 March, 1977.
24. *Ibid.*, 10 June, 1977.
25. *Pakistan Horizon* (Karachiv).
26. *Kabul Times* 7 March, 1978.
27. *Ibid.*
28. For full text see, *Pakistan Horizon.*
29. *Afghanistan Annual 1974* (Kabul, 1974), p. 126.
30. *Afghanistan Annual 1975* (Kabul, 1975), p. 164.

31. *Ibid.*
32. *Ibid.*, p. 165.
33. *Ibid.*
34. *Ibid.*, p. 168.
35. *Ibid.*, p. 170.
36. *Afghanistan Annual 1974*, p. 28.
37. *Ibid.*, p. 31.
38. *Ibid.*, pp. 28-29.
39. *Ibid.*, p. 31.
40. Speech of Daoud cited in Hasan Kakkar, "The Fall of the Afghan Monarchy in 1973", *International Journal of Middle Eastern Studies*, Vol. 9, No. 2, May, 1978, p. 214.
41. Fred Halliday, "Revolution in Afghanistan", *New Left Review*, No. 112, November-December 1978, p. 29.
42. Kabul Radio, 27 April, 1978 in *FBIS/ME*, 28 April, 1978, p. 51.
43. Kabul Radio. 9 May, 1978, *FBIS/ME*, 10 May, 1978, p. 51.
44. Thomas T. Hammond, *Red Flag Over Afghanistan* (Boulder: Westview Press, 1985), p. 82.
45. Department of State Memorandum, 30 April, 1978 in *Declassified Documents 1978* (Washington, 1981).
46. *Ibid.*
47. Theodore L. Eliots, Jr., "The 1978 Afghan Revolution: Some Internal Aspects", *Fletcher Forum*, Vol. 3, No. 4, Spring 1979, p. 61.
48. *Ibid.*
49. Steven R. Galster, "Rivalry and Reconciliation in Afghanistan: What Prospects for the Accords?", *Third World Quarterly* (London), October 1988, p. 1518.
50. Cyrus Vance. *Hard Choices: Critical Years in America's Foreign Policy* (New York: Simon and Schuster, 1983), p. 385.
51. Quoted in Hammond, No. 44, p. 63.
52. Zbigniew Brzezinski, *Power and Principle* (New York: Farrar-Straus, 1983), p. 73.
53. Quoted in Hammond, No. 44, p. 63.
54. Vance, No. 50, p. 386.
55. US Embassy in Kabul to the Secretary of State, No. 3242, 27 April, 1978, *Declassified Documents* (Washington, 1981).

56. From Secretary of State to various US Embassies, No. 108913, 28 April, 1978. *Ibid.*
57. Zalmay Khalilzad, "The United States and War in Afghanistan", in Leo N. Rose and N.A. Hussain, *United States-Pakistan Forum: Relations with the Major Powers* (Lahore : Vanguard, 1987), p. 178.
58. *New York Times*, 5 May, 1978.
59. Drew Middleton, "How Afghans Government, into Soviet Global Strategy", *Ibid.*, 24 June, 1976.
60. Leon B. Poullada, "The Failure of American Diplomacy in Afghanistan", *World Affairs* Washington), Vol. 145, 1 No. 3, Winter 1982/83, p. 247.
61. Crzezinski, No. 52, p. 218.
62. J. Bruce Amstutz, *Afghanistan: The First Five Years of Soviet Occupation* (Washington: National Defence University, 1986), p. 40.
63. UK, *Afghanistan: The Soviet Invasion and its Consequences for British Security* (London: Her Majesty's Stationary Office, 1980), p. 6, Also see, *Washington Post*, 6 May, 1978.
64. Henry S. Bradsher, *Afghanistan and the Soviet Union* (Durham, N.C.: Duke Press, 1983), p. 84.
65. *FBIS Trends*, 3 May, 1978. p. 2.
66. *Tass*, 3 May, 1978 in *FBIS/US*, 4 May, 1978, p. 11.
67. *Pravda*, 6 May, 1978 in *FBIS/US*, 9 May, 1978, p. J1.
68. *Tass*, 19 May, 1978 in *FBIS/US*, 19 May, 1978, p. J1.
69. Kabul Radio, 11 July and 21 August, 1978, in *FBIS/ME*. 27 July, and 23 August, 1978, pp. 51 and 53.
70. The text of this agreement in *Afghanistan*, 'Appendix A.
71. For text of the Treaty see, *FBIS/US*, 6 December, 1978, pp. J10-13.
72. *Ibid.*
73. *Ibid.*
74. *FBIS Trends*, 13 December, 1978, p. 6.
75. Moscow Radio, 5 December, 1978, in *FBIS/US*, December 1978, p. J2.
76. Khalilzad, No. 57, p. 178.
77. *Ibid.*

78. US Embassy in Kabul to the Secretary of State, No. 3805, 18 May, 1978, reproduced in Government of Islamic Republic of Iran, *Documents of the Den of Espionage*, Vol. 29 (Tehran, 1981), pp. 64-67.

79. US Department of State, *The Kidnapping and Death of Ambassador Adolph Dubs: Summary of Report of Investigation* (Washington, D.C., 1980).

80. *Ibid.*

81. Richard P. Cronin, *Afghanistan, Soviet Invasion and US Response* (Washington, 1981), p. 4.

82. Beverley Male, *Revolutionary Afghanistan: A Reappraisal* (London: Croom Helm, 1982), p. 151.

83. *Kabul Times*, 15 February, 1979.

84. *New York Times*, 23 February, 1979.

85. *Ibid.*, 24 July, 1979.

86. Cronin, No. 81, p. 4.

87. *Ibid*

88. Leon B. Poullada, "The Road to Crisis, 1919-1980—American Failures, Afghan Errors and Soviet Success", in Rosanne Klass, *Afghanistan: The Great Game Revisited* (New York: Freedom House, 1987), p. 56.

89. *Kabul Times*, 16 September, 1979.

90. *Pravda*, 18 September, 1979, *FBIS/US*, 19 September, 1979, p. D1.

91. Halliday, No. 41, pp. 34-35.

92. On 14 September, 1979, four minister, Major Sherjan Mazdooryar, Colonel Mohammed, Aslam Watanjar, Colonel Syed Mohammad Gulabzoy and Asadullah Sarwari were dismissed by Amin and after the shoot out incident, they reportedly took refuge in Soviet Embassy in Kabul. See Hammond, No. 44. p. 83.

93. Cable No. 07444 from NS Embassy in Kabul to State Department, 11 October, 1979, *ibid.*, p. 86.

94. *Kabul Times*, 1 December, 1979.

95. *Ibid.*, 23 July, 1979.

96. *Ibid.*, 21 July, 1979.

97. Male, No. 82, p. 184.

98. *Ibid.* Also see Bradsher, N. 64, p. 116.

99. *FBIS Trends*, 3 October, 1979, pp. 15-16.

100. Brzezinski, No. 52, p. 427.
101. Khalilzad, No. 57, p. 180.
102. *Den of Espionage*, No. 78, Vol. 30, pp. 68-70.
103. Cable No. 05789 from Kabul to State Department, 11 September, 1979, p. 1, cited in Hammond, No. 44, p. 87.
104. Cable No. 07218 from Kabul to the State Department, 27 September, 1979, p. 1, *ibid*, p. 87.
105. Cited in Male, N. 82. p. 200.
106. US, Department of State, *Country Reports on Human Rights for 1979* (Washington, D.C.: Government Printing Press, 1980), pp. 707-12.
107. Cable No. 07726 from Kabul to State Department, 28 October, 1979, pp. 1-3, cited in Hammond, No. 44, p, 287.
108. Cable No. 282436, State Department to US Embassy in Islamabad, 29 October, 1979, p. 1, *ibid.*, p. 87.
109. *Den of Espionage*, No. 78, Vol. 30, pp. 9269-76.
110. Poullada, No. 60. p. 248.
111. Hammond, No. 44, p. 9.
112. Afghanistan, No. 62, pp. 37-38.
113. US, Department of State *Chronology of Recent Developments Related to Afghanistan* (Washington, D.C., 1980), p. 4.
114. *The Economist* (London), 17 November, 1979, pp. 68-69.
115. Patrick J. Garrity, "The Soviet Military Stake in Afghanistan 1956-1979", *Journal of the Royal United Services Institute for Defence Studies* (London), Vol. 125, No. 3, September 1980, pp. 35-36.
116. *Ibid.*
117. *Kabul Times*, 1 December, 1979.
118. Hammond, No. 44, p. 98.
119. Detailed account appeared in *New York Times*, 2 January, 1980.
120. *Tass*, 27 December, 1979, in *FBIS/US*, 28 December, 1971 pp. D1-2.
121. Kabul Radio, 27 December, 1979 in *FBIS/ME*, 28 December, 1979, p. 52.

122. *Pravda* 31 December, 1979, *FBIS/US*, 31 December, 1979, pp. D7-10.

123. Jamir Phillips, "The Soviet Invasion of Afghanistan", *Backgrounder* (Washington, D.C.: Heritage Foundation, 1980), p. 3.

124. *Presidential Documents* (Washington, D.C.), No. 16, 14 January, 1980, p. 41.

125. *Ibid* , No. 15, 31 December, 1979, p. 2. Also see *New York Times*, 29 December, 1979.

126. *Presidential Documents*, No. 16, 14 January, 1980, p. 25.

127. *Ibid.*

128. *New York Times*, 30 December, 1979.

129. *Ibid.*, 1 January, 1980.

130. *Presidential Documents*, No. 16, 28 January, 1980, p. 111.

131. *Ibid.*, No. 16, 25 February, 1980. pp. 386-87.

132. *Pravda*, 8 January, 1980, in *FBIS/US*, 10 January, 1980, pp. A7-8.

133. *Presidential Documents*, No. 16, 3 March, 1980, p. 387.

134. Hammond, N. 44, p. 105.

135. *Time* (New York), 24 April, 1978, p. 20.

136. *Ibid.*, p. 21.

137. Quoted in Hammond, N. 44, p. 107.

138. *Ibid.*

139. *New York Times*, 22 December, 1979.

140. *Ibid.*

141. *Ibid.*

142. US Congress, House of Representatives, Sub-Committee on Europe and the Middle East, 96th Congress, *East-West Ralations in the Aftermath of Soviet Invasion of Afghanistan* (Washington, D.C., Government Printing Office, 1980), p. 115.

143. *Ibid.*, p. 118.

144. Hammond, No. 44, p. 112.

145. *Presidential Documents*, No. 16, 14 January, 1980, p. 41.

146. *Ibid.*, No. 16, 28 January, 1980, p. 166.

147. *Ibid.*, p. 185.

148. *Ibid.*, p. 197.

149. *Department of State Bulletin* (Washington, D.C.), October 1979.

150. *Ibid.*

151. *Ibid.*

152. *Ibid.*

153. *Ibid.*, December 1979.

154. *Ibid.*

155. *Ibid.*

156. *Ibid.*

157. *Ibid.*, January 1980.

158. US, House Sub-Committee on Europe and the Middle East, *An Assessment of the Afghanistan Sactions: Implications for Trade and Diplomacy in the 1980s* (Washington, 1981), p. 8.

159. *Ibid.*

160. *Ibid.*

161. *Tass*, 6 January, 1980, in *PBIS/80*, 2 January, 1980, pp. A1-4.

162. *Pravda*, 13 January, 1980, in *PBIS/80*, 14 January, 1980, pp. A1-8.

163. *Ibid.*

164. United States International Communication Agency (USICA), *Chronology of Afghanistan Events: A Retrospective* (New Delhi, 1980), p. 2.

165. *Ibid.*

166. *Ibid.*

167. USICA, *Press Release* (New Delhi), 23 May, 1981.

168. USICA, *Backgrounder* (New Delhi), 12 August, 1981.

169. *Ibid.*

170. *Department of State Bulletin*, January 1982.

171. *Ibid.*

172. USICA, "President Reagan calls for Soviet Withdrawal from Afghanistan", *Official Text* (New Delhi), 29 December, 1981.

173. *Ibid.*

174. USICA, "President Reagan's Afghanistan Day Proclamation", *Official Text*, 11 March, 1982.

175. *Ibid.*

176. Thomas T. Hammond, "Afghanistan: The Road to the West", *The Washington Post*, 20 January, 1983.

177. *Congressional Record* (Washington), Vol. 129, No. 52, 21 April, 1983, p. 1857.

178. *Ibid.*

179. *Ibid.*, Vol. 129, No. 133, 6 October, 1983, p. S. 13791.

180. *Ibid.*

181. *Ibid.*

182. USICA, "US Unalterably Opposes Soviet Invasion of Afghanistan", *Official Text*, 15 December, 1983.

183. *Ibid.*

184. *Department of State Bulletin*, December, 1984. Also see USICA, *US Ambassador Cites Resolution on Afghanistan* (New Delhi, 1984), p. 10.

185. USICA, "Reagan Calls Afghan Crisis as Impediment to US-USSR Ties", *Official Text*, 27 December, 1984.

186. *Ibid.*

187. *Ibid.*

188. *Ibid.*

189. *Ibid.*

190. *Congress Record*, 99th Congress, First Session, Vol. 131, No. 117, p. E 4089.

191. *Ibid.*, Vol. 131, No. 131, 26 September, 1985, p. E. 4209.

192. *Congressional Record—Senate*, 99th Congress, First Session, Vol. 131, No. 133, 8 October, 1985, p. S. 12925.

193. *Ibid.*, Vol. 131, No. 142, 23 October, 1985, p. E. 4763.

194. *Ibid.*, Vol. 131, No. 148, 31 October, 1985, p. H. 9559.

195. *Department of State Bulletin*, May 1986.

196. *Ibid.*

197. *New York Times*, 9 September, 1986.

198. USICA, *Recent Developmenis in Afghanistan* (New Delhi, 1986),

199. *Ibid.*, p. 12.

200. *Ibid* , p. 13.

201. *Ibid.*, p. 15.
202. *New York Times*, 31 October, 1986.
203. USICA, No. 206, p. 16.
204. USICA, *Backgrounder*, 6 November, 1986, p. 3.
205. *Ibid.*, p. 5.
206. *Ibid.*, p. 6.
207. *New York Times*, 19 November, 1986.
208. USICA, No. 206, p. 19.
209. USICA, *Official Text* (New Delhi), 30 December, 1986, p. 1.
210. *Ibid.*, p. 2.
211. *Ibid.*
212. *Ronald Reagan: In Search of Peace with Freedom, Selected Speeches* (Washington, 1987), p. 69.
213. *Ibid.*, p. 70.
214. *Ibid.*, p. 76.
215. *USSR-US Summit: Documents and Materials* (Moscow, 1987), p. 71.
216. USIS, *Backgrounder* (New Delhi), 9 April, 1988, p. 1.
217. *Ibid.*
218. *Ibid.*
219. *Ibid.*
220. USIS, *Backgrounder*, 12 April, 1988, p. 1.
221. *Ibid.*, p. 2.
222. USIS, "Geneva Signing, Shultz's Comments", N E 4060414, 14 April, 1988, p. 4.
223. *Ibid.*
224. *Ibid.*, p. 5.
225. *Ibid.*
226. USIS, *Backgrouuder*. 20 May 1988.
237. *Ibid.*, 24 June, 1988.
228. *Ibid.*, p. 2.
229. *Ibid.*, 2 November, 1988, p. 1

230. *Ibid.*, p. 2.

231. *Ibid*, 3 November, 1988, p. 1.

232. *Ibid.*, 5 November, 1988, p. 1.

233. *Ibid*, p. 2.

234. These countries were: Bangladesh, Jamaica, Nigeria, the Philippines, Tunisia and Zambia.

235. K.P. Saksena, "Afghanistan Conflict and the United Nations", *International Studies*, Vol. 19, No. 4, October-December 1980, p. 665.

236. Soviet Union and German Democratic Republic (GDR) voted against it.

237. Those who voted against were: Afghanistan, Angola, Bulgaria, Byelorussia, Cuba, Czechoslovakia, Democratic Yemen, Ethiopia, GDR, Grenada, Hungary, Laos, Mongolia, Mozambique, Poland, the Ukrainian SSR, Soviet Union and Vietnam.

238. General Assembly resolution ES-6/2, 14 January, 1980.

239. UN, *Official Records of the General Assembly* (*hereafter*) *GAOR*), Thirty-fifth session, Resolution 35/37, 20 November, 1980. p. 17.

240. UN Doc. A/36/653, 6 November, 1981.

241. *Ibid.*

242. *Ibid.*

243. *GAOR*, Thirty-sixth session, Resolution 36/34, 18 November, 1981, p. 18.

244. *Ibid.*

245. For Full text see, USICA, "US Resolution on Afghanistan", *Official Text*, 6 December, 1982.

246. A.R. Pazhwak, "The Basic Way for the Political Solution of Afghan Problem", *Afghan Mujaheed* (Peshawar), December 1982.

247. *Ibid.*

248. For text of the resolution see, UN Information Centre, *The UN Weekly Newsletter* (New Delhi), Vol. 35, No. 4, 4 December, 1984, p. 1.

249. *Ibid.*

250. *Ibid.*

251. *The UN Weekly Newsletter*, 25 Novemder, 1985.

252. *Ibid.* 30 November, 1986.

253. UN Doc. A/37/482, 27 September, 1982.

254. Munawar Noorani, "Afghanistan Negotiations: Implications for the US of an Impasse", *Journal of South Asian and Middle Eastern Studies* (Villanova), Vol. IX, No. 3, Spring 1986, p. 9.

255. "An Accord in Offing", *Far Eastern Economic Review* (Hong Kong), 9 June, 1983, p. 28.

256. *New York Times*, 29 June, 1985.

257. Larry Jagan, "Summit Surprise?", *Economic and Political Weekly* (Bombay), Vol. XXI, No. 4, 23 August, 1986, p. 1473.

258. David B. Ottaway, "U.S. Missiles Alter War in Afghanistan", *Washington Post*, 19 July 1987.

259. Cited in Alvin Z. Rubenstein, "The Soviet Withdrawal from Afghanistan," *Current History*, October 1988, p, 334.

260. *Foreign Broadcast Information Service* (PBIS). *Soviet Union*, 8 February, 1988, p. 34.

261. For full text see, US, Senate Committee on Judiciary, Sub-Committee on Immigration and Refuges Affairs, *Afghanistan: Peace and Repatriation* (Washington: 1988), pp. 33-35.

262. A.R. Pazhwak's interview with the *Voice of America*, as reproduced in *Afghan Mujahid* (Peshawar), No. 18, December 1982.

263. *Ibid.*

264. For full text of the resolution see, UN Doc. A/35/109, 21 February, 1980, pp. 16-19.

265. *Ibid.*, p. 17.

266. *Ibid.*

267. *Ibid.*, p. 18.

268. *Ibid.*

269. *Ibid.*, p. 19.

270. Cited in Richard P. Cronin, *Afghanistan, [Soviet Invasion and US Response* (Washington, D.C.: Congressional Research Service, 1986), p. 5.

271. *Ibid.*, p. 6.

272. For full text, see, UN Doc. A/36/138, 31 March, 1981, pp. 36-39.

273. *Ibid.*, p. 36.

274. *Ibid.*, p. 38.

275. *Ibid.*

276. UN Doc. A/36/236, 7 May, 1984, p. 3.

277. *Ibid.*, p. 4.

278. For full text see, UN Doc. A/39/133, 19 March, 1984, pp. 47-50.

289. *The Times* (London), 8 February, 1986.

280. *Pakistan Times*, 22 March, 1989.

281. UN Doc. A/36/153, 30 March, 1981.

282. *Ibid.*

283. *New York Times*, 28 March, 1982.

284. *Ibid.*, 14 May, 1983.

285. UN Doc. A/38/261, 17 May, 1983.

286. *Ibid.*

287. UN Doc. A/40/PV. 71, p. 53.

288. *Ibid.*, p. 58.

289. *Ibid.*, p. 57.

290. Government of India, *Twenty-Five Years of the Non-aligned Movement* (New Delhi, 1986), Vol. I, p. 507.

291. *Ibid.*

292. *Ibid.*, p. 571.

293. Government of India, *Twenty-Five Years of the Non-aligned Movement* (New Delhi, 1986), Vol. II, p. 33.

294. *Ibid.*

295. *Ibid.*

296. *Ibid*, pp. 118-19.

297. *Ibid.*, p. 184.

298. *Ibid.*, p. 291.

299. Government of India, *Ministerial Meeting of the Coordinating Bureau of the Non-aligned Countries, New Delhi, April 1986* (New Delhi, 1986), p. 45.

300. *New York Times*, 14 September, 1986.

CONCLUSION

The Soviet invasion of Afghanistan in December 1979 and the continued presence of Soviet troops on Afghan soil for about a decade and their departure by February 1989 presents an unprecedented instance in the annals of international relations. Afghanistan is an ancient country, whose history dates back to over 5000 years. Since its emergence as a modern political entity about 25 decades back, Afghanistan has been the nerve centre of Super Power rivalry. The geo-strategic location of Afghanistan makes it share border with the Soviet Union. Despite the severe pressures of Anglo-Russian rivalry prior to the Second World War and Soviet-United States (US) rivalry in the post-war period, Afghanistan has always warded off the overtures of Super Powers by pursuing the policy of strict neutrality and genuine non-alignment. Thus, it also managed to safeguard its independence, sovereignty and territorial integrity. Afghanistan had pursued this smooth course for centuries and even the change of regime did not affect the basic tenets of Afghan foreign policy.

However, the Soviet invasion of Afghanistan in December 1979 changed the entire course of Afghan history and an in dependent and non-aligned country became a "satellite of Soviet Empire." The background of Soviet invasion was laid down during the last week of April 1978 when the People's Democratic Party of Afghanistan (PDPA) seized power, with Soviet help, by overthrowing and simultaneously killing Sardar Mohammad Daoud. Between April 1978 and December 1979, the Soviet military advisers, and troops had started reaching Afghanistan for a virtual takeover. The PDPA regime had departed from the traditionl path of genuine non-alignment and Afghanistan was gradually pushed into the Soviet orbit. The Soviet invasion in the last week of December finally sealed the fate of Afghanistan as an independent non-aligned and sovereign country. Today's Afghanistan is a client and satellite state of Soviet Union.

The existing norms and practices of international relations and International law as well as the principles enshrined in the Charter of the United Nations are opposed to the invasion and occupation of one country by another country. Afghanistan throughout the course of its history has always pursued the policy of strict neutrality and genuine non-alignment. Besides, the pursuit of peace and friendly relations have always been the main bulwark of Afghan foreign policy. It had never harboured territorial designs against any country, especially its neighbours. Rather, Afghanistan had been the victim of foreign aggression, three times by the British and three times by Soviet Union, prior to the Second World War and again by Soviet Union in December 1979.

Even during the hey days of Anglo-Russian rivalry, Afghanistan never fell a prey to either Soviet or British overtures nor it allowed its territory to be used by either side against the other. The Afghan rulers were convinced that they could retain the independence and territorial integrity of Afghanistan by pursuing a policy of strict neutrality. Even during its hostilities with the British, Afganistan never accepted the Soviet help but defended itself with its own indigenous resources. In the immediate aftermath of the conclusion of the Second World War, the Soviet-US rivalry for winning newly independent countries to their respective "spheres of influence" gave rise to the emergence of cold war which was followed by the founding of military alliances. Afghanistan remained aloof from the power politics of the cold war and did not join any military alliance. It pursued the policy of genuine non-alignment.

In the wake of these developments, the Soviet invasion and its consequent occupation of Afghanistan for a decade was very perplexing and unwarranted. There was not even a slightest provocation on the part of Afghanistan which could prompt the Soviets to invade Afghanistan. Moscow for long had been cherishing the goal of reaching the "hot waters" of the Indian Ocean through the Indian subcontinent or through Persian Gulf. The strategic location of Afghanistan was most congenial for Soviet Union to fulfil its centuries old dream. The Soviet action proves that Moscow, for long, had been harbouring territorial designs on Afghanistan and was looking for an opportunity which came in April 1978 and culminated in fulfilling Soviet aspirations in December 1979.

By invading Afghanistan, Soviet Union violated its bilateral agreements with Afghanistan, violated the principles of the United Nations Charter and defied the world public opinion. But for the December 1978 Soviet-Afghan treaty, all earlier treaties signed in 1921 and 1926 between Moscow and Kabul had reiterated Soviet affirmation in the independence and territorial integrity of Afghanistan. The Treaty of Neutrality and Non-aggression signed between Moscow and Kabul on 31 August, 1926 enjoined upon both the contries to maintain neutrality in case either of them was involved in a military conflict with a third country. It also provided that both countries would refrain from interfering in the internal affairs of each other. Before the advent of communist regime in Kabul in April 1978, the Afghan policy towards Russia had been based on good neighbourliness, mutual respect, and principles of peaceful coexistence. This policy was vigorously pursued by different regimes in Afghanistan. All the joint statements and joint communiques issued by the two countries prior to April 1978 had reiterated the faith of two countries in these principles. The Afghan-Soviet friendship treaty signed on 5 December, 1978 envisaged under Article IV that both countries sought continually to develop cooperation in the military field on the basis of appropriate agreements and also provided for consultations between the two countries and for the initiation of appropriate measures by mutual consent to ensure their security, independence and territorial integrity.[1] It was under the pretext of this clause that the Soviets justified their invasion of Afghanistan. The Soviets claimed that they had been "invited" by the Kabul regime to defend Afghanistan against the "foreign intervention." It is worth noting that the advent of the Soviet-backed communist government in Kabul in April 1978 was followed by exodus of Afghans opposed to the communist takeover from Afghanistan into neighbouring Pakistan and Iran. The people of Afghanistan also organized themselves into resistance groups to launch armed struggle against the Soviet occupation. Thus the Russian-backed communist regime in Kabul was almost near collapse and Moscow also saw an opportunity to fulfil its long-cherished ambition of reaching the hot waters of the Indian Ocean by occupying Afghanistan. Consequently, the Soviet Union invaded Afghanistan in the last week of December 1979 using the Soviet-Afghan Treaty of 1978 as a pretext.

The resolutions passed by the General Assembly called for the immediate and total withdrawal of "foreign troops" from Afghanistan. But the Soviet Union did not care to comply with those resolutions which were only recommendatory in nature. Moscow, being the permanent member of the Security Council, had already vetoed a resolution on Afghanistan on 7 January, 1980 and could veto any such resolution which it deemed detrimental to its interests. However, in the General Assembly where Moscow could not influence every member, passed several resolutions calling for the withdrawal of Soviet troops from Afghanistan and even condemned the Soviet invasion on Afghanistan. This showed that the Soviet action in Afghanistan was in utter violation of the principles of the UN Charter and Moscow had remained unconcerned about what the General Assembly had called for.

Besides, the Soviet Union had also shown utter disregard for the international public opinion. The Soviet invasion and continued occupation of Afghanistan had been widely condemned by the non-aligned Summit Conferences held in New Delhi in 1983 and at Harare in 1986, by the Organization of Islamic Countries, European Economic Community (EEC) and other regional organizations like ASEAN, Arab League,

OPEC etc. The salient points common to the resolutions passed by these organizations had called for the immediate and total withdrawal of Soviet troops from Afghanistan, the return of the Afghan refugees to their homes with honour and dignity and the restoration of the independent and non-aligned status of Afghanistan. All such urgings and appeals had fallen flat on Soviet ears.

Under the contemporary international relations, act of one Super Power can be counter balanced by the other Super Power. After all the countries of the Third World have been the victim of the Super Power rivalry which threatens their existence. The United States could have definitely helped in entangling the Afghan knot much earlier had it acted more sincerely and tactfully. The reaction of Washington to the developments in Kabul between April 1978, and December 1979 had been lukewarm. The Carter Administration also took time in imposing US sanctions against the Soviet Union. However, the US was itself engaged in the US hostages' affair in Iran during that period. These sanctions were softened by the Reagan Administration.

The advent of diplomatic relations between Kabul and Washington dates back to early 1940s but efforts in this direction were initiated as early as the second half of the second decade of the present century. The lukewarm US response to the Afghan endeavours to establish diplomatic relations between the two countries during 1920s and 1930s did not deter Kabut which continuously availed every opportunity to convince the policy markers in Washington of Afghanistan's anxiety and eagerness to establish diplomatic relations between the two countries.

The establishment of diplomatic relations between Afghanistan and the United States in 1942 coincided with the zenith of the Second World War. The United States was involved in the war. However, Afghanistan maintained the policy of strict neutrality throughout the period of the Second

World War. The Afghan policy of strict neutrality during the war period was highly appreciated by the Allied powers, especially in the United States.

The post-Second World War period witnessed the growth of cordial and friendly relations between Kabul and Washington. Afghaniston got economic and technical assistance from the United States which proved helpful in the economic and industrial development. In the wake of onset of cold war hotly chased by the United States and the Soviet Union to win over the newly independent countries to their respective "spheres of influence,'' Afghanistan pursued a genuinely non-aligned policy and maintained an independent posture in international affairs. Keeping in view the cold war situation and Afghanistan's proximity to the Soviet Union, the United States failed to properly appreciate the geo-political significance of Afghanistan for US strategy. The UN foreign policy under the influence of the Secretary of State John Foster Dulles ignored Afghanistan. Afghanistan's requests for US arms during 1950s were also ignored.

Pakistan, with which Afghanistan had differences over the issue of Pakhtunistan, was given added significance by the policy makers in Washington. As and when Kabul approached Washington for arms assistance for self-defence, it was straight-away rejected and on occasions Kabul was told to compromise with Pakistan on the issue of Pakhtunistan and then pay for cash to procure arms. Pakistan's bilateral military and defence agreement with the United States and its active membership of the US sponsored regional defence pacts like SEATO and CENTO and continued supply American arms and rejection by Washigton to meet even the minimum defence requirements of Afghanistan were such hard facts which irritated the ruling elite in Kabul. The United States even ignored Afghan offers of mediating between Pakistan and Afghanistan on the question of Pakhtunistan.

Moscow seized this opportunity to win Afghan favour by providing increased economic aid especially after mid-1950s.

This does not mean that Afghanistan abandoned its traditional policy of genuine non-alignment and toed the Soviet line. But more enlightened US foreign policy during the Dulles period could have made Afghanistan less dependent on Soviet Union for economic and military assistance.

The Afghanistan-US relations remained almost friendly since the beginning of early 1940s till the advent of Russian-backed communist *coup* in Kabul in April 1978 on the basis of mutual respect for each other, non-interference and peaceful coexistence. The United States provided economic and technical assistance to Afghanistan during this period. There had been exchange of visits by the leaders of the two countries. Both countries shared common views on global and regional issues. Afghanistan had great admiration for US role in maintaining international peace and security while the United States greatly valued Afghanistan's policy of genuine non-alignment. Had the United States used its good offices in mediatiating between Pakistan and Afghanistan on the Pakhtun issue and Afghanistan's genuine defence requirements, the pattern of the Afghan relations would have been different and increase of Russian influence could have been properly checked.

However, the lukewarm reaction by the United States to the advent of pro-Moscow communist regime in Kabul in April 1978 allowed the developments to take a decisive turn in December 1979 when Soviets invaded Afghanistan. A stern action in the form of diplomatic and economic sanctions against Moscow and stern warning to Moscow not to interfere into the internal affairs of Afghanistan could have prevented Soviet Union from invading Afghanistan in December 1979.

In the wake of Soviet invasion of Afghanistan, Carter Administration took belated measures by imposing sanctions against the Soviet Union and warning the latter to "keep hands off from the Persian Gulf". By the time US sanctions were announced, the tens of thousands of Russian troops had entrenched their position in Afghanistan. An early and immediate strong action by Carter Administration could have saved the situation from further deterioration.

Though the United States under Reagan Administration rendered valuable humanitarian assistance to the people of Afghanistan in their just struggle against Soviet invasion and Washington also condemned the Soviet act of aggression in the United Nations and its consistent stand on Afghan issue which helped in boosting the morale of Afghan freedom fighters, but it was not enough.

Despite the diplomatic and humanitarian assistance rendered by the US to the Afghan Mujahideen, yet this alone had not been sufficient to drive the Soviets out of Afghanistan. The US should have taken more tough stand in the United Nations and other international for a against the Soviet Union so that the latter could realize that its action in Afghanistan would strain its relations with the United States. Besides, the Reagan Administration should have given direct economic and other types of assistance to Afghan Mujahideen and not through any third party. It is worth mentioning here that it was the tough stand of Washington which compelled Moscow to withdraw its troops from Iran in 1946. The SoViet Union should have been made to realize that it would not be allowed to usurp Afghanistan. The US could have re-imposed severe diplomatic and economic sanctions against the Soviet Union in order to pressurize Moscow to vacate the aggression of Afghanistan, which the latter did only after a decade. In case the Reagan Administration and the US State Deparment had acted in unison as per the advice of the US Congress and followed a more rigid and practical policy towards Moscow, the Russians would not have taken to pull out their troops from Afghanistan. The American started supplying strategic weapons like Sdinger missiles to the Afghan freedom fighters only in late 1986 which really turned the tide in favour of the Mujahideen in their liberation war against the occupation forces. Supply of such strategic weapons in the beginning of 1980s could have borne more fruitful results.

Another hope of defusing the Afghanistan crisis is the United Nations. Afghanistan is one of the founding members of the UN. It has played very active and constructive role in strengthening the world body. The moral support rendered by Afghanistan to the United Nations in tackling the crucial global issues has been instrumental in consolidating the constructive role of the world body in maintaining international peace and security. But when one of its members—Afghanistan—had been invaded by another powerful member—Soviet Union—the world body failed in discharging its basic duty of safeguarding the independence, sovereignty and territorial integrity of Afghanistan.

The First resolution passed by the General Assembly in January 1980 condemned the Soviet Union by name for invading Afghanistan and called for the "withdrawal of Soviet troops" from Afghan soil. But the subsequent resolution passed by the General Assembly beginning with November 1980 resolution became mild in their condemnation of Soviet Union and called for the "withdrawal of foreign troops" from Afghanistan. It seemed that Moscow succeeded in influencing the functioning of the General Assembly which was reflected in the softening tone of UN resolutions on Afghanistan. If such a state of affairs is allowed to continue the faith of the countries in the UN would be eroded.

The resolutions so far passed by the General Assembly on the situation in Afghanistan have suffered from many weaknesses. In the first instance, the invader (Soviet Union) was not mentioned by name. The Soviet troops were stationed on Afghan soil and the reference in the resolution to "withdrawal of foreign troops" defeated the very purpose of the resolutions. Instead, reference should have been made to "immediate, complete and unconditional withdrawal of Russian troops from Afghanistan."[2]

REFERENCES

1. For full text of the treaty see, *Soviet Review* (New Delhi), Vol. 15, No. 58, 21 December, 1978, pp. 31-34.
2. A.R. Pazhwak, "Basic Way for the political Solution of Afghan Problem", *Afghan Mujahid* (Peshawar), Special Issue, No. 18, Decembes 1982.

APPENDIX A

Amir Amanullah Khan of Afghanistan to President Harding

To My Great Friend Mr. President of the United States of America

Expressing my friendly feeling to Your Excellency, I intend to inform Your Excellency's high Government about my coronation.

After the tragic death of my father His Majesty Amir Habibullah Khan who was killed during his Royal Territorial excursion, I came to the throne of Afghanistan, as it was my right and all public desire of Afghan nation.

For the expression of friendly feelings of my Government, I sent one of my Generals G. Mahammad Wali Khan as Extraordinary Ambassador to Your Excellency's high Government.

As I used to have the sincere wish to establish a permanent friendly relation between Afghanistan and high Government of the United States, I expect that Your Excellency's High Government may be satisfied with the keeping of this friendly relation too.

Sending to Your Excellency my sincere greeting I beg to express herewith to Your Excellency and Your Excellency's High Government by highest esteem.

AMIR AMANULLAH KHAN

President Harding to Amir Amanullah Khan of Afghanistan

GREAT AND GOOD FRIEND: I have received from the hands of G. Mohammad Wali Khan, the letter by which Your Majesty advised me of the death of your father, his late Majesty Amir Habibullah Khan, and of your ascension to the throne of Afghanistan, as well as of your desire to establish diplomatic relations between the United States and Afghanistan.

While I have learned with sorrow of the tragic death of Your Majesty's father, and offer to you my sincere sympathy in this great affliction, I congratulate your Majesty on your ascension to the throne and trust that your reign will rebound to your Majesty's glory and the prosperity of Afghanistan.

It is my wish that the relations between the United States aad Afghanistan may always be of a friendly character and I shall be happy to cooperate with your Majesty to this end. I am constrained, however, to confirm to your Majesty what was stated orially to G. Mohammad Wali Khan, that with respect to the United States the question of the creation of a Diplomatic Mission and of the appropriate action to that end by the Congress of the United States must be reserved for future consideration.

In thanking Your Majesty for your friendly sentiments, I desire to assure you of my good wishes four personal happiness and for the prosperity of your country.

Your Good Friend,

Washington, July 29, 1921. WARREN G. HARDING

Source: US *Paper Relating to the Foreign Relations of the United States 1921*, Vol. 1 (Washington, D.C.: Government Printing Office, 1936), pp. 260-61.

APPENDIX B

Afghanistan-Soviet Union Treaty: 28 February, 1921

With the intention of strengthening the friendly relations existing between Russia and Afghanistan and to protect the real independence of Afghanistan, F.S.F.S.R. on the one hand, and His Majesty's Government of Afghanistan on the other, decided to make the following Treaty themselves. And to this end they have appointed as their plenipotentiaries the following:

For His Majesty's Government of Afghanistan:

Mohammad Wali Khan, Mirza Mohammad Khan and Gholam Seddigh Khan;

For the R.S.F.S. Government of Russia:

Georgy Vassilievich Chicherin, and Lev Mikhailovich Kara Khan.

These plenipotentiaries have agreed as follows:

I. Each of the High Contracting Parties recognizes the independence of the other and undertakes to respect it and enter into proper political relations with the other.

II. Each of the High Contracting Parties undertakes not to enter into any military and political agreement with a third government that may be against the interest of the other of the High Contracting Parties.

III. The legations and consulates of the High Contracting Parties will equally and respectively possess the customary and international political privileges.

First explanation of the above:

(a) The right to fly a government flag.

(b) The immunity of the listed members of the legations and consulates.

(c) The immunity of political despatches and of courtier services and any mutual assistance in this connection.

(d) The right of telegraphic, telephonic and wireless communications, in accordance with the privileges of diplomatic representatives.

(e) The legation and consular buildings of each of the High Contracting Parties on the territory of the other will possess extraterritorial privileges, but cannot become an asylum for those persons who are considered outlaws by the local government.

Second explantation: The legations of High Contracting Parties will each have a military attache.

IV. The High Contracting Parties agree that the R.S.F.S. Government of Russia will have five consulates in the territory of Afghanistan and His Majesty's Government of Afghanistan will have seven consulates in the Russian territory including five consulates in Russian Middle Asia.

Explanation: The High Contracting Parties will be free to open other consulates in the territory of each other, in addition to the number mentioned above, after special agreement.

V. The Russian consulates will open in the towns of Herat, Mazar-i-Sherif, Kandhar, Kaznein and Meimeneh. The Consulate General of Afghanistan will be opened at Tashkent, and the consulates in Petrograd, Kazau, Khokand, Samarkand, Merv, and Krashavodsk.

Explanation: The manner and the time of the actual opening of the Russian consulates in Afghanistan and the Afghan consulates in Russia will be fixed according to a special agreement in each instance.

VI. Russia consents to free and uninterrupted transit of all goods going to Afghanistan from Russia including goods brought in Russia through governmental departments as well as those bought abroad direct.

VII. The High Contracting Parties agree to respect the freedom of the nations in the East on the basis of plebiscite and self-government.

VIII. In accordance with article VII of the present document the High Contracting Parties recognize the independence and freedom of the Government of Bukhara and Khiva under any form of government that may be desired by their nationals.

IX. In order to accomplish the promise given by the R.S.F.S. Government of Russia through its President, Mr. Lenin, to the Minister of His Majesty's Government of Afghanistan, which promise being to the effect that the Government of Russia agrees to return to Afghanistan all the lands situated in the frontier zone, and which had belonged to Afghanistan in the past century, it is hereby agreed that a separate agreement will be signed by the plenipotentiaries of the High Contracting Parties on the basis of the plebiscite of the nationals living in those lands.

X. In order to further the friendly relations existing betbeen the High Contracting Parties, the R.S.F.S. Government of Russia undertakes to give material and financial assistance to the Government of Afghanistan.

XI. This Treaty is written in Persian and Russian texts, each of which shall have equal validity.

XII. This Treaty will become effective after it is ratified by the respective Governments of the High Contracting Parties, and the exchange of ratifications will take place in Kabul.

***Source*: Leonard Shapiro (ed.), *Soviet Treaty Seires, 1917-1928*, Vol. 1 (Washington, D.C.: The Georgetown University Press, 1950), pp. 96-97.**

APPENDIX C

Afghan-Soviet Treaty of Neutrality and Non-Aggression 1926

The Government of USSR and the exalted Government of Afghanistan, with the object of confirming the friendly relations, and of strengthening the neighbourly ties which fortunately exist and on the basis of the Treaty signed in Moscow on 28 February, 1921—said Treaty to preserve its force in all its parts, irrespective of the continuance or cancellation of the present Treaty—both exalted Parties have authorized: His Excellency Mr. Leonid Stark, Minister Plenipotentiary of USSR in Afghanistan and His Excellency Mr. Mohammad Beg Khan Tarzi, Minister for Foreign Affairs of the exalted Government of Afghanistan, who. . . with the object of strengthening the friendly relations and insuring the peace between the two Governments, have framed and signed the Articles below:

I. In case of war or military action between one of the Contracting Parties and one or more third powers, the other contracting Party undertakes to observe neutrality towards the first party.

II. Each of the Contracting Parties undertakes to abstain from all kinds of aggression, against the other and will not, on the territory under its own occupation, take any such steps which may cause political or military injury to the other contracting government. In particular, each of the Contrating Parties undertakes not to join any other state or states in any political or military alliance or union directed against the other. In addition, should the policy of a third state or states be hostile in its action to either of the Contracting Parties, the other Contracting Party shall undertake not only to abstain from assisting such hostile policy, but also to prevent the said policy and hostile actions and their inception within its own territory.

III. The High Contracting Parties, mutually recognizing the sovereignty and integrity of the other, undertake to abstain from all kinds of armed and unarmed interference in the internal affairs of the other Contracting Party and also not join or assist any other state or states which may take steps against or interfere with the other contracting state.

The Contracting Parties will not permit any groups or individuals in their own territories to establish or to prosecute activities detrimental to the other Contracting Party; to take steps for the subversion of the established Government of the other Contracting state; to take any action against the integrity of the territory of the other Contracting Party; to mobilize or collect armed forces against the other Contracting Party; and will prevent them from taking said actions. Similarly the Parties will not countenance the transit through their territories of any armed forces, arms, firearms, ammunition or the supply of any kind of war materials intended for use against the other Contracting Party and likewise will take active steps to prevent the same from passing through its territory.

IV. The Contracting Parties agree that within four months they will enter into discussions to determine principles for the solution of differences which may arise between them, which cannot be settled through the ordinary diplomatic channels.

V. Each of the Contracting Parties outside the limits of undertakings the conditions of which are defined in this Treaty, has freedom of action in taking steps to form any kind of relations and any kind of agreement with other states.

VI. This Treaty will have the force of law and will remain in force for three years following the date of ratification which should take place within three months following the date of signature of the present Treaty. After the expiration of the said period it will be understood that the Treaty will continue in force for an additional year automatically unless either of the Contracting Parties had notified the other that it desires to terminate the enforcement of this Treaty six months before the expiration of that period.

VII. Two copies of this Treaty have been written in Persian and in Russian and both texts will have equal force.

Source: Leonard Shapiro, *Soviet Treaty Series, 1917-1928*, Vol. I (Washington, D.C.: The Georgetown University Press, 1950), pp. 322-23.

APPENDIX D

Agreement Between the United States of America and the Kingdom of Afghanistan in Regard to Friendship, Diplomatic and Consular Representation, Juridical Protection and Commercial Relations: 1935

I. There shall be a firm and enduring peace and sincere friendship between the United States of America and its citizens and His Majesty, the King of Afghanistan, his successors and subjects, throughout all their territories and possessions.

II. The diplomatic representatives of each country shall enjoy in the territories of the other, the privileges and immunities derived from generally recognized international law. The consular representative of each country, duly provided with exequater, will be permitted to reside in the territories, they shall enjoy the honorary privileges and the immunities accorded to such officers by general international usage; and they shall not be treated in a manner less favourable than similar officers of any other foreign country.

III. Subjects of His Majesty, the King of Afghanistan in the United States of America, its territories and possessions, and the nationals of the United States of America, its territories and possessions, in the King of Afghanistan shall be received and treated in accordance with the requirements and practices of generally recognized international law. In respect of their persons, possessions and rights, they shall enjoy the fullest protection of the laws and authrities of the country, and they shall not be treated in regard to their persons, property, rigths and interests, in any manner less favourable than the nationals of any other foreign country.

IV. In respect of import, export and other duties and charges affecting commerce, as well as in respect of transit warehousing and other facilities, the United States of America, its territories and possessions, will accord to the Kingdom of Afghanistan, and the King of Afghanistan will accord to the United States of America, its territories and possessions, unconditional most-favoured nation treatment. Every concession with respect to any duty, change of reuglation, affecting commerce now accorded or that may hereafter be accorded by the United States of America its territortes and possessions, or by the Kingdom of Afghanistan to any foreign country will become immediately applicable without request and without compensation to the commerce of the Kingdom of Afghanistan and of the United States of America, its territories and possessions respectively.

V. The stipulations of this agreement shall not extend to the treatment which is accorded by the United States of America to the commerce of Cuba under the provisions of the Commercial Convention concluded between the United States and Cuba on December 11, 1902 or the Reciprocal Trade Agreement concluded on August 24, 1929, or the provisions of any other Commercial Convention, which hereafter may be concluded between the United States of America and Cuba. Such stipulations, moreover, shall not extend to the treatment which is accorded to the commerce between the United States of America and the Panama Canal Zone or any of the dependencies of the United States of America or to the commerce of the dependencies of the United States of America with one another under existing or future laws.

Nothing in this agreement shall be construed as a limitation of the right of either Government to impose, on such terms as it may see fit, prohibitions or restrictions of a sanitary character designed to protect human, animal or plant life or regulations for the enforcement of police or revenue laws.

Nothing in this Agreement shall be construed to affect existing statutes of either country in relation to the immigration of aliens or the rights of either Government to enact such statutes.

VI. The present stipulations shall become operative on the day of signature thereof and shall remain respectively in effect until the entry into force of a definitely treaty of commerce, or until thirty days after notice of their termination shall have been given by the Government of either country but should the Government of the United States of America be prevented by future action of its legislature from carrying out the terms of these stipulations, the obligations thereof shall thereupon lapse.

VII. In witness whereof the undersigned, duly authorized thereto by their respective Governments, have signed this agreement, in duplicate, at Paris this......day of......one thousand nine hundred and thirtyfive.

Source: United States, *Foreign Relations of the United States*: *Diplomatic Papers, 1935* (Washinton, D.C.: Government Printing Office, 1953), pp. 557-59.

APPENDIX E

The Treaty of Friendship, Good Neighbourliness and Cooperation, 5 December, 1978

ARTICLE 1

The High Contratcting Parties solemnly declare their determination to strengthen and deepen the inviolable friendship between the two countries and to develop all-round cooperation on the basis of equality, respect for national sovereignty, territorial integrity and non-interference in each other's internal affairs.

ARTICLE 2

The High Contracting Parties shall make efforts to strengthen and broaden mutually beneficial economic, scientific and technical cooperation between them. With these aims in view, they shall develop and deepen cooperation in the fields of industry, transport and communications, agriculture, the use of natural resources, development of the power-generating industry and other branches of economy, to give each other assistance in the training of national personnel and in planning the development of the national economy. The two sides shall trade on the basis of the principles of equality, mutual benefit, and most-favoured nation treatment.

ARTICLE 3

The High Contracting Parties shall promote the development of cooperation and exchange of expertise in the fields of science, culture, art, literature, education, health services, the press, radio, television cinema, tourism, sport and other fields. The two sides shall facilitate the expansion of cooperation between organs of State power and public organizations enterprise, culture and scientific institutions with a view to making a deeper acquaintance of the life, work experience and achievements of the peoples of the two countries.

ARTICLE 4

The High Contracting Parties, acting in the spirit of the traditions of friendship and good neighbourliness, as well as the UN Charter, shall consult each other and take by agreement appropriate measures to ensure the security, independence and territorial integrity of the two countries. In the interests of strengthening the defence capacity of the High Contracting Parties, they shall continue to develop cooperation in the military field on the basis of appropriate agreements concluded between them.

ARTICLE 5

The USSR respects the policy of non-alignment which is pursued by the DRA and which is an important factor for maintaining international peace and security. The DRA respects the policy of peace pursued by the USSR and aimed at a strengthening friendship and cooperation with all countries and peoples.

ARTICLE 6

Each of the High Contracting Parties solemnly declares that it shall not join any military or other alliance or take part in any groupings of states as well as in actions or measures directed against the other High Contracting Party.

ARTICLE 7

The High Contracting Parties shall continue to make every effort, to defend international peace and security of the peoples, to deepen the process of relaxation of international tension, to spread it to all areas of the world, including Asia, to translate it into concrete forms of mutually beneficial cooperation among states and to settle international disputed issues by peaceful means. The two sides shall actively contribute towards general and complete disarmament including nuclear disarmament, under effective international control.

ARTICLE 8

The High Contracting Parties shall facilitate the development of cooperation among Asian states and the establishment of relations of peace, good neighbourliness and mutual confidence among them and the creation of an effective security system in Asia on the basis of joint efforts by all countries of the continent.

ARTICLE 9

The High Contracting Parties shall continue their consistent struggle against machinations by the forces of aggression, for the final elimination of colonialism and racism in all their forms and manifestation. The two sides shall cooperate with each other and with other peace-loving states in supporting the just struggle of the peoples for their freedom, independence, sovereignty and social progress.

ARTICLE 10

The High Contracting Parties shall consult each other on all major international issues affecting the interests of the two countries.

ARTICLE 11

The High Contracting Parties state that their commitments under the existing international treaties do not contradict the provisions of the present Treaty and undertake not to conclude any international agreements incompatible with it.

ARTICLE 12

Questions which may arise between the High Contracting Parties concerning the interpretation or application of any provisions of the present Treaty, shall be settled bilaterally in the spirit of friendship, mutual understanding and respect.

ARTICLE 13

The present Treaty shall remain in force within 20 years of the day it comes into effect unless one of the High Contracting Parties declares six months before the expiration of this term of its desire to terminate the Treaty it shall remain in force for the next five years until one of the High Contracting Parties warns in writing the other Party, six months before the expiration of current five year term, about its intention to terminate the Treaty.

ARTICLE 14

If one of the High Contracting Parties expresses the wish in the course of the 20-year term of the Treaty to terminate it before its expiration date, shall notify in writing the other Party, six months before its suggested date of expiration of the Treaty, about its desire to teminater the Treaty before the expiration of the term and may consider the Treaty terminated as of the date thus set.

ARTICLE 15

The present Treaty shall be ratified and take effect on the day of exchange of the instruments of tatification, which is to take place in Kabul.

Done in Duplicate, each in the Russian and Dari languages, both texts being equally authentic.

Done in Moscow on 5th December, 1978.

For the USSR	For the DRA
L. Brezhnev	N. Mohammad Taraki

Source: *Kabul Times*, 6 December, 1978.

BIBLIOGRAPHY

PRIMARY SOURCES

Official Publications of the United States

Afghanistan: *A Year of Occupation* (Washington, D.C.: Department of State, February 1981),

Afghanistan: *Two Years of Occupation* (Washington, D.C.: Department of State, December 1981).

Afghanistan: *Three Years of Occupation* (Washington, D.C.: Department of State, 1982).

Afghanistan: *Four Years of Occupation* (Washington, D.C.: Department of State, 1983).

Background Notes: *Afghanistan* (Washington, D.C.: Department of State, April 1980).

Chronology of Afghanistan Events: *A Retrospect* (Washington, D.C.: Department of State, 1980).

Cronin, Richard P., *Afghanistan*: *Soviet Invasion and Response* (Washington, D.C.: Congressional Research Service, 1982).

Department of Devence, *Soviet Military Power* (Second edn.) (Washington, D.C.: Government Printing Office, March 1983).

Department of State Bulletin (Washington), 1939-86.

Department of State, *Afghanistan*: *Soviet Invasion Attacked in U.N.* (Washington, D.C.: Department of State, 6 January, 1980).

Documents on American Foreign Relations (Boston: World Peace Foundation), 1934-78.

East-West Relations in the Aftermath of Soviet Invasion of Afghanistan (Washington, D.C.: Government Printing Office, 1980).

Foreign Relations of the United States: Diplomatic Paperd (Washington, D.C.: Department of State), 1914-54.

Soviet Dilemmas in Afghanistan (Washington, D.C.: Department of State, June 1980).

Soviet Invasion of Afghanistan (Washington, D.C.: Department of State, April 1980).

The Global Significance of the Occupation of Afghanistan by the USSR (New Delhi: USICA, 1983).

United States Policy and United States—Soviet Relations, 1979 (Washington, D.C.: Government Printing Office, 1979)

US Congress, House of Representatives Committee on Foreign Affairs, Subcommittee on Europe and the Middle East, *An Assessment of the Afghanistan Sanctions: Implications for Trade and Diplomacy in the 1980s* (Washington, D.C.: Government Printing Office, April 1981).

US House, 84th Congress, Second Session, Subcommittee of the Committee on Appropriation, *Hearings on Mutual Security Appropriation for 1957* (Washington, D.C., 1957).

US House, 96th Congress, First Session, Committee on Foreign Affairs, Subcommittee on Asian and Pacific Affairs, *Hearings on the Crisis in the Subcontinent: Afghanistan and Pakistan* (Washington, D.C.: Government Printing Press, 1979).

United States International Aid for Development (USAID), *Afghanistan: A Briefing Book* (Kabul: USAID, 1970).

———, *A Summary of US Assistance to Afghanistan* (Kabul: USAID, 1968).

United States International Communication Agency (USICA), *Backgrounder* (New Delhi: US Embassy), 1978-86.

———, *Official Texts* (New Delhi: US Embassy), 1978-86.

US Senate, Committee on Foreign Relations, *Restrictions on Appointment of an Ambassador to Afghanistan* Washington, D.C., 1979).

Official Publications of the United Nations

Official Records of General Assembly (*GAOR*), 1946-88.

Official Records of the Security Council (*SCOR*), 1946-86.

UN Monthly Chronicle (New Delhi: UN Information Centre), 1960-86.

UN Weekly Newsletter (New Delhi: UN Information Centre), 1980-86.

Yearbook of the United Nations (New York), 1945-83.

Official Publications of Afghanistan

Afghanistan (London: Afghan Embassy), 1954-74.

Afghanistan News (Kabul), 1957-62.

Democratic Republic of Afghanistan Annual 1979 Kabul:) Government Printing Press, 1979).

On the Saur Revolution (Kabul: Government Printing Press, 22 May, 1978).

Second Five Year Plan (Kabul: Ministry of Planning, 1968).

Survey of Progress, Annual (Kabul), 1960-70.

Government of Soviet Union

The Truth About Afghanistan—Documents, Facts, Eyewitness Reports (Moscow: Novosti Press, 1980).

Miscellaneous

Aitchison, C.U., ed., *A Collection of Treaties, Engagements and Sanads Relating to India and Neighbouring Countries*, Vol. II (Calcutta: Government Printing Press, 1919).

Great Britain, House of Commons Foreign Affairs Committee, *Afghanistan, the Soviet Invasion and Its Consequences for British Policy* (London: Her Majesty's Stationery Office, 1980).

Khrushchev, Nikita, *Khrushchev Remembers* (Boston: Little Brown, 1970).

SECONDARY SOURCES

Books

Adamec, Ludwig, W., *Afghanistan, 1900-1923: A Diplamatic History* (Berkeley: University of California Press, 1967).

———, *Afghanistan's Foreign Affairs to the Mid-Twentieth Century: Relations with the USSR, Germany and Britain* (Tuscon: University of Arizona Press, 1974).

Agabekov, Georges, *OGPU: The Russian Secret Terror* (New York: Brentano's, 1931).

Akhramovich, R.T., *Outline History of Afghanistan After the Second World War* (Moscow, 1966).

Amstutz, J. Bruce, *The First Five Years of Soviet Occupation* (Washington, D.C.: National Defense University, 1986).

Arnold Anthony, *Afghanistan: The Soviet Invasion in Perspective* (Stanford, Calif: Hoover Institutions Press, 1981).

———, *Afghanistan: Two Party Communism, Parcham and Khalq* (Stanford: Hoover Institution Press, 1983).

Aspaturian, Vernon *et. al*, *The Soviet Invasion of Afghanistan: Three Perspectives* (Los Angeles: University of California Press, 1980).

Banuazizi, Ali and Weiner, Myron, *The State, Religion and Ethnic Politics in Afghanistan, Iran and Pakistan* (New York: Syracuse University Press, 1986).

Barmine, Alexander, *One Who Survived: The Story of a Russian Under the Soviets* (New York: Putnam's, 1945).

Becker Seymour, *Russia's Protectorates in Central Asia: Bukhara and Khiva, 1865-1924* (Cambridge: Harvard University Press, 1968).

Benningsen, Alexander and Broxup Marie, *The Islamic Threat to the Soviet State* (New York: St. Martin's Press, 1983).

Bhargava, G.S., *South Asian Security After Afghanistan* (Texas: Lexington Books, 1983).

Bilgrami, S.A.H.R., *Afghanistan and British India, 1793-1907* (New Delhi, 1972).

Bradsher, Henry S., *Afghanistan and the Soviet Union* (Durham, N.C.: Duke Press, 1965).

Brown, Archie, and Michael Kaser, eds, *The Soviet Union Since the Fall of Khrushchev* (New York: Free Press, 1976).

Brown, J.F., *Relations Between the Soviet Union and Its Eastern European Allies* (Santa Monica: Rand Corporation, 1975).

Brzezinski, Zbignew, *Powers and Principle: Memoirs of the National Security Adviser, 1977-81* (New York: Farras and Straus, 1983).

———, *The Soviet Bloc* (Cambridge, Mass: Harvard University Press, 1967).

Caroe, Olaf, *The Pathans: 550 B.C. to A.D. 1957* (London, 1959).

Carter, Jimmy, *Keeping Faith* (New York: Bantam Books, 1982).

Chaliand, Gerald, *Report From Afghanistan*, Translated by Tamar Jacoly (New York: Viking, 1982).

Cleveland, Harlan and Goodpaster, Anerew J., *After Afghanistan—The Long Hand* (Boulder: Westview Press, 1980).

Collins, Joseph J., *The Soviet Invasion of Afghanistan: A Study in the Use of Forces in Soviet Foreign Policy* (Lexington, Mass.: Lexington Books, 1985).

Cottrell, Alvin S., ed., *The Persian Gulf State* (Baltimore, Md.: Johns Hopkins University Press, 1980).

Dallin, David J., *The New Soviet Empire* (New Haven: Yale University Press, 1951).

Davis, Colin, *The Problems of North West Frontier, 1890-1908* (Cambridge: Cambridge University Press, 1972).

Dornberg, John, *Brezhnev: The Mask of Power* (New York: Basic Books, 1974).

Dupree, Louis and Albert Linette, eds., *Afghanistan in the 1970s* (New York: Praeger, 1974).

Dupree, Louis, *Afghanistan* (Princeton, N.J.: Princeton University Press, 1980).

Dzie Wanowski, M.K., *A History of Soviet Russia* (New Jersey: Prentice Hall, 1979).

Edwards, Michael, *Playing the Great Game* (London: Hamish Hamilton, 1975).

Elphinstone, Mountstuart A., *Account of the Kingdom of Cabul* (London, 1815).

Eudin, Xenia J. and North, R.G., *Soviet Russia and the East, 1920-27: A Documentary Survey* (Stanford, Calif., Stanford University Press, 1957).

Farr, Grant M. and John G. Merriam, *Afghan Resistance: The Politics of Survival* (Boulder: Westview Press, 1987).

Fischer, Louis, *The Soviets in World Affairs* (London: Jonathan Cape, 1930), 2 volumes.

———, *Men and Politics: An Autobiography* (New York: Duell, Sloan and Pearce, 1941).

Fix, Ernest, *Travels in Afghanistan* (New York, 1943).

Fletcher, Arnold, *Afghanistan: Highway of Conquest* (Ithaca: Cornell University Press, 1965).

Francis, Peter, *Afghanistan Between East and West* (Washington, D.C.: National Planning Association, 1960).

Fraser-Tytler, W.K., *Afghanistan: A Study of Political Developments of Central and Southern Asia* (Third edn.).

Freedman, Robert O., *Soviet Policy Toward the Middle East Since 1970* (New York: Praeger, 1975).

Fukuyama, Francis, *The Future of the Soviet Role in Afghanistan: A Trip Report* (South Monica, Calif.: Rand Corporation, 1980).

———, *The Security of Pakistan: A Trip Report* (Santa Monica, Calif: Rand Corporation, 1980).

Fullerton, John, *The Soviet Occupation of Afghanistan* (Hong Kong: Far Eastern Economic Review, 1983).

Gall, Sandy, *Behind Russian Lines: An Afghan Journal* (London: Sidgwick and Jackson, 1983).

Garthoff, Raymond L., *Detente and Confrontation* (Washington, D.C.: The Brokings Institution, 1985).

Ghaus, Abdul Samad, *The Fall of Afghanistan* (Washington: Pergamon Brassey, 1988).

Girardet, Edward R., *Afghanistan: The Soviet War* (New Delhi: Selectbook Service Syndicate, 1986).

Goldman, Marshall I., Soviet Foreign Aid (New York: Praeger, 1967).

Goodwin, Ian, Caught in the Crossfire (New York: E.P. Dutton, 1987).

Gregorian Vartan, *The Emergence of Modern Afghanistan* (Stanford, Calif.: Stanford University Press, 1969).

Griffith, William E., *The Soviet Empire: Expansion and Detente* (Massachusetts: Lexington Books, 1976).

Hammond, Thomas T., ed., *The Anatomy of Communist Takeover* (New Haven: Yale University Press, 1975).

———, *Red Flag Over Afghanistan: The Communist Coup, the Soviet Invasion and the Consequences* (Boulder: Westview Press, 1984).

Heathcote, T.A., *The Afghan Wars 1839-1919* (London: Osprey Publishing Ltd., 1980).

Helmanek, Allen and Whelar, Joseph C., *Afghanistan Invasion: The Soviet Muslim Factor* (Washington, D.C.: Library of Congress, Congress Research Service, 1980).

Hussain, S.S. *et. al.*, *Afghanistan Under Soviet Occcupation* (Islamabad: World Affairs Publications, 1980).

Hyman, Anthony, *Afghanistan Under Soviet Domination* (London: Macimillan, 1984).

James C. Hsiung and Winberg Ghai, eds., *Asia and US Foreign Policy* (New York: Praeger, 1981).

Jones, Low, *South Asia: Afghanistan, Pakistan, India and Ceylon: A Survey* (Washington, D.C., 1957).

Kakar, Hasan K., *Government and Society in Afghanistan* (Austin: University of Texas Press, 1979).

Kamrany, Nake. M., *Peaceful Competition in Afghanistan: American and Soviet Models for Economic Aid* (Washington, D.C.: Communication Service Corporation, 1969),

Kanet, Roger E., ed., *Soviet Foreign Policy in the 1980s* (New York: Praeger, 1982).

Kaplan, Stephen S., *Diplomacy of Power: Soviet Armed Forces as a Political Instrument* (Washington, D.C.: Brookings Institution, 1981).

Kapur, Harish, *Soviet Russia and Asia, 1917-1927: A Study of Soviet Policy Towards Turkey, Iran and Afghanistan* (Geneva: Michael Joseph, 1966).

———, *The Soviet Union and the Emerging Nations* (Geneva: Michael Joseph Ltd., 1972).

Khan, Mir Munshi Sultan Mohammad, ed., *The Life of Abdur Rahman, Amir of Afghanistan* (London, 1900), 2 volumes.

Krine, David, *Afghanistan: David Krine's Report from Behind Rebel Lines on the Resistance to Moscow's Aggression* (Chicago: Call Publications, 1980).

Laqueur, Walter Z., *The Soviet Union and the Middle East* (New York: Praeger, 1959).

Lessing, Doris, *The Wind Blows Away Our Words* (London: Pan Books, 1987).

Mackintosh, Malcolm, *Strategy and Tactics of Soviet Foreign Policy* (London: Oxford University Press, 1963).

Male, Beverley, *Revolutionary Afghanistan: A Reappraisal* (New York: St. Martin's Press, 1982.)

Miller, Charles, *Khyber: British Inida's North-West Frontier* (New York: Macmillan, 1977).

Misra, K.P., ed., *Afghanistan Cirisis* (New Delhi: Vikas Publishing, 1981).

Monks, Alfred L., *The Soviet Intervention in Afghanistan* (Washington, D.C.: American Enterprise Institute, 1981).

Nayar, Kuldip, *Report on Afghanistan* (New Delhi: Allied Publishers, 1981).

Neil, Mac Farlance, *Soviet Intervention in Third World Conflict* (Geneva: PSIS Occasional Papers, 1983).

Newell, Nancy P. and Newell Richard S., *The Struggle for Afghanistan* (Ithaca, N.Y.: Cornell University Press, 1981).

Newell, Richard S., *The Politics of Afghanistan* (Ithaca, N.Y.: Cornell University Press, 1972).

Nollau, Guenther and Wiebe, H.J., *Russia's South Flank* (New York: Praeger, 1963).

Pazhwak, A.R., *Ariana: The Ancient Afghanistan* (London: Royal Afghan Embassy, 1952).

———, *Pakhtunistan* (London: Royal Afghan Embassy, 1967).

Poullada Leon B., *Reform and Rebellion in Afghanistan, 1919-29* (Ithaca, N.Y.: Cornell Univeristy Press, 1973).

Ramazani, R.K., *The Northern Tier, Afghanistan, Iran and Turkey* (New York: Van Nostrand, 1966).

Roi, Yaacov, ed., *The Limits to Power* (London: Croom Helm, 1979).

———, ed., *The USSR and the Muslim Warld: Issues in Domestic and Foreign Policy* (London: George Allen and Unwin, 1984).

Rubinstein, Alvin Z., *Soviet Policy toward Turkey, Iran and Afghanistan* (New York: Praeger, 1982).

———, ed., *The Great Game: Rivalry in the Persian Gulf and South Asia* (New York: Praeger, 1983).

Ryan, Nigel, *A Hitch or Two in Afghanistan: A Journey Behind Russian Lines* (London: Weidenfeld and Nicolson, (1983).

Scalpino, Robert A., *Asia and the Road Ahead: Issues for the Major Powers* (Berkeley: University of California Press, 1975).

Shah, Sardar Ikbal Ali, *Afghanistan of the Afghans* (Quetta: Pakistan Press, 1978).

Shahrani, M. Nazif and Canfield, Robert L., *Revolutions and Rebellions in Afghanistan* (Berkeley: University of California, 1984).

Shapiro, Leonard, *Soviet Treaty Series 1921-28*, Vol. I (Washington, 1950).

Steele, Jonathan, *World Power* (London: Michael Joseph, 1983).

Valenta, Jiri, *Soviet Intervention in Czechoslovakia 1968: Anatomyof a Decision* (Baltimore, Md.: Johns Hopkins University Press, 1979).

Van Dyk Tere, *In Afghanistan: An American Odyssey* (New York: Coward-McCann. Inc., 1985).

Vance, Cyrus, *Hard Choices: Critical Years in America's Foreign Policy* (New York: Simon and Schuster. 1983).

Weinland, Robert G., *An (The?) Explanation of the Soviet Invasion of Afghanistan* (Alexandria, Ba: Center for Naval Analysis, May 1981).

———, *The Soviet Invasion of Afghanistan: To What Extent Does it Represent a Harbinger of Things to Come in South West Asia* (Alexandria: Va: Center for Naval Analysis, June 1980).

Wilber, Donald N., *et. al.*, *Afghanistan, Its People, Its Society, Its Culture* (New Haven, Conn.: Human Relations Area Files, 1962).

Articles

Amin, A. Rasul, "A General Reflection on the Sealthy Sovietization of Afghanistan", *Central Asian Survey*, Vol. 3, No. 1, 1984, pp. 47-61.

Amin, Tahir, "Afghan Resistance: Past, Present and Future", *Asian Survey*, Vol. 24, April 1984. pp. 373-99.

Armstrong, Hamilton F., "North of the Khyber", *Foreign Affairs*, Vol. 34, No. 4, pp. 610-24.

Aspaturian, Vernon V., "Superpower Manoeuvres—Moscow's Afghan Gamble", *The New Leader*, Vol. 63, 28 January 1980, pp. 7-13.

Aspinall, Richard, "Broken Window in Central Asia Afghanistan", *Australian Outlook*, Vol. 10, No. 1, March 1956, pp. 42-56.

Assifi, Abdul Tawab, "The Russian Rope: Soviet Economic Motives and the Subversion of Afghanistan", *World Affairs*, Vol. 145, No. 3, Winter 1982/83, pp. 253-66.

Barry, Michael, "Afghanistan: Another Cambodia", *Commentary*, August 1982, pp. 29-38.

Beck, William T., *et. al.*, "Afghanistan: What Impact on Soviet Tactics?", *Military, Review* Vol. 62, March 1982, pp. 2-11.

Bennigsen, Alexandre, "The Soviet Union and Muslim Guerrilla Wars, 1920-1981: Lessons for Afghanistan", *Conflict*, Nos. 2-4, 1983, pp. 301-24.

Bernstein, Carl, "Arms for Afghanistan", *The New Republic*, No. 125, 18 July, 1981, pp. 8-10.

Bernstein, Richard, "Remaking Afghanistan in the Soviet Image", *The New York Times Magazine*, 24 March, 1985.

Bhattacharya, Sauri P., "Soviet Nationality Policy in Afgnanistan",*Asian Affairs*, June, 1984, pp. 125-37.

Biermann, John, "Russia's Afghan Enemy", *The New Republic*, 6 June, 1981, pp. 10-11.

Blechman, Barry M., "The Afghan Anglo: Where Detente?" *Washington Quarterly*, No. 3, Autumn 1980, pp. 1000-8.

Bodansky, Yossef, "The Bear on the Chessboard: Soviet, Military Gains in Afghanistan", *World Affairs* Vol. 145. No. 3, Winter 1982/83, pp. 273-98,

Bradsher, Henry S., "Afghanistan", *Washington Quarterly* Summer 1984, pp. 42-55.

Bree, Betsy, "The Soviet Soldier", *Review of the Soviet Ground Forces*, April 1982, pp. 29-32.

Broseup, Marie, "The Soviet in Afghanistan: The Anatomy of a Takeover", *Central Asian Survey*, April 1983, pp. 83-108.

Caroe, Olaf, "The Russian View of Afghanistan", *The Round Table*, July 1981, pp. 276-79.

Chadda, Maya, "Afghan Peace Prospects and the Regional Environment", *Transnational Perspectives*, Vol. 8, No. 1, 1983, pp. 6-11.

Chaffetz, David, "Afghanistan in Turmoil", *International Affairs* (London), Vol. 56, No. 1, January 1980, pp. 15-36.

Charpentier, C.J., "One Year After the Saur Revolution", *Afghanistan Journal*, No. 4, 1979, pp, 117-20.

Charters, David "Coup and Consolidation: The Soviet Seizure of Power in Afghanistan", *Conflict Quarterly*, No. 292, Spring 1981, pp. 41-42.

Chubin, Shahram, "The Northern Tier in Disarray", *World Today*, Vol. 35. December 1979, pp. 474-80.

Coldren, Lee O., "Afghanistan in 19 4: The Fifth Year of the Russo-Afghan War", *Asian Survey*, February 1985, pp. 169-79.

Collins, Joseph, "Soviet Military Performance in Afghanistan: A Preliminary Assessment", *Comparative Strategy*, Vol. 4, No. 2, 1983, pp. 147-67.

Collins, Joseph J., "The Use of Force in Soviet Policy: The Case of Afghanistan"; *Conflict Quarterly*, Vol. 3, Spring 1983, pp. 20-47.

———, "The Soviet Military Experience in Afghanistan", *Military Review*, Vol. 65, May 1985, pp. 16-28.

Curren, James B. and Karber, Phillip A., "Afghanistan's Ordeal Puts a Region At Risk", *Armed Forces Journal International*, March 1985, pp. 78-105.

Cynkin, Thomas M., "Aftermath of the Saur Revolution: Insurgency and Counter-insurgency in Afghanistan", *The Fletcher Forum*, Spring 1982, pp. 269-98.

Dawisha, Karen, "The USSE in the Middle East: Superpower in Eclipse?", *Foreign Affairs*, Vol. 61, Winter 1982/83, pp. 438-52.

Dil, Shaheen F., "The Cabal in Kabul: Great Power Interaction in Afghanistan", *American Political Science Review*, Vol. 71, June 1977, pp. 468-76.

Donaldson, Robert H., "Soviet Involvement in South Asia and the Indian Ocean Region", in Reger E. Kanet, ed., *Soviet Foreign Policy in the 1980s* (New York: Praeger, 1982), pp. 330-49.

Dunbar, Charles, "Inside Wartime Kabul", *Asia*, November-December 1983, pp. 26-31.

Dupree, Louis, "The Mountains Go To Mohammad Zshir", *Reports (AUFSR)*, Vol. 4, No. 6 (1960), South Asia.

———, "The Decade of Daoud Ends: Implications of Afghistan's Change of Government", *AUFSR*, vol. 7, No. 9, 1963, South Asia.

———, "A Note on Afghanistan: 1974". *AUFSR*, Vol. 12, No. 8 (1974), South Asia.

———, "Afghanistan 1977: Does Trade Plus Aid Guarantee Development", *AUFSR*, Vol. 21, No. 3, August 1977, South Asia Series.

———, "Towards Representative Government in Afghanistan —Part II", *AUGSR*, 1978/mo. 14, Asia.

———, "The Democratic Republic of Afghanistan. 1979", *AUFSR*, No. 32, 1979, Asia.

———, "Red Flag Over the Hindu Kush: Leftist Movements in Afghanistan—Part I", *AUFSR*, No. 44 1979, Asia Series.

———, "Red Flag Over the Hindu Kush: The Accidental Coup or Taraki in Blunderland—Part II", *AUFSR*, 1978/ No. 45, Asia.

———, "Red Flag Over the Hindu Kush: Rhetoric and Reforms or Promises? Fpromises?"—Part III, *AUFSR*. 1980/ No. 23, Asia.

———, "Red Flag Over the Hindu Kush: Foreign Policy and the Economy—Part IV", *AUFSR*, 1980/No. 27, Asia.

———, "Red Flag Over the Hindu Kush: Repression or Security Through Terror Purges—Part V", *AUFSR*, 1980/ No. 28, Asia.

———, "Militant Islam and Traditional Warfare in Islamic South Asia." *AUFSR*, No. 21, 1980, Asia Series.

———, "Afghanistan: 1980", *AUFSR*, No. 37, Asia 1980.

———, "Afghanistan under the Khalq", *Problems of Communism*, Vol. 28, No. 28, July-August 1979, pp. 34-50.

———, "Inside Afghanistan: Yesterday and Today: A Strategic Appraisal" *Strategic Studies* (Islamabad), Vol. 2, Spring 1979, pp. 64-83.

———, "Afghanistan in 1983 and Still No Solution", *Asian Survey*, Vol. 24, No. 2, February 1983, pp. 229-39.

Eiva, Andrew L., "The Russian Invasion of Afghanistan: The Facts behind the Takeover," *Islamic Defence Review*, No. 1, 1981, pp. 5-12.

Eliot, Theodore L. Jr., Afghanistan After the 1978 Revolution," *Strategic Review*, Vol. 7, Spring 1979, pp. 57-62.

———, "The 1978 Revolution: Some Internal Aspects", *The Fletcher Forum*, Vol. 3, Spril 1979, pp. 82-87.

Foot, Rosemary, "The Changing Pattern of Afghanistan's Relations with its Neighbours", *Asian Affairs* (London), Vol. 67, Fall 1980, pp. 55-62.

———, "Sino-Soviet Rivalry in Kabul", *The Round Table*, October 1980, pp. 434-42.

Freedman, Robert O., "Soviet Policy Towards the Middle East Since the Invasion of Afghanistan," *Joural of International Affairs*, Vol. 34, Fall/Winter 1980/81 pp. 283-310.

Freistetter, Franz, "The Battle in Afghanistan: A View from Europe", *Strategic Review*, Vol. 9, Winter 1981, pp. 36-43.

Froam, Joseph, "Cold War in Remotest Area", *US News and World Report*, 3 December, 1948, pp. 3-5.

Fromkin, David, "The Great Game in Asia', *Foreign Affairs*, Spring 1980, pp. 946-51.

Frumkin, Si, "Untold Stories", *National Review*, 2 November, 1984, pp. 42-43.

Fullerton, John, "A Rift Among Rebels", *Far Eastern Economic Review*, 29 October, 1982, pp. 20-22.

Fullerton Romey, "Cordovez Starts Over", *Far Eastern Economic Review*, 12 April, 1984, pp. 26-27.

Furlong, R.D.M., and Winkler Theodor, "The Soviet Invasion of Afghanistan", *International Defense Review*, Vol. 13, No. 2, March 1980, pp. 168-69.

Garrity, Patrick J., "The Soviet Military Stake in Afghanistan", *Journal of the Royal United Services Institute for Defence Studies*.

Goldman, Minton F., "Soviet Military Intervention in Afghanistan: Roots and Causes", *Policy*, Spring 1984, pp. 384-403.

Granwald, Hemy, "Foreign Policy and Reagan—II", *Foreign Affairs*, Winter 1984/85, pp. 219-39.

Griffith, Willian E., "The Implications of Afghanistan", *Survival*, July-August 1980, pp. 146-51.

Haggerty, Jerome J., "Afghanistan: The Great Game", *Military Review*, Vol. 60, August 1980, pp. 37-44.

Ha'liday, Fred, "Revolution in Afghanistan", *New Left Review*, No. 112, November-December 1978, pp. 3-44.

———, "Afghanistan—a Revolution Consumes Itself", *The Nation*, No. 229, 17 November 1979, pp. 492-95.

———, "The Arc of Revolution: Iran Afghanistan, South Yemen, Ethiopia," *Race and Class*, Vol. 20, Spring 1979, pp. 373-90.

———, "War and Revolution in Afghanistan", *New Left Review*, No. 119, January-February 1980, pp. 20-41.

Harrison, Selig S, "Nightmare in Baluchistan", *Foreign Policy*, No. 32, Fall 1978, pp. 136-60.

———, "Dateline Afghanistan: Exit Through Finland?", *Foreign Policy*, No. 41, Winter 1980/1981, pp. 163-87.

———, "Fanning Flames in South Asia", *Foreign Policy*, No. 45, Winter 1981-1982, pp. 84-102.

———, "A Breakthrough in Afghanistan", *Foreign Policy* Summer 1983, pp. 3-26.

Hart, Douglas M., "Low-Intensity Conflict in Afghanistan: The Soviet View", *Survival*, March-April 1982, pp. 61-67.

Hauner, Milan, "The Significance of Afghanistan: Lessons from the Past", *The Round Table*, July 1980, pp. 240-44.

Heller, Mark, "The Soviet Invasion of Afghanistan", *Washington Quarterly*, No. 3, Summer 1980, pp. 36-59.

Hough, Jerry F., "Why the Russians Invaded", *The Nation*, No. 230, March 1980, pp. 232-34.

Hutchison, John M.,"Scorched—Policy: Soviet in Afghanistan, *Military Review*, Vol. 62, April 1982, pp. 29-37.

Hyman, Anthony, "Afghanistan's Unpopular Revolution", *The Round Table*, No. 275, July 1979, pp. 222-26.

———, "The Struggle for Afghanistan", *World Today*, Vol. 40. July 1984, pp. 276-84.

Jacobs, G., "The Years of Soviet War Operation Evaluated", *Asian Defence Journal*, December 1982, pp. 34-45.

Kakar, Hassan, "The Fall of the Afghan Monarchy in 1973", *International Journal of Middle Eastern Studies*. Vol. 9, May 1978, pp. 195-214.

Kamlin, Muhammad, "Russia in Afghanistan: Piercing a Window or Bursting the Floodgates?" *Asia Pacific Community*, Spring 1980, pp. 67-93.

Kamrang, Nako M., Afghanistan under Soviet Occupation", *Current History*, Vol. 81, May 1982, pp. 219-22.

Khalilzad Zalmay, "Soviet Occupied Afghanistan", *Problems of Communism*, Vol. 29, November-December 1980, pp. 23-40.

———,"The Struggle for Afghanistan", *Survey*, Vol. 28, Spring 1980, pp. 189-216.

———, "Afghanistan and the Crisis in American Foreign Policy", *Survival*, Vol. 22, No. 4, July-August 1980.

———, "The Soviet Dilemma in Afghanistan", *Current History*, Vol. 84, October 1985, pp. 334-37.

Klass, R.T., "The Tragedy of Afghanistan", *Asian Affairs* (New York), Vol. 7, Summer 1979, pp. 1-7.

Klass, Rosanne, "Missing in Action: Treasures of Afghanistan", *Asia*, March-April 1981, pp. 27-35.

Krakowski, Elie D., "Defining Success in Afghanistan", *Washington Quarterly*, Vol. 8, No. 2, April 1985, pp. 37-46.

Lerniercier-Cruelguejay, Chautal and Alexandre Bennigsen, "Soviet Experience of Muslim Guerrilla Warfare and the War in Afghanistan", in Haavov Ro'i, ed., *The USSR and the Muslim World: Issues in Domestic and Foreign Policy* (London: George Allen and Unwing, 1984), pp. 206-14.

Leventhal, Todd, "Terror and Propaganda: The Two Pillars of Soviet Policy in Afghanistan", *Political Communication and Persuasion*, No. 3, 1984, pp. 277-82.

Luttwak, Edward N., "After Afghanistan, What?", Commentary, Vol. 69, April 1980, pp. 40-49.

Lynch, Kevin, "Afghanistan: War on a Shoestring", *National Review*, 21 January, 1983, pp. 40-41.

Maley, William, "Prospects for Afghanistan", *Australian Outlook*, Vol. 39, December 1985, pp. 157-64.

Malhuret, Claude, "Report from Afghanistan", *Foreign Affairs*, Winter 1983-84, pp. 426-35.

Malik, Hafeez, "The Afghan Crisis and Its Impact on Pakistan", *Journal of South Asian and Middle Eastern Studies*, Spring 1982, pp. 40-52.

Medvedev, Roy, "The Afghan Crisis", *New Left Review*, No. 121, May-June 1980, pp. 91-96.

Mehta, Jagat S., "A Neutral Solution", *Foreign Policy*, No. 47, Summer 1982, pp. 139-53.

Mukerjee, Dilip, "Afghanistan Under Daud: Relations with Neighbouring States", *Asian Survey*, Vol. 15, No. 4, April 1975, pp. 301-12.

Muraka, Dev, "Afghanistan: The Russian Intervention: A Moscow Analysis", *The Round Table*, April 1981, pp. 122-39.

Naby, Eden, "The Ethnic Factor in Soviet Afghan Relations", *Asian Survey*, Vol. 20, No. 3, March 1980, pp. 237-56.

Negaran, Hannah, "The Afghan Coup of April 1978: Evolution and International Security", *Orbis*, Vol. 23, Spring 1979, pp. 93-113.

———, "Afghanistan: A Marxist Regime in a Muslim Society", *Current History*, Vol. 76, April 1979, pp. 172-75.

Nelson, Denny R., "Soviet Air Power: Tactics and Weapons Use in Afghanistan", *Air University Review*, January-February 1985, pp. 32-43.

Newell, Richard S., "Revolution and Revolt in Afghanistan", *The World Today*, Vol. 35, No. 11, November 1979, pp. 432-42.

———, "Soviet Intervention in Afghanistan", *The World Today*, Vol. 36, No. 7, July 1980, pp. 250-58.

Noorani, A.G., "Afghanistan and the Rule of Law", *International Common Jurists Review*, January 1980, pp. 37-52.

O'Ballance, Edgar, "Soviet Tactics in Afghanistan", *Military Review*, Vol. 60, August 1980, pp. 45-52,

Oren, Stephen, "The Afghan Coup and the Peace in Northern Tiet", *The World Today*, Vol. 30, No. 1, January 1974, pp. 26-32.

Overhoet, William H., "The Geopolitics of the Afghan War", *Asian Affairs* (New York), Vol. 7, March-April 1980, pp. 205-17.

Pipes, Richard and George F. Kenan, "How Real Is the Soviet Threat?", *US News and World Report*, 10 March, 19‹0, pp. 33-39.

Poullada, Leon B, "Afghanistan and the United States: The Crucial Years", *The Middle East Journal*, Vol. 35, Spring 1981, pp. 178-90.

———, "The Failure of American Diplomacy in Afghanistan", *World Affairs*, Vol. 145, Winter 1982/83, pp. 230-52

Ramazani, R.K., Afghanistan and the USSR", *The Middle East Journal*, Vol. 12, 1958, pp. 144-52.

Reincourt, Amaury de, "India and Pakistan in the Shadow of Afghanistan", *Foreign Affairs* (New York), Vol, 61, Winter 1982/83, pp. 416-37.

Rubinstein, Alvin Z., "Soviet Imperialism in Afghanistan", *Current History*, Vol. 79, October 1980, pp. 80-83.

———, "Afghanistan: Embraced by the Bear", *Orbis*, Vol. 26, Spring 1982, pp. 135-53.

———, "The Last Years of Peaceful Coexistence: Soviet-Afghan Relations 1963-1978", *Middle East Journal*, Vol. 36, Spring 1982, pp. 1-13.

———, "The Soviet Union and Afghanistan", *Current History*, Vol. 82, October 1983, pp. 318-21.

———, "Afghanistan at War",*Current History*, Vol. 85, March 1986, pp. 117-20.

Saikal Amin, "The Afghanistan Crisis: A Negotiated Settlement?", *World Today*, Vol. 40, November 1984, pp. 481-89.

Simes, Dimitri K., "The Death of Detente", *International Security*, Vol. 5, Summer 1980, pp. 3-25.

Simour, Lewis M. "Standoff in Afghanistan", *The New Republic*, No. 187, 16-23 August 1982, pp. 23-25.

Singleton, Seth, "The Soviet Invasion of Afghanistan", *Atlantic Community Quarterly*, Vol. 19, Summer 1981, pp. 186-200.

Smolanky, O. M., "Soviet Policy in Iran and Afghanistan", *Current History*, Vol. 80, October 1981, pp. 321-24.

Summerscale, Peter, "Eastern Europe in the Wake of Afghanistan", *World Today*, (London), Vol. 36, No. 6, May 1980, pp. 172-79.

Tahir-Kheli, Shirin, "The Soviet Union in Afghanistan: Benefits and Costs", in Donaldson Robert M., ed., *The*

Soviet Union in the Third World: Successes and Failures (London: Westview Press, 1981), pp. 217-31.

Taussing, H.C., Afghan Neutralism", Eastern World, Vol. 15, No. 12, December 1961, pp. 9-11.

Valenta, Jiri, "From Prague to Kabul: The Soviet Style of Invasion", *International Security*, Vol. 5, Fall 1980, pp. 114-41.

———, "The Soviet Invasion of Afghanistan: The Difficulty of Kowning Where to Stop", *Orbis*, Vol. 24, Summer 1980, pp. 201-18.

Van Prangh, David, "The Greater Game: Implications of the Afghan Coup", *International Perspective*, March-April 1979, pp. 12-16.

Vertzberger, Yaacov, "Afghanistan in China's Policy", *Problems of Communism* Vol. 31, May-June 1982, pp. 1-23.

Wafadar, K., "Afghanistan in 1980: The Struggle Continues", *Asian Survey*, February 1981, pp. 172-80.

———, "Afghanistan in 1981: The Struggle Intensifies", *Asian Survey*, February 1982, pp. 147-54.

Weeks, Albert L., "The Soviet Assault on National Sovereignty", *Freedom At Issue*, May-June 1980, pp. 5-9.

Wimbush, S. Enders and Alexiev, Alex, "Soviet Central Asian Soldiers in Afghanistan", *Conflict*, Nos. 2-4, 1983, pp. 325-37.

Yolalarsky, Michall, "First Step in Soviet Diplomacy toward Afghanistan, 1917-1921", in Yaavoc Ro'i, ed., *The USSR and the Muslim World: Issues in Domestic and Foreign Policy* (London: George Allen and Unwin, 1984) pp. 215-25.

Ziring, Lawrence, "Soviet Policy on the Rim of Asia", *Asian Affairs* (New York), Vol. 9, January-February 1982, pp. 135-46.

Journals and Periodicals

Asian Survey (Berkeley).

American Political Science Review (Washington).

Current History (Philadelphia).

Central Asian Survey (London).

Foreign Affairs (New York).

Foreign Policy (New York).

International Affairs (London).

International Security (Harvard).

Middle East Journal (Washington).

Newsweek (New York).

Orbis (Philadelphia).

Problems of Communism (Washington).

Survival (London).

The Economist (London).

The Far Eastern Economic Review (Hong Kong).

The New Left Review (London).

The Round Table (London).

US News and World Report (Washington).

Newspapers

Anis (Kabul).

Islah (Kabul).

Kabul Times (Kabul).

Mujahid Wollas (Norway).

The Christian Science Monitor (Paris).

The International Herald Tribune (Paris).

The Los Angeles Times (Los Angeles).

The New York Times (New York).

The Times (London).

The Washington Post (Washington).

Wall Street Journal (London).

Index